When

THE

Piano

Stops

A MEMOIR *of* HEALING
FROM SEXUAL ABUSE

CATHERINE McCALL

SEAL PRESS

When the Piano Stops
A Memoir of Healing from Sexual Abuse

Copyright © 2009 by Catherine McCall

Published by
Seal Press
A Member of the Perseus Books Group
1700 Fourth Street
Berkeley, California 94710

Library of Congress Cataloging-in-Publication Data

McCall, Catherine.
When the piano stops : a memoir of healing from sexual abuse /
Catherine McCall.
p. cm.
ISBN-13: 978-1-58005-267-2
ISBN-10: 1-58005-267-3
1. Child sexual abuse--United States--Psychological
aspects--Biography. 2. Adult child sexual abuse victims--United
States--Biography. I. Title.
HV6570.2.M39 2009
362.76092--dc22
[B]
2008051789

Cover design by Susan Koski Zucker
Cover photo by © Joe Mikos/Getty Images
Interior design by Tabitha Lahr
Printed in the United States of America
Distributed by Publishers Group West

Dedicated to the well-being of children.

There are stories no one wants to tell, because they are stories everyone wants to deny are true. And yet, the integrity of life compels one to give testimony as another bears witness to the truth. The gospel truth.

Author's Note

I have written this memoir in solidarity with those who have endured sexual abuse, their partners, children, and therapists. The narrative of my story is structured in the sequence in which the events happened, rather than that in which I remembered them. Although I remembered my parents' drunkenness, my father's erratic mood swings, and periods when my siblings and I lived in terror because of his unrelenting psychological abuse, I did not remember episodes of him sexually abusing me, which are described in Part One, until I was forty years old. My mother was dying, and as a result of a constellation of triggering events described in Part Two, memories of the sexual abuse began to emerge through flashbacks. This phenomenon is often characteristic of post-traumatic stress disorder and the nature of traumatic memory.

Many children who are repeatedly abused sexually may have no memory of these experiences. This may vary depending on when and how they are abused, their level of cognitive development, personal and family dynamics. How can they believe what they cannot imagine? How can they name that for which they have no words? And what child doesn't prefer to believe that the abuse did not happen? Denial, dissociation, and repression allow children to go on living life with the illusion of normalcy, though they may have a sense that they made something awful happen, and their capacity to stand up for themselves is often undermined. In my case, I felt that my mere existence was a source of profound pain for the people I loved the most.

The traumatic nature of abuse often resets a child's physiology from fight to freeze. Thus, she or he becomes captive to the perpetrator's wishes. The child's ability to accommodate to these circumstances is amazing, and its effect on her or his development is powerfully influenced by the child's full context—innate personality, physical stamina, early nurturing, immediate and extended family dynamics, school, community, faith, friends, teachers, culture, and physical surroundings.

The experience of sexual abuse by incest is the most profound violation of personal boundaries imaginable and creates a ripple effect of pain throughout the survivor's life and family. There are many forces at work to keep the child and, later, the adult s/he becomes, quiet about her or his victimization. When I decided to write and publish my story I did so with the full support of my husband, Peter, though it contains a detailed account of how my history and his affected our marriage, including our sex life. My writing style is an outgrowth of our commitment to truth-telling without evasion. Intimate stories of monogamous marriage are rare in our culture of sexual exploitation and frequent media attention to the infidelities of politicians and celebrities. Our hope is that other couples struggling to heal and to love can learn from our experiences.

I realize that in telling my story, I am also telling my family's story, both past and present. My siblings have encouraged and respected my commitment to the telling of my perspective about our childhood. Issues relevant to Peter and me and our own children carry a different sensitivity. I have worked hard to chisel a narrative that keeps our daughters and their stories out of my memoir as much as possible, to protect their privacy. Their names and those of many people and places in my family's history have been changed for the same reason.

Contents

PART ONE:

The Biology of Evil and the
Psychology of Grace

PART TWO:

The Geography of Trauma and the History of Redemption

Prologue

Mother had her lucid moments during those final months in the nursing home. But Mary Anne, my therapist, had warned me that the time would come when such moments would cease to be. In anticipation of that day, I went through all the old family Kodachrome slides—and there were many, as photography had been Dad's hobby. I selected thirty-five favorites and had them made into prints, arranged them in an album, and took a morning off from work to deliver my gift.

When I arrived, I found Mother in her wheelchair, lined up against the wall with other patients. She was frail and scrawny, wearing a pink-and-white striped blouse, white polyester pants, and running shoes. Her thin, shoulder-length white hair was parted on the side and held back with a baby blue barrette.

At the sight of me, she began waving and calling my name, trying to stand up on those spindly legs that had been paralyzed for four months. I walked toward her quickly, smiling and returning the waves, until I was close enough to bend over and embrace her, kissing her soft,

1

drooping cheek, as she smiled and the almond scent of Jergen's lotion welcomed me into her space.

I wheeled her into the privacy of the sunlit visiting room, and told her I had made her a special gift.

"Oh, goody!" she exclaimed. "I love presents."

When I opened the album to the first picture—of her and Dad during their engagement, dressed in their Sunday best—a wave of dementia seemed to roll across her face, as if the mere sight of it had flipped a switch deep inside her. Determined to penetrate the stone stare that only moments earlier had held warmth and awareness, I sat beside her and discussed each page, in monologue: "Look, Mom, here you are at Buck Hill Falls with Dad and your friends. Do you remember? . . . And look at this other page. Here's your favorite picture of the four of us. Andrew looks about eleven, I'm about eight, Lucy, five, and Paul looks not quite two. Isn't he cute?" But there was no recognition on her part at all. Absolutely none.

I sat teary-eyed, with remnants of our past gazing up at me in living color, while Mother stared out the window, eyes glazed, Revlon-red lips pursed together, appearing resolute to do nothing except wait to be delivered to the other side.

But not for long. Mother motioned and grunted to me, as if I were a nursing home attendant, that she wanted to be wheeled back to her room. Immediately. My body stiffened. This was the attitude the staff had so often complained about. Though multi-infarct dementia—Binswanger's disease, as the doctor had called it—caused her arteries to become more and more narrowed, decreasing the blood supply to her brain, apparently the cells that made her so demanding were still intact.

My irritation evaporated, however, when I looked up and noticed that she had slumped over and was rubbing her eyes. Of course she wanted to be wheeled back to bed. She needed a nap, and she needed it now.

I eased her wheelchair toward the exit of the visiting room, but she suddenly stopped it with her hands and motioned for me to come around and bend over close to her. She grabbed my arm with surprising strength and spoke to me as her daughter again.

"Catherine, please, promise me you'll write a book someday and tell them all about it," she said. "Tell them in a way that will make it all make sense. Tell them in a way that will make some good of it. Please." Then the cloud moved over her face once more, this time to stay.

I was forty-two years old when she died, on Mother's Day 1990. And now, at fifty-nine, as I enter the final decades of my life, the time has come for me to fulfill my promise to my mother, to keep my promise to myself.

Make some good of it. *Please.*

PART ONE:

The Biology of Evil and the Psychology of Grace

How can we explain the hate that burns in so many homes?
—Elie Wiesel, All Rivers Run to the Sea: Memoirs

Shame is a highly negative and painful state that also results in the disruption of ongoing behavior, confusion in thought, and an inability to speak . . . Shame can cause memory loss.

—Michael Lewis, Shame: The Exposed Self
(from pages 75 and 121)

. . . I want to go up to them and say Stop, don't do it—she's the wrong woman, he's the wrong man, you are going to do things you can not imagine you would ever do, you are going to do bad things to children, you are going to suffer in ways you never heard of . . .
—Sharon Olds, "I Go Back to May 1937"

Chapter 1

Christmas 1973. Peter and I, both twenty-five, have just completed our three-year tour of duty with the Army in Heidelberg, Germany. Having seen my parents only twice during that time, we are eager for our children to visit their grandparents. Claire is almost three, Beth is two, and Annie, seven months. At nine thirty in the morning, after an overnight flight from Frankfurt to New York on a military-chartered plane, we arrive at my parents' house, 763 Montgomery Place, a brownstone mansion in the Park Slope neighborhood of Brooklyn.

Peter is holding Annie and her blanket, a diaper bag, and a sack of the children's toys. Although it's a cold winter's day, he's wearing only a sweater over his tall, lean body, which turned muscular during his four years at West Point. Heart pounding, I stand beside him shivering in my parka, while Claire and Beth, in red snowsuit jackets and mittens, lean against the oak-framed, glass-paneled front door, peering at their reflections and giggling.

"Well, Cath, here goes," Peter says as I reach for the doorbell. "Let's hope for a good visit."

Dad answers the door almost immediately. His gray hair is parted neatly on the side, he's wearing silver-rimmed bifocals and a navy velvet dinner jacket with burgundy ascot, and he's holding a martini.

"Cath, dear. And Peter . . . how delightful it is to see you both," he says, stepping back to lead us from the vestibule into the first-floor foyer. I watch his slow pace, distrusting his calm demeanor. My stomach tightens as his blue green eyes, now appearing icy, meet mine. "Oh, yes, and the girls, how lovely!" he continues in a sarcastic tone, eyes focused on me.

Hesitant, I glance at Peter, and he nods that we should go in. Reassured by his decisiveness, I clutch Claire's hand, simultaneously lifting Beth into my other arm. She's chubby, so lifting her isn't easy, but she's also one whose need to explore can get the best of her in any new situation. And this moment feels rife with danger.

I walk through the vestibule and kiss Dad's cheek automatically. My heart sinks. He reeks of alcohol. Peter follows, opting for a handshake. I look first into the room on the right, behind Dad, which had been the waiting room for his ophthalmology patients during much of my childhood. The chairs, tables, lamps, and magazine racks are covered with sheets and plaster chunks. I look up to see that large sections of the fourteen-foot ceiling have caved in. Slabs of the ceiling are strewn throughout the room, and it looks like it's been that way for a while. When did this happen?

I turn to the left, staring into what had been my father's secretary's room. The beautiful mahogany Steinway baby grand his mother had left him when she died is wedged in front of the secretary's desk with a huge chunk of ceiling on its closed top. Beside it, the broken arms and legs and ripped upholstery from the Victorian rocking chair I inherited from my maternal grandmother, Ammy, are stacked in a pile on the floor. Jaws clenched, my body tenses. What I am seeing is hard to absorb. Ammy had told me that she cherished memories of my running into her living room and planting myself in this chair at the beginning of each visit, rocking to my heart's content. I had left it at Mom and Dad's because I feared the move might damage it.

"What happened to my rocking chair?" I gasp.

He smiles; raises his eyebrows. "Can't you tell by looking at it, dear? I destroyed it with a hammer," he says matter-of-factly.

Beth looks at me, her hazel eyes widening, then nestles her head of thick, shiny black hair into my chest. Claire squeezes my fingers. "Mommy, I don't like this man," she whispers. I look down at her, cup her head in the palm of my hand, ease her against my leg, and stare at my father. *You are scaring my children. You are scaring me.* "Where's Mom?" I ask.

"Oh, don't you see her, dear?" He turns and points. Beads of perspiration appear on the upper lip of his sinister grin. "She's right up there . . . right at the head of the stairs. Your mother has had a slight accident, so she can't come down. She hurt her ankle. She'll have to be in a wheelchair until it heals."

I look up. There she sits, leaning forward, smoking a cigarette, waving madly. She appears to be drunk. Her thick black hair is now streaked with gray, and she has gained weight. Her fifty-one-year-old body stretches to the limits of the size 20 charcoal gray dress I recognize from years before. One of her feet is wrapped in an elastic bandage reaching to mid-calf, and she wears an athletic sock on the other.

"Hi, Cath! . . . Hi, girls! . . . Hi, Peter! Come on up, all of you! We have a Christmas tree and some presents for the girls."

I feel reluctant but drag myself up the stairs with Claire and Beth. I cannot kiss Mom; she reeks of gin. I guide my family into the living room, walking right by her.

"I need to go potty," Claire whispers, fidgeting with her pink corduroy pants.

"Okay. I'll take you in just a few minutes," I whisper back, hoping one of the bathrooms is clean enough to use.

As I finish my sentence, I hear Dad telling Mom he's going to the kitchen to refill his martini glass and find her another pack of cigarettes. I motion to Peter to keep an eye on Beth, along with Annie, who has fallen asleep in his arms, and then I head down the hall with Claire. I'm relieved to see that even though old newspapers are stacked high in the bathtub, the toilet is usable.

When we return, I deposit Claire with Peter and follow Dad to the kitchen. I'm intent on preparing lunch for the girls, but the sight of the kitchen weakens me. I am amazed by the density of dirt, grease, and grime on the counter, sink, and cabinets. The sticky filth of the floor grabs like glue at the soles of my shoes. I look down and say, "This place is an absolute shithole."

"Oh, *really*, dear?" Dad says, pouring his cocktail. He grabs a rancid dishtowel and wipes the counter. "So, it doesn't meet with your approval, sweetheart?"

Hell, no, I think, but it's useless to reply. It's clear that he has been on a drunken binge for days, and so has Mom.

I open the refrigerator to find something for my family to eat. All I see is a container of orange juice and a six-pack of beer. No food in the cabinets, either. Only roaches. Big, fat New York roaches.

"We thought you'd go to the grocery store for us, Cath. Your mother and I haven't been feeling up to it," I hear him say from behind me, but I'm already halfway down the hall, headed for Peter.

"There's no food," I tell him. "They were expecting *me* to get groceries, and probably to clean the house, too. This place isn't fit for children. I want to leave. Now."

"I'll tell you what, Cath," he says, turning toward the staircase. "You wait here with the girls, and I'll go upstairs and check to see what condition the bedrooms are in."

I hate it when Peter questions my intuition, but he leaves before I can protest.

Moments later he returns. "I never want you to lay eyes on your bedroom again, Cath," he says.

"That bad?"

"Trust me. It's worse."

"Let's get out of here," we say in unison.

Peter gathers all the children's things in one arm, maneuvering without awakening Annie, who is still asleep in his other. I hold Claire's hand and reach for Beth's, but she flails into a temper tantrum. Peter drops the kids' belongings, spanks her little behind, then lifts her and their things and heads toward the staircase. I am furious. The grandparents deserve the spanking, not our two-year-old.

Dad reenters the living room just as I'm saying goodbye to Mom, who is begging me to stay.

"What's *this?* Just what do you think is going on here, Catherine?" His tone is hostile, authoritative.

"Great question," I respond, without editing the sarcasm from my voice.

Suddenly I'm distracted. His piano. His second Steinway baby grand—this one ebony—is destroyed, too. Splinters are strewn randomly on the keyboard and the floor underneath. Large pieces of wood lie on the strings. He's smashed the top in. The hammer is still there, on the piano bench. Thank God he isn't standing near the hammer now.

I don't notice him come closer until Claire yanks my hand, looking at me with urgency.

"Mama, Claire no lika dat man." My articulate firstborn, who is almost three, is so frightened her speech pattern regresses twelve months. I lift her into my arms.

"Mommy, that man is going to hurt you," she says, pointing.

I can't let him anywhere near me or my children.

"Get out of my way!" I shout, pushing him aside. I run down the stairs with Claire and hurry through the front door after Peter, the still-crying Beth, and Annie, while Dad yells after me.

"Go ahead, Catherine, leave! *Go* with Peter! Do like your precious Bible says, *leave* your mother and father and cling to your husband, *even* if your poor mother's in a *wheelchair!* Why should *you* care? Ha! You'll see how wonderful your life will be!"

I race to the car, holding Claire securely against my chest.

between my legs. He's pulling my panties out and peeling and tugging around.

Chapter 2

I am six. We are sitting on the piano bench. Daddy's wearing his undershorts. That's all. I'm wearing my white underpants. That's all. Daddy is smiling at me.

"Play 'Never Never Land,' Daddy, *please?*" I beg.

"Ah, yes, Catherine," he says. "You fell in love with Peter Pan, didn't you? There will be many more Broadway shows for us to enjoy, sweetheart." He's putting his hand on the keys. His thumb is on middle C. He winks at me. "We're going to make beautiful music together, Catherine Girl," he says.

It doesn't *feel* like we're going to make beautiful music.

He's on the floor now, kneeling in front of me and looking between my legs. He's pulling my panties out, and peeking and touching around.

"Why are you doing that, Daddy?"

"Because I'm giving you an examination, dear."

"But Mommy already took me to the doctor. He said I'm a perfectly healthy first-grader. Please, stop it, Daddy." He's not stopping. I want to fly away. I wish Tinker Bell would come and sprinkle fairy dust on me.

13

I have a baby brother. His name is Paul. Daddy picked it out because of St. Paul's epistles. Mommy thought he had a good idea. She likes St. Paul. Maybe someday my baby brother will be a saint. I have a little sister, too, Lucy. She's three. She's upstairs in bed already. And I have a big brother, Andrew. He's nine, and he's watching TV in the room next to the nursery. But I like Baby Paul the best.

Daddy is downstairs playing the piano, "To a Wild Rose." It's one of his favorite's; Mommy's, too. Me and Mommy are in the kitchen. Our kitchen is blue and white and the wallpaper has windmills on it and pictures of people wearing wooden shoes and funny hats, carrying milk. Mommy says it's because they're Dutch. Our milkman doesn't wear funny hats and wooden shoes. He's American.

Mommy is busy making bottles for Baby Paul. She better hurry, 'cause he just started crying. His voice shakes when he cries, and it scares me because maybe he got hurt.

"Catherine, run in and talk to him very softly until I finish up, will you please, dear? Tell him I'll be there in one minute."

I run down the hall into the nursery and lean on the bassinet, reach in, and give him one of my fingers, just like Mommy and Daddy taught me to. He likes to hold it, but he's still crying.

"Shh, Baby Paul . . . Mommy's coming. She's bringing your bottle . . . it will be okay."

Here she is. She's picking him up and carrying him to her chair. He's getting quiet, except for the sucking sound. I go stand by them. Mommy smiles at Baby Paul with her pretty red lipstick on. I'm smiling, too, and giving him my finger to hold again while he drinks his milk.

"Our mommy loves you, Baby Paul," I say in my soft voice, looking down at him. "And she loves me, too."

"Very true, Cath, very true," Mommy says. "I'm glad you know that."

"I know it's true because Daddy told me. He said you have Andrew love, Catherine love, Lucy love, and Paul love, and he does too."

I'm eight. It's a beautiful fall afternoon, a Saturday. The sun is out, the sky is a deep shade of blue, and I gaze out the bay window of our music room, watching the light dance among red and yellow leaves. Andrew is eleven, and he has gone to his friend's house for the afternoon. Lucy is five and Paul is two. They are both upstairs taking naps and so is Mommy. Mommy says only little ones have to take a nap on Saturdays. I get to play with Daddy while they're sleeping. Daddy's doing one of my favorite things. He's teaching me about the great composers and their masterpieces.

"Isn't this lovely, Cath?" he asks. "It's Chopin's *Heroic Polonaise,* opus 53," he says as the first chord booms over my head. I'm lying under the piano, watching the hammers move as his fingers press the keys.

"I know, Daddy," I reply confidently.

I love it, all of it—the way the piano looks, the way it works, the way it sounds, and best of all, the way my daddy and I have so much fun together.

"Play opus 40, number 1, Daddy! . . . I like that one!" I'm showing off. I'm proud of myself for remembering the name of the piece.

He starts playing it. I like it when he plays whatever you want so fast like that. I can hear him humming while he's playing. It's funny. He hums out of tune, but he plays perfectly in tune.

Now he's playing Chopin's *Revolutionary Étude,* opus 10, my favorite, and he knows it. The hammers dance all over the wires, and his feet get very busy going up and down and back and forth on the pedals. I don't know which to watch first, the hammers or Daddy's feet. I love his feet. He has on those wingtip shoes. When I grow up and get married, I hope my husband wears wingtips like Daddy.

"Listen to this, Cath," he says. "It's by Debussy. It's called 'Clair de Lune.' Lie still and close your eyes and just listen . . . Isn't it delightful? . . . Doesn't it *sound* like what you would expect the moonlight over a peaceful lake to *look* like, Cath, dear?"

I close my eyes and remember visiting my cousins last summer in Spring Lake, New Jersey. I imagine I'm sitting in the moonlight, on the grass in front of Saint Catharine's Church there, looking at the lake.

He stops playing.

"Why'd you stop, Daddy? We were having fun."

"We can have more fun!" he says, smiling and laughing as he crawls under the piano toward me, reaches his arm out, and tickles my stomach.

I hate being tickled. I'm begging him to stop, but he keeps tickling me anyway. It's weird, because I'm laughing but I'm not happy.

He's kissing me now. His saliva is getting all over my face and all over my lips. It tastes yucky and it smells disgusting.

Now he's undoing my play pants. He's pulling them down and licking me down there. I talk to God in my head.

> *Please take my mind to Jesus' house,*
> *where everyone is quiet as a mouse,*
> *and Mary and Joseph*
> *are always kind to children.*

It isn't helping. "Stop it, Daddy! Stop it! I *hate* this!"

"Okay, dear . . . in just a few minutes."

He licks a little bit more and then he starts pulling my pants up, but I kick him.

"I can do my own pants! Leave me alone!"

I run upstairs to the third floor, straight into Mommy's room. She's in bed, still taking her nap. She opens her eyes.

"Mommy! Get up right this minute. *Please.* And *please* go downstairs and stay with Daddy. I *hate* him! He's bothering me! *Please,* promise me you'll stay with him."

"Catherine, what on earth is the matter? How could your father be bothering you? He's been in a very happy mood."

"Just go, Mommy, please!"

She gets up, brushes her hair, and puts her red lipstick on. She adjusts her blouse and skirt, looks at me like she can't figure me out, and heads for the stairs.

"You stay up here for a while," she says.

I watch down the stairwell until I can tell they're both in the music room.

"There's nothing to worry about, dear," my father yells up at me. "Your mother and I are having a lovely time."

I run into my bedroom and get my statue of the Blessed Mother, a change of clothes, and my bubble bath, and then run into the bathroom and close the door. I am safe. I can hear Daddy playing Liszt's *Hungarian Rhapsody,* number 2 in the background. I put Mary on the sink facing the tub, so we can look at each other while I take a bath. I wash all his licking and kissing off me. Mary tells me to. It's a good thing I know about the Mother of God. My teacher, Sister Mary Aquila, told my class that the Blessed Mother can help people who have something bad happen to them. What do children do who don't know about her?

Chapter 3

My father, George Albert Graham, was born on April 23, 1912, in Queens, New York. His mother, whom we children called Nana, climbed out of her bedroom window to marry my grandfather and to spite her parents the night she turned eighteen. Ten months later, Dad was born. Nana named him George after my grandfather, and Albert after her older brother and only sibling. She liked the royal flavor of my father's names. He was her prince.

She didn't like pregnancy and childbirth, however, and even decades later pleaded ignorance of sex. "I didn't know how in the world it happened," she would lament each holiday, referring to becoming pregnant with Dad, "but once I figured it out, I never did *that* again."

Nana loved to brag about how intelligent and good-looking Dad was. "Why, he could go to the cabinet and pick out the sheet music for any one of Chopin's Études by the age of three," she would often say, "and he could play them by the time he started school. He had a genius IQ. He was a child prodigy."

"Just look at what a beautiful set of teeth he has—not a single cavity. There's only one way that happens—breast milk," she proclaimed

19

during one of Mom and Dad's Christmas parties. I was passing around a tray of snacks to the adults. "Your father nursed until he was five years old, anytime, anyplace. Why, he was such a good little fella, he would just come up and open my blouse and suck on my nipples no matter where we were or who was looking."

"Shut your goddamn mouth!" Dad yelled, stomping out of the music room. "Where's Pop? . . . Pop, get Mom to stop all this nonsense talk. I've heard about all I can stand! . . . How about another Manhattan? . . . I'm going in the kitchen and make everyone more cocktails. . . . Shut that goddamn woman up!"

My mother, Catherine Bridget O'Connor, was born on February 20, 1918, in Princeton, New Jersey. Mom, whom everyone called Cate, was named Catherine after both her grandmothers, who had fled the potato famine in Ireland with her grandfathers and settled in Princeton.

My grandmother Bridget—we children called her Ammy—had been training to become a concert pianist when she fell in love with my grandfather, who was working as a director of the family's funeral business. She dropped her career ambition to marry him, but continued playing piano at home and sang in church for weddings and funerals. Mom inherited Ammy's rich first-soprano voice, and her family spent many evenings and holidays gathered around the piano.

Mom had two brothers—Kevin, eight years older, and Sean, eight years younger. She loved them both, but had a special fondness for Uncle Sean.

My parents met during the Christmas holidays at the Inn at Buck Hill Falls, in the Poconos of Pennsylvania. Dad, twenty-four years old and shopping for a mate, spotted Mom at a social and thought she was beautiful. He invited her to play a round of Ping-Pong, then offered to take her back to her room. On the way up the stairs, he leaned over and kissed her. As they would later tell us, this angered Mom, and with the quick reflexes of an eighteen-year-old, she slapped

Dad across the face. This reaction perplexed him. Since he liked her, he felt entitled to kiss her. She felt that he hadn't earned the right. But he continued to pursue Mom, sending her notes and flowers, traveling to New Jersey to take her out to dinner and movies, expressing an interest in her family, and he gradually won her affection. At the time, Mom's father was suffering from a terminal cancer that had begun in his eye. I've often wondered if Dad's studying to become an ophthalmologist was part of what made him attractive to her.

After four years of courtship, Mom and Dad grew impatient to marry. Dad was in medical school and financially dependent on his parents, who threatened to discontinue support if he married before receiving his MD. Determined to gain independence, he wrote several piano pieces and got an appointment to audition at Paramount on 42nd Street in New York City. He hoped his music might be purchased for the score of a Broadway show. By this time, he was an accomplished pianist and had been composing music since high school. Everyone who met him was impressed by his talent. At the close of Dad's audition, the committee accused him of plagiarizing a famous composer. "Who are you, *really?*" they kept asking. "Is this a practical joke? Who sent you here to play a trick on us?" Unfortunately for Dad, Paramount didn't buy his work. He did, however, gain a story that would feed his grandiosity for decades.

Mom and Dad married in 1941, and moved into an apartment near Fort Dix, New Jersey. It was during the war, and Dad was a lieutenant in the Medical Corps, assigned to Fort Tilden General Hospital, where as a new ophthalmologist he worked closely with the neurologist, writing up evaluations. Mom told me she was happy that, unlike many new brides of that era, she wouldn't have to be separated from her husband. Their blissful start came to a shocking halt, however, when Dad had a psychotic break six months later.

He came in to work one day with a bunch of evaluations that were written illegibly, in very large handwriting. None made any sense. When colleagues questioned him, Dad pulled out elaborate plans he had drawn up for airplanes for the U.S. military to design. He explained, as if his description made sense, that the planes were to be built with mirrors, so that the enemy would only see their reflections, and therefore not shoot. The next day, his colleagues drove him to Walter Reed Army Hospital on the pretense that he would be giving an ophthalmology presentation. Once there, he was put in a straitjacket and committed. This event was a family secret for decades.

Because of the state of mental health care at that time, Mom wasn't included in any aspect of treatment though he was hospitalized for over two months. She told me a year before her death that all she could draw from during that time was her commitment to their marriage vows and her loyalty to the Catholic Church, which taught that once you marry you are thereafter responsible for the salvation of your spouse's soul. She decided to do everything she could to keep Dad from "getting so upset" ever again. And she carried on in a state of denial about his mental illness, colluding with the delusions of grandeur he had expressed in a letter to his parents: "It was all a big mistake. The Army is just not used to having people as brilliant as I am in their midst. My disposition board is to call within ten days, and I'm to be honorably discharged because of a nonclassifiable diagnosis of hyperactive energy output unsuited to routine administrative management in the Army."

We will never know the Army's treatment recommendations, however. His inpatient records, along with those of sixteen to eighteen million others who served from 1912 to 1960, were burned in the National Personnel Records Center fire in St. Louis in 1973.

After Dad's discharge from the Army, he and Mom moved into an apartment at 40 Prospect Park West, on the corner of Garfield Place in Park Slope, Brooklyn. Dad opened his ophthalmology practice in a rented office across the street, and Mom, who had a college degree in French, worked as his secretary and was active in the Junior League. They spoke fondly of those days. Mom used to brag about how their first, and for quite some time only, piece of furniture was their black Steinway baby grand. She said it wasn't difficult to sacrifice other things, because she believed Dad's special talents required a fine instrument. It wasn't until just before the onset of her dementia that she confessed the anguished truth to me: She was terrified he would go crazy again. Before I came along, music seemed to be the only thing that could calm him when she could not.

Chapter 4

I'm ten. My mother is in the hospital with pneumonia, so it's up to me to put my little sister and brother to bed. Lucy is seven and Paul, four. Andrew is thirteen. He's in his room with the door closed. He spends a lot of time there. Daddy's at the hospital, either making rounds or visiting Mommy. I don't know which. Probably visiting Mommy. He's lucky he gets to visit. Children aren't allowed.

I'm wearing my nightgown and slippers, ready to put myself to bed, but I miss Mommy too much. I tiptoe into my parents' bedroom and close the door. I go over to her dresser, open her jewelry box, and try on every piece, separately and together. I hope it will make me feel close to her. It does for a minute, and then I start missing her all over again, worse. I cry, very hard.

I kneel beside Mommy's bed and pray to the Sacred Heart, staring at His picture on the wall beside her dresser. I pray with all my might, like Mommy taught me when I was a little girl. I pray that she will get well very soon and come home, but I'm scared she's gonna die and never come home, so I start crying again and keep praying, only now I'm praying for me and my sister and brothers.

I get into Mommy's bed so I can keep looking at the kindness on Jesus' face, and I cry myself to sleep thinking, Please *come home, Mommy,* please. *I'll take good care of you,* promise!

Much later I wake to hear Daddy close the vestibule door. My heart is beating fast. I fell asleep in Mommy's bed and I'm not supposed to be here. I'm scared. He doesn't stop to play piano before he comes upstairs. He might be in a *very bad* mood.

I'm under the covers, listening. He doesn't go into my brothers' and sister's rooms to check on them or kiss them goodnight. Why not?

I hear the floor crack. My heart beats even faster. I keep under the covers and pretend I'm asleep. He's in the closet now, taking his clothes off. He's lonely. He has nobody to talk to. Maybe if I just ask how Mommy is, he'll be able to talk about it and feel better. I sit up, brave-like.

"So, Dad, how's Mommy?" I ask.

I'm sorry I said anything. His face is white, like chalk. And he's bare naked.

"So, you want to know how your mother is, do you? Well, I'll show *you.*"

He yanks at my legs 'til I'm lying down, pulls up my nightgown, rips my underpants off.

He's on top of me now. I leave, but I'm there.

"And *this* is for *you,* Catherine! . . . And *that's* for your *mother!* . . . and *that's* for your *grandmother!* . . . and *that's* for your *other* grandmother! . . . and *that's* for your brothers and that sister of yours!"

My mind jumps over to the picture of the Sacred Heart: into the bloody part, where Jesus' heart is glowing with love even though there's a crown of thorns wrapped around it. I make a song in my head for Jesus:

> *When I grow up this house*
> *will be an*
> *orphanage for*
> *children like me.*

I'll keep them safe
and fed and warm,
never bring them any harm.

He's sitting on the bed, putting my underpants on me. He's talking to me very calmly and gently and kindly. His face isn't white anymore. My whole body is white. And stiff like a dead body in Ammy's freezer in the basement of the funeral home she owns. But I'm not dead. I'm an alive child. And I probably have the face of a crazy person. *His* crazy. He squirted it right into me.

He's lifting me out of the bed. He's talking to me, but I don't hear a word he says. He's carrying me to my own bed in my own room, just like a normal daddy would do to his little girl. But *he's* not a normal daddy.

I'm very relieved to lie in my own bed. I hear him talking again.

"It's okay, Cath. There's nothing to be afraid of. Nothing happened. And if you think anything did, you're wrong. It's all in your imagination, sweetheart. You must never talk about this to anyone. Do you understand? . . . Of course you understand. . . . It's okay, Cath. Everything's fine. Your mother's fine. You're fine. I'm fine. Everything's fine. Goodnight, Cath."

I made a big mistake. I must do everything I can to please him. Forever.

I put my thumb in my mouth and curl up like a tiny baby.

She'll never sleep in her mommy's bed again.

I wake up in my own bed the next morning, but I don't know how I got there. The last thing I remember is tucking Lucy and Paul into their beds.

I smell bacon and toast and I hear Daddy and Andrew and Lucy and Paul in the kitchen, but I don't want to be in their family anymore. I want to be Shirley Temple.

I hum "On the Good Ship Lollipop" while I get dressed in my uniform—a royal blue jumper and white short-sleeved blouse with Peter Pan collar. And then I spend a long time in Mommy's bathroom looking in the mirror, practicing Shirley Temple smiles, pulling the rubber bands out of my hair, brushing out the braids, wetting sections, twisting them and holding them in place with Mommy's bobby pins.

I have long, thick, straight brown hair. Mommy braided it every morning until she got sick. She would pull it real tight and neat looking. I loved the way she did it. Daddy's been fixing it while she's been in the hospital, but I hate the way he does it.

"You don't need your daddy to braid your hair today," I say to the little girl in the mirror. "Today, you're wearing ringlets."

When it's time to leave for school I remove the bobby pins, but I'm afraid that because my hair is still wet, brushing it might take the curl out, so I don't brush it. I skip through the vestibule, convinced that I could win a Shirley Temple look-alike contest. Outside, my hair bounces when I walk. I love that. It's still damp, so my head is chilly, but I figure it'll have plenty of time to dry during my walk to school.

My class has to line up outside the rectory until the morning bell rings. I take my place in line, expecting compliments from my friends and teacher, but I hear the giant-size rosary beads hanging from Sister Annice's belt clang as she waves her hands in the air, pushing the other children aside so she can get to me.

"Miss Graham! Who in God's holy name do you think you are, coming to school like that? Your mother would never let you out of the house looking so ridiculous. Why, if she knew, it would break her heart. You look like an imbecile."

Everyone in the class is staring at me. Who in God's holy name do I think I am? Shirley Temple. I always wanted to be her, and I was almost positive I was. But I'm wrong. I'm not Shirley Temple. I'm not even Catherine Graham. I'm *Miss* Graham. Imbecile.

My heart is beating very fast, like a little animal living inside my stupid, disgusting Miss Graham chest, in my ugly Miss Graham body. Sister Annice is right. Mommy would never let me come to school looking so ridiculous. If she knew—thank God and His Holy Name she doesn't—it really might break her heart. *Poor* Mommy. I want to hide. But I'm right out in public, on the corner of Sixth Street and Eighth Avenue, and I have to stay at school. It's the law.

Mommy just got home from the hospital. I thought she was gonna be all better, but she looks pale and weak. Daddy's holding her hand and telling her to walk up the stairs slowly. I'm standing by the second-floor staircase, watching. They stop at both landings, so she can sit and rest for a few minutes.

Mommy has on her penny loafers, navy-blue knee socks, gray flannel Bermuda shorts, a starched white blouse, and a white wool blazer with a pretty gold, red, and navy blue emblem on it. She smells like Chanel No. 5. She looks like she washed and set her hair and she's wearing makeup, with her pretty red lipstick. She sees me. I start to cry.

"Mommy! Oh, Mommy! You're home! You're home!" We're hugging each other tight.

"Leave your mother alone, Catherine!" Daddy's pushing me away from her. "Now, get in the TV room with your brothers and sister and wait for your mother to sit down before you bother her. She's very weak, and she doesn't need to be exposed to any germs."

I run into the other room with Andrew and Lucy and Paul, but I can't be still. I'm too excited. She walks over to the wing-back chair, her favorite. I run behind, and just as she starts to sit down, I pull it out from under her, thinking I'm making a funny joke for everyone so that we can be one big happy family now that we have our mommy back.

Mommy's on the floor in pain. I hurt her.

"Go straight to your room and stay there, young lady!" Daddy yells.

Lucy and Paul are crying. "You mean and stupid person!" Andrew screams. "You could have, might have paralyzed her!"

I run into my room and close the door. *Imbecile.* I lie down on my bed and cry. Then I get up and turn the crucifix on the wall backward, so Jesus won't have to see me. Who in God's holy name do I think I am? I walk over to the statue of Mary on my bookshelf, and turn her around too. I cry out loud for a long time. And when I stop I hear them all laughing. Mommy is still alive. Not paralyzed. Not going back to the hospital.

I hear her talking to Daddy all stern-like. "No, George, stop." Her voice is loud and almost strong.

"What do you mean, Cate? This girl needs some sense put into her. Who does she think she is?"

"No, I want to talk to her. She didn't mean to hurt me."

"How do you know, Cate?"

"I just do. She was all excited. I've never seen her look that way before. Like she had so many feelings all at once." I love my Mommy's voice.

It seems like hours before Mommy comes to my room. She knocks on my door and opens it at the same time. She sits on my bed slowly, like she's hurting somewhere inside her body.

"I missed you so much, Mommy . . . I missed you so much!" The tears pour out of my eyes like a waterfall.

"And I missed you, Cath." She's crying, too.

Mommy puts my pillow against the headboard, leans back, and then guides my head onto her chest. It's soft and warm. The best in the world.

"I'm sorry, Mommy. I didn't mean to hurt you. My friends and I do that all the time and we just giggle. Nobody gets hurt."

"I know . . . I know, dear. You didn't mean to hurt me. . . . It's okay. . . . But just don't do it again, even with your friends. People can get hurt from that kind of thing."

I kneel beside my bed and say my night prayers. I thank God for Mommy, and I promise to attend daily Mass for the rest of my life. I set my alarm for six o'clock in the morning so I can start tomorrow.

We live seven blocks from St. Saviour's Catholic Church and Mass is at six thirty. I get up, wash my face, brush my teeth, put on my uniform, and I'm out the door by six fifteen. I'm scared to be walking the streets alone, especially when I see a strange man come toward me, but I hold my head up and walk fast, praying all the way that my guardian angel will protect me.

I love being at Mass. I sit in the back of church where I can see everything and everyone, especially the nuns. They sit in front of the statue of the Blessed Virgin. I wonder what mysterious holy things go on behind the big iron door that leads to their convent. I pray for a vocation so that I can become a nun myself one day and find out.

Mass is in Latin. I love knowing that the same Mass is being said in one language, all over the world: *Agnus Dei, qui tollis peccata mundi, miserere nobis. Agnus Dei, qui tollis peccata mundi, miserere nobis. Agnus Dei, qui tollis peccata mundi, dona nobis pacem.* I imagine children like me, spiritual pen pals, attending Mass in other countries like Brazil and France and Ireland.

When I leave church and head home for breakfast, the streets are busy with people going to work. My mind is filled with stories of love and hope, from the Gospel and Epistle. I believe that Jesus is in my heart and in my body because I received Holy Communion. I feel safe.

Chapter 5

I'm twelve. Mom and I are putting our packages down on the dining room table. I hear Dad coming up the stairs from seeing his afternoon patients. He stands in the hallway and stares at us. He's tall, with dark, wavy hair, black and silver–rimmed glasses, and he's wearing a navy blue pin-striped suit, red and blue striped tie, and black wingtips. Just because he was the ophthalmologist for the Brooklyn Dodgers and is on staff at several hospitals, he thinks he's such a fancy doctor. But I know he's really not. He's really a slob. His office is a mess. There are books and journals piled high on his desk, next to it, and behind it. Papers and prescription pads with his scribbling on them are scattered around, too. Some of the nuns at school and a couple of my friends are his patients, and it's so embarrassing that they see it. Mom says people know it's a sign of his genius and for me to remember how much his patients love him, that every day they wait for hours to see him, because they know that once they're in his office, he'll take special care of them and spend as much time answering their questions as they need.

Now she's telling him what a big day it is, that I have just gotten my first bra. "Stand up straight and turn around so Daddy can see how pretty you look in your new bra, Catherine," she says.

I think this is weird. I'm sure none of my friends have to show their fathers when they get their first bras. Mom reads too much Taylor Caldwell. I wish she'd get over this "dear and glorious physician" thing, this idea that just because Dad's a doctor it's normal for him to be so interested in my body.

"Why do I have to? Maybe I just won't," I say to her, looking at her like I wish she were dead. And I do. I wish she'd drop dead right in front of me.

"Don't give me that sass," she says, "and stand up straight and tall for your father."

I hate her guts, but I do what she tells me to anyway because I want to go outside with my friends. The faster I obey, the faster I can leave.

Dad's looking me over. I don't think he's noticing the new blue and white striped blouse I picked out, or the monogram on the collar Mom treated me to. No, he's looking straight at my breasts, and it feels as if I don't even *have* a blouse on.

Later that night I feel his hands touching my breasts under my nightgown. His hands are warm and gentle, and I like how they feel. I'm sleeping when the pleasure awakens me, and I sense him kneeling beside my bed. I wonder if I'm just dreaming—if girls have accidental dreams like this about their fathers sometimes. But then I hear his voice: "Nothing's happening, Cath, and if you think there's anything happening, then you're crazy."

I'm glad I'm not crazy. I just had a weird dream.

It's Valentine's Day, time for dinner and fun at our house.
Dad loves celebrations, and what could be better than a day to celebrate love? Andrew is in a play at school and they're rehearsing, so he won't be home until later, but the rest of us are here. I helped Mom set the table

with a Valentine's Day tablecloth, matching napkins, and plates. They don't match the earth colors in the design of birds, branches, and flowers on the wallpaper of our formal dining room, but Mom doesn't seem to care about that tonight. She doesn't seem to care that she and Dad aren't having their usual cocktail hour before dinner, either, and neither does Dad, even though he's been telling her, ever since she had pneumonia, that she needs a cocktail every night for medicinal purposes.

Mom's dressed up in her white blouse, navy blue skirt, pearl necklace and earrings. Dad's wearing his glen plaid suit, a red and white striped bow tie, and he's carrying a bag of gifts. Every room of the house smells delicious. We're having a rib roast, roasted potatoes, carrots, and peas for dinner.

After we seat ourselves, Dad walks around the table and kisses the back of each of our heads just like he does every other night, only tonight, after the kiss, he places a big heart-shaped box of assorted chocolates on each of our plates. Lucy's is first. She's next to Mom on Mom's right, and she's sitting up especially straight. "Thank you, Father dear," she says, smiling sweetly, and then looks at me. I stare back, a blank stare, to make eye contact with her without letting on to Mom or Dad that something's up between us. Earlier, she and Paul and I decided to be on our best behavior tonight, hoping Dad would stay in a good mood, because for the last five days he's been in bed and we weren't even allowed to ask why.

Mom is next in line and Dad hands her a little red box tied with a white ribbon and bow. "The best things come in small packages, dear," he says in a jolly tone.

She sighs, "You shouldn't have. . . . " But when she opens it—a 14 carat gold pin of several hearts spaced in a circular pattern, each with one pearl in it—she squeals, "Oh . . . this is beautiful, George . . . just beautiful . . . thank you, dear!"

"Our love is a pearl of great price, sweetheart," he says with a chuckle as he leans over to kiss her on the lips.

Next, he turns toward Paul, who is on Mom's left, next to me. Paul, too, says, "Thank you, Father dear," as Dad places the box on his plate. Then, with raised eyebrows and a smile, he looks across the table at Lucy and holds his candy-filled heart up for her to see. "Mmm . . . " he adds. Paul is in first grade now, tall and skinny, not at all like the chubby baby he used to be, but he's still my favorite.

Dad kisses my head, placing the last heart-shaped box in front of me. "Catherine Girl, Happy Valentine's Day, sweetheart," he says, patting my shoulder, then sits at the head of the table—to the left of me, and opposite Mom. He spreads a napkin on his lap, and that's our cue that we can begin eating.

Toward the end of dinner Dad does magic tricks with his hands. He has double-jointed thumbs, so the contortions he can create are pretty funny. Paul and Lucy are in hysterics laughing, and I'm clearing the table for Mom, so that we can get the kitchen cleaned up and gather around the piano.

Lucy excuses herself to go to her room and study for a test, and Paul, Dad, and I move downstairs into the music room.

The music room is large, paneled in a dark wood. There's a bay window overlooking our small back yard, and a dark green tile–inlaid fireplace to the left of the bay window. Above the mantel hangs a print framed in black and gold, of hunters riding horses, with their hound dogs following. Dad's ebony baby grand is along the wall opposite the fireplace and there are two chairs arranged near the piano. Dad's tape recorder is on a table to the left of him, and a professional microphone stands on the ledge of the piano to the right of the sheet music.

Paul pulls up a chair and puts in his first request, for me to sing "Somewhere Over the Rainbow." Dad plays the introductory chords, while I, fascinated by his talent, watch his short, stubby fingers strike the keys. Mom often says it's a wonder he can perform eye surgery with those fingers. I move into position, projecting my voice into the mike, which Dad has adjusted at just the right angle, facing me. At the end of the song, Paul claps and cheers.

"It sounds lovely, Cath . . . quite lovely," Mom says, coming in from behind me and sitting in the chair next to Paul.

"What would you like to sing next, dear heart?" Dad asks, glancing at me while continuing to play chords.

"How about 'Someone to Watch over Me,' Dad?"

"Ah, yes, dear . . . lovely . . . you take the lead, and I'll follow . . . remember, you're the singer; I'm only the accompanist."

My heart, filled with delight, blossoms into song: "There's a somebody I'm longing to see, I hope that he turns out to be, someone to watch over me. . . . "

Afterward, Mom suggests that we sing our duet. She and Dad both love jazz and Mom is a big fan of Ella Fitzgerald, so they put together an arrangement of one of Ella's songs as a duet for Mom and me to sing: "The End of a Beautiful Friendship."

"Ah, listen to that vibrato," Dad comments, as Mom starts the song. She's got a lot of rhythm, and she expresses it in the way she sways her body with the music and belts out the melody: "That was the end of a beautiful friendship, it ended a moment ago; that was the end of a beautiful friendship I know for my heart told me so." I join in a little later, because my voice is higher and softer: "We were always like sister and brother, until tonight when we looked at each other. That was the end of a beautiful friendship, and just the beginning of love."

After our duet, Mom excuses herself to get Lucy and Paul ready for bed, and I flip through Dad's music books until I find "You've Gotta Have Heart," from Rogers and Hammerstein's *Damn Yankees.* The lyrics are perfect for the occasion, because I'm worried about Dad. He's happy and fun tonight, but when he's in his dark moods, like last week, I'm afraid he'll kill one of us or himself. And I feel sorry for his patients, his secretary, and the ladies at his answering service. Sometimes they call the house to see where he is and Mom tells us to say that the doctor is not in and hang up, immediately. I hate it; it's so mean. And I'm surprised that his patients come back at all.

"Here, Dad, play this." I spread the sheet music before him, and he's playing the introduction before I've even finished my sentence. Using all the peppy feelings I can find in my love for him, I sing the lyrics with expression: *"You've gotta have heart, all you really need is heart. When the odds are saying you'll never win, that's when the grin should start. You've gotta have hope . . . mustn't sit around and mope. . . . Mister, you can be a hero of course, just keep that old horse before the cart. . . "*

Afterward, when I'm upstairs getting ready for bed, I hear Dad playing a medley of Broadway tunes downstairs, with Mom singing along. I nestle under the covers smiling, and drift off to sleep.

Weeks later, everyone is asleep except Dad. He hasn't been home for days, at least when any of us are awake and would see him. Mom's been sneaking gulps of beer during the afternoons and while she's making dinner. She hides it behind a bowl in the kitchen cabinet, above the sink. She's getting sloppy, and she goes to bed early. Whenever one of us asks where Dad is, she just says, "Your father is making rounds at the hospital," which sounds like a lie to me. I wonder if he's so mad at all of us for some reason he hasn't told us about yet, that he won't come home until he knows he won't kill us, or if maybe he's in love with another woman.

He wakes me up and turns on the light. He has on a suit and a tie.

"Hello, Catherine. There's nothing to worry about, dear. Everything's fine."

Oh, no. I'm doomed. The words are nice, but his voice is very low, like he's furious angry. And he's squinting, sneering. His face looks like there's a devil living inside him.

He takes off his tie. His suit jacket. His shirt. His pants. His sleeveless undershirt. He only has on his drawers, and he's getting into bed with me.

I was wearing my pink flannel nightgown while I was sleeping, but I don't have anything on now. I don't know how I got this way. All

I know is I'm in bed, paralyzed, but I'm over on the other side of the room, too, and Dad's talking.

"Nothing's happening, Catherine. Nothing's happening. And if you think anything is happening then you're crazy."

"I know, Dad. You're right. I'm not crazy. I know nothing's happening." I don't want to be crazy. *I don't want to be like you!*

He's on top of me. If I concentrate on Jesus—very, very hard—this will all be over. It won't be over fast, because if it were going to be over fast it would *be* over, but if I *concentrate,* he will finish. He's putting his thing between my legs where my hair is. His thing is very warm. Hot, now. And slimy. He's gushing it around.

Maybe if I look at the mirror it will help—the one over my dressing table. He bought me that dressing table when we decorated my room, so I could play beauty parlor. And he let me pick out any wallpaper I wanted. I picked this one—pink, with ballerinas on it. I'm not really the ballerina type, but I picked it and I like it.

He's getting dressed now. It won't be long 'til he's out of the room. He already has his shirt on. It's filled with pens and his ophthalmoscope. They look like they're gonna fall out. I wish they would—on his stocking feet. I wish his brains would fall out, too.

He's actually looking in the mirror to do his bow tie. And using my hairbrush to fix his hair all dapper-like. How professional of him! He wants to go right upstairs to his wife and look like he just got in from making rounds at the hospital. And that's just what she'll think. She'll never know about this. Nobody will. Go ahead upstairs to your wife, Dad. I hate your guts.

I feel guilty for hating him, and I hate her too. She says I'd be a lovely girl if I wasn't so angry and disrespectful much of the time. I take my glow-in-the-dark rosary beads out from under my pillow. I'm fascinated with their pure light. It soothes me. I want to be pure and holy. Pure and holy and kind and respectful. In the morning all I can remember is praying the rosary and asking Our Lady to help me become more like her.

Chapter 6

It's a pretty spring day. I'm in my room doing things—
twelve-year-old things, puttering—arranging my hair bands, lining
up my Nancy Drew books, sharpening my pencils, and I'm thinking
about my science class. Sister Daniel teaches it, and she's *so* weird.
She's always yelling at the boys, "Boys, your mind is where your motion is! Stop that, or I'll tell the girls what you're doing!" We know
what they're doing. They're scratching their balls. I figure some of
them can't help it. They're growing. Maybe their balls hurt like my
breasts did right before I needed a bra, or maybe they get uncomfortable in their underwear. Some of the boys do it just for the attention,
just to show us girls they have a thing. And some of them are just plain
sleazeballs. They want to go all the way, and they wouldn't even care if
they got a girl pregnant.

Not Peter McCall. He's *so* nice. He sits next to me and I *really*
like him. He never puts his hands down there, and his face gets red
when Sister Daniel says that, like he's so embarrassed he could just
die. I know exactly how he feels, because that's how I look when my
friends see Mom drunk. Peter's the tallest boy in the class and the

shiest and the best athlete. We crack jokes together, and yesterday I got in trouble for laughing so hard. I didn't care. It was worth it. I think he likes me. I noticed him peeking at me, and at the end of class he said, "Your hair is pretty, Catherine." His face got red again when he said it, and he had to swallow in the middle of one of the words. My insides lit up like it was Christmas morning, and I smiled and said, "Thanks" in a low, sweet voice I didn't recognize.

Dad just came into my room, whistling. It's a Saturday. No office hours. He's wearing a short-sleeved white shirt and khaki shorts, white socks, and penny loafers with shiny new pennies in them. He smells like Old Spice cologne, and his hair is slicked back like Cary Grant's, but he actually looks more like Spencer Tracy.

"Catherine Girl," he says, "we are home alone today, so there's no reason to close the door." He leaves the door open, rubs his hands together. I stand there and look at him. Why are we home alone? Where are Mom and Andrew and Lucy and Paul? My heart thumps in my chest. Something's up. I wonder what.

"Today's a special day, Catherine dear. Today I'm going to give you a biology lesson."

Biology lesson? I don't want a biology lesson. But he loves biology, so I'd better pretend I'm interested.

"Do what I say, Catherine, and there won't be any trouble." Trouble means he might kill me. The best thing to do is to hang on his every word as if they're jewels flowing from his mouth. He likes it when I do that.

"Now, take your clothes off and lie down on your bed. I'm going to teach you some basic anatomy, sweetheart."

I take off my white sleeveless blouse and my Maidenform bra; my brown, orange, and yellow madras plaid shorts; and my white cotton underpants with the little blue buds on them. I'm relieved I don't have my period; I don't have one of those belts on, and a pad.

He gets into bed next to me.

"Catherine Girl, you are very special, and I'm going to teach you about all the special parts."

I hate the way he says I'm special.

"You're becoming a woman, and I'm going to teach you all the things a woman needs to know."

I don't want to learn what a woman needs to know. I don't think I'm gonna like being a woman. Mom's a woman. She doesn't act like she thinks it's so great.

But something feels cozy and warm. His skin. That's what it is—his skin against mine. And he's talking in a soft voice. That's sort of nice.

Uh-oh. He's holding his thing.

"This is my penis, and this is the head of my penis . . . and this is my scrotum . . . and this is my pubic hair. . . . "

He's rolling over. He's touching me, pointing.

"And this is your pubic hair."

"Thank you, Daddy, for teaching me the name of that hair. I haven't had it very long, and I didn't know it had a special name." I'm lying. My friend Jill told me about it one day on the way home from school.

"I'm going to teach you what mommies and daddies do to make babies. You've been curious about that for a long time."

"No!" I protest. My heart is racing. He's not smiling any more. He looks mean. It feels like he's turning into the devil.

"Oh, yes, dear. Don't be frightened. All good fathers teach their daughters these things. How else would they acquire the proper knowledge?"

"I don't know. I don't want to know." It's no use. He's getting on top of me anyway, and he's pointing his penis at my pubic hair. At least I can yell.

"No! . . . Stop it! . . . Get off me! . . . Stop it!"

His hands are pinning me down. I'm wiggling and squirming, fighting him with every ounce of strength I have.

"Stop it! . . . Leave me alone!"

He slaps me across the face.

"You be quiet, young lady!"

I'm still screaming, even though his hand is covering my mouth. I'll never stop. I don't care *what* he says.

He takes his hand off my mouth, pulls out a knife, flips it open, and holds the sharp edge across my throat.

"You keep your mouth quiet, young lady, or I will slit your throat. Do you understand? . . . And no one will believe I did it. Everyone will think you committed suicide. Think of what that will do to your mother." He smiles. "Think of how she will feel her whole life that Catherine, the daughter who gets up early and goes to Mass every morning, ended her own life. Think of how painful that will be for her, Catherine. Am I making myself clear?"

"Yes, Father. Please put the knife down."

He's putting it on the other pillow, I think, but I'm not sure. My heart is beating too hard to be sure of anything, except that he might kill me.

"Now, shall we proceed, Catherine dear?"

"Yes, Father."

"Stare at the mantelpiece, Catherine. You're a smart girl. I see you concentrate on your schoolwork. Concentrate on the mantel."

I look at the mantel. It's painted white and plain, except for a design of tied ribbons formed with plaster along the front. I like the tile inlays below it better. They surround the fireplace and extend in front of it on the floor. A pretty, deep-blue edge of each tile lightens into a soft shade of baby blue in the center. Blue is my favorite color. I stare at the tiles. I concentrate on their beauty.

But he's hurting my hole, and I think it might be bleeding. It feels warm and creamy. And my legs are tingling, like the blood in them is clogged and can't get through to the rest of me. And I can hardly breathe.

He's getting up now, and going in the bathroom off my room, on the other side of my night table.

Here he comes back with a wet washcloth in his hand. He has his drawers on. He leans over and washes me off.

"There now," he says. "You must never tell anyone about this."

He stuffs the washcloth into his pocket and pulls out the knife, opens it. Sunlight reflects on the blade.

"Am I making myself *crystal* clear?" He looks back and forth between the blade and my eyes. He's snickering. He has made himself crystal clear but I don't tell him, because my vocal cords are not working.

"Now my advice to you, Catherine, is that you pull the covers over your head, and roll over and go to sleep for a long nap and forget anything ever happened, dear. Just think about the mantel, and remember how heartbroken your mother would be to find out that you had committed suicide."

I would *never* kill myself. I want to grow up, and get *out* of this house, and make something *good* of my life.

I pray.

> *Hail Mary, full of grace*
> *the Lord is with thee.*
> *Blessed art thou among women*
> *and blessed is the fruit of thy womb, Jesus.*
>
> *Holy Mary, Mother of God,*
> *pray for us sinners now,*
> *and at the hour of our death.*
> *Amen.*

You're the only one who helps me, Mother, I say to Our Lady.

I put my clothes on and go into the bathroom where the memory of his biology lesson disappears. All I can think about is Peter McCall. I want to be pretty for Peter. I brush my hair for one hundred strokes and then one hundred strokes again. I want it to be beautiful. I want it to shine.

Chapter 7

It is a very good day. Mom's not drinking. She's wearing a flowered blouse, royal blue linen shorts, white socks, and white Keds. She has red lipstick on and her dark brown hair is held back with two bobby pins, and curled. She's even wearing Chanel No. 5 perfume. I love days like this.

"Come with me," she says, smiling. She's grabbing my hand and leading me to the third floor. "I've been saving something for you in my dresser drawer."

The dark shades are drawn because it's August, but her room is still beautiful. The mantel, tiles surrounding the fireplace, and molding around the room are a deep green, and the background of the wallpaper is ivory, covered with large bouquets of roses. Mom and Dad ordered it from England.

"What? How come you never told me about it?" I ask, following her.

"I wanted to wait until I thought you were old enough to wear and take care of jewelry, Cath. Some friends of ours gave this to you as a gift on your christening day, because St. Catherine Laboure, the saint whom Our Lady instructed to make these medals, is your patron saint. It's called a miraculous medal, and it's very beautiful." She looks through her top dresser drawer and pulls out a small, old-looking box. My heart feels very happy. She opens the box, and there's a tiny blue-velvet envelope inside. "I thought that one day it might become very important to you, so I wanted to make sure it didn't get lost. Our Lady has promised that those who wear this medal will receive special graces," she says.

I can hardly stand still, but I feel like I'm in the presence of the Blessed Sacrament, so I try to behave as if I'm in church. She opens the envelope and hands me the medal. It's small and oblong, deep blue, with a thin gold outline.

"You're almost a teenager now. I think it's time for you to have this, Cath. But wait until we can get a good chain before you wear it."

I carry it to my room, close the door, find a safety pin in my top dresser drawer, and pin the medal to the inside of my bra. I can't wait to receive the great graces, and I want them to spill into my breasts. I'm privately beginning to love them, and I need my heavenly Mother to keep them safe.

Mom and Dad later give me a gold chain. I wear the medal around my neck all the time, and when Mom's drunk I rub it like an Aladdin's lamp and beg Our Lady to help me be okay. To help my whole family be okay.

The world outside of my family is becoming more important to me, especially the world of boys, and Peter McCall in particular. We're in eighth grade now, and our crowd of friends from school plans boy-girl parties almost every Saturday night. The first kissing game starts early in the evening: Everyone picks a dance partner, somebody flicks off the lights, and you kiss the one you're with. But none of the guys kiss me, and they rarely even ask me to dance.

"So, Catherine, how's it going?" they ask me from the sidelines. "Where's Pete?"

I shrug my shoulders and smile, holding back tears. My girl-friends do some detective work for me. "The guys say you're Pete's girl, and they'd never betray him 'cause they respect him so much," they tell me.

I like that he's so highly thought-of by his friends, and I'm excited to learn that they consider me his girl, but I leave each party depressed because he never shows up; the only time I get to see him is at school. What's the fun in that, after I've spent hours primping, longing to be held in his arms, curious about what it would be like to kiss him? Unlike some girls in my class, I have had no experience with boys, and I don't want to be left out. I also wonder if the guys are lying. Maybe they think there's something weird about me, something so ugly that no boy will ever want to kiss me.

Dad picks me up from the parties at eleven o'clock, before the more serious games start. I beg him to let me stay, but he says trouble starts when it gets close to midnight. In a way, I'm grateful to have a good excuse to leave, because the next day, when my friends huddle together and talk about the guys tongue-kissing them and touching their breasts, it sounds so impure, so sinful, and dangerous. What if they accidentally got pregnant? And besides, I think I might have a vocation to the religious life. I want to dedicate my life to God.

Dad's in my room. He has my desk drawer open. I walk up behind him, but he doesn't hear me. He doesn't even know I'm home. My body tenses, teeth clench. What's he snooping around for?

Oh, no. He's reading the period chart Mom gave me. It's none of his business.

"Hi, Dad!" I make it sound cheery. I'm trying to act like Patty Duke, the star of my favorite TV show. I hope that if I act cute and carefree he'll get out of my room and leave my stuff alone. But he doesn't. He stays.

"Hello, Catherine Girl. Mother tells me your stomach has been upset lately. Is that true, dear?"

"Yes, it's true, but what are you looking at my chart for?" My voice is monotone.

"I see here that you had no period in October, and so far you're late for November. It's nothing to be worried about, dear. Irregularities like this are common for girls your age." He turns around and walks out the door.

The next day Mom checks me out of school.

"We're going over to your father's office, dear," she says, glancing at me out of the corner of her eye.

"Why, what's going on?"

"You need a very simple procedure. Your father says it's nothing to worry about, and he can do it himself right in his office, so you won't feel uncomfortable."

At this time, Dad's office is in the first floor of an apartment building, 35 Garfield Place, on the corner of Prospect Park West, only a block from our house. His secretary is on vacation, and the office is dark and spooky.

"There you are, sweetheart. We have the whole office to ourselves," he says. He's wearing scrubs, even the hat over his hair. "Nobody will disturb us," he continues, in a jolly tone, "and your own mother and father will take care of you." He drools slightly, like a dog awaiting a chunk of beef.

He's leading me into the back room. "Just lie down here on this table, and your mother will hold your hand."

"I didn't know you had an examining table in your office. What do you need it for? I thought your patients just sat in that special chair while you tried lenses on them."

"Well, that's true, dear. But the doctor who used to rent this office had left it. I knew it would come in handy, just like those wonderful pictures on the wall. Aren't they fascinating, Cath?"

No. The three framed prints on the wall next to the examining table are scary: a dentist pulling a man's tooth, a surgeon performing an appendectomy, an obstetrician performing a caesarean. The doctors look like they're concentrating on what they're doing. But the patients remind me of corpses—except for the guy getting his tooth pulled, and he looks like he's screaming.

My heart beats very fast. I look to Mom for reassurance, while Dad goes into the other room to get something. She's wearing a yellow shirtwaist dress—Dad's favorite—and she's standing erect, like she feels important, but I smell beer on her breath.

"Everything will be fine, Catherine. I'm right here with you," she says. "Now let me help you take your clothes off, and strap your legs into these stirrups."

"Stirrups? Stirrups are for riding horses. Why are they on this examining table?"

"It's very common, Cath, dear. Whenever a woman gets examined she has to put her legs in stirrups, and you're becoming a woman."

"Well, I don't like it, and I don't want to."

"I know, dear. I don't like it either, but it's the best way. Your father's just going to see if you're developing properly, that's all. It will only take a couple of minutes."

"Does this have anything to do with my period chart?"

"No, why would that have anything to do with it? Daddy just learned about a new procedure for girls your age that he felt was very important for you to have, that's all."

"None of my friends had a *procedure*. Why do I have to?"

"Maybe their parents don't know about it, Cath. I trust your father 100 percent about these things. He's brilliant when it comes to practicing medicine."

"I don't care. I don't want to be here. How come he's wondering if I'm developing properly? What's wrong with me?"

He's back in the room. "You calm down, young lady, or I'll give you a shot in the behind that'll calm you down, and it will sting so hard you'll wish I hadn't."

"I *hate* you!" I cross my arms and make my body stiff. I squint my eyes, staring at him.

"We'll not have that," he says, adjusting his glasses. "Cate, get over here and help me strap her arms to the table."

"Yes, George." Mom tries to fasten the straps, not looking at me, but I squirm and swing my arms, putting up a fight.

"No! No! *Please! Why* are you doing this, Mom? Take me to another doctor, *please!* Make him stop. Get me out of here. My stomach doesn't hurt anymore. I want to go back to school!"

They have me strapped. Mom's standing behind me now; Dad's preparing the needle. "Mom . . . " I say through my sobs.

"It's okay, Catherine. Your father is far more intelligent than any other doctor we could take you to. It's best that he do it. I'll be right here, watching. We love you, dear."

Was it hours, or only a moment ago? I don't know. I'm wrapped in a blanket and my parents are leading me up the stairs of our stoop. I'm yawning, very sleepy.

Mom covers me with more blankets when we get to my room, and tucks me into bed. Dad brings me pills every few hours. I sleep a lot for a few days, and have my period, with big balls of blood in it. I guess that's what was wrong with my development. I never had big balls of blood before, and I was supposed to.

It's the night before I go back to school, and the phone rings. I answer it; it's Ammy. Mom rushes behind me. "Don't say *anything* about being home from school," she whispers. "Your grandmother doesn't need to know about it all."

"I can't wait to see you, Ammy," I say, speaking of the plans for her to come for Christmas. "Here, let me give Mom the phone. I have to study for exams."

I run into my bedroom, close the door, lie down on my bed, and stare at the ceiling. I hate being only thirteen. I wish I were old enough to leave. I'd pack my suitcase right now and go live with Ammy.

I roll over to stare out the window. Rays of moonlight dance across the radiator, just below the sill. They remind me of summer. I get to spend two weeks visiting Ammy next summer, and I'll love every minute of being with her. She would never let anyone hurt me.

Chapter 8

*Summer has finally arrived, and Ammy and I are spend-*ing two weeks together at the Tremont Hotel in Sea Girt, New Jersey.

"I'm worried about your mother," Ammy tells me one afternoon, while we sit in rockers on the front porch of the hotel. "She's gotten very heavy and she doesn't look happy. What's going on, Catherine? Do you know?"

"No, Ammy, I don't." I can't tell her that she's right, that Mom is never happy anymore, that she gets drunk a lot.

Ammy rocks, resting her freckled hand on the arm of the chair. I stare at her piano fingers and red nail polish, then notice *The Wall Street Journal* folded on her lap. She teaches me about the stock market each day, but I don't concentrate on what she says about the numbers. Instead, I memorize her kind brown eyes behind wire-rimmed glasses, her thin grey hair with the blue rinse in it, her pearl earrings, her big nose, the movement of her mouth full of the false teeth she leaves in a glass near the sink at night. She breathes through her mouth a lot and it makes a slight whistling noise. This morning I could hear it, but this afternoon I can't. All I can hear is the sound of waves hitting the shore across the street, and the green awnings above us rippling from the sea breeze.

"Take a deep breath of that ocean air," she tells me. "It's good for you." I love the smell of the ocean, and I love the smell of Ammy's house, even the funeral parlors in it. But I don't like how Mom smells anymore.

One day as I walked up to the second floor on my way in from school, I heard banging in the kitchen, and Mom's voice, "Ah, hell's bells! . . . hell's bells!" Slam! Bang!

"Mom?" I called, trying to get in. "Is something the matter?"

The door swung open and the stench of beer mixed with Easy-Off oven cleaner smacked me in the face. "Oh, Catherine? . . . her royal highness? . . . how nice to see you, dear," she said, standing before me with dirty bare feet, wearing a yellow and orange housecoat with snaps down the front, half of which were open—the top half.

Her large breasts were stuffed into a dingy bra, her black hair looked almost as greasy as the inside of the oven, her eyes were bloodshot, and she was weaving back and forth. Three beer cans sat on grimy paper towels in the sink, and another one rolled along the kitchen floor. Two lighted Chesterfield cigarettes were in view—one in an ashtray on the table and one resting on the edge of the yellow formica countertop.

"Here, *you* take over, dear . . . you're such a *competent* child," she said, then weaved up the stairs, and collapsed into bed.

I walked down the hall. Lucy and Paul were watching TV, each holding a package of saltines. Paul's face was wet with tears. Lucy was trying to cheer him up.

It would break Ammy's heart to know this.

One night, Andrew called a meeting in his room, for the four of us children. He sat in a desk chair in front of us. I noticed he had a lot of acne, but he was a cute teenage guy. He looked a little like Ricky Nelson, but he didn't have a girlfriend yet. Or at least he hadn't told us, if he did. I sat on the floor in front of him; Lucy to my right, and Paul to my left.

"It's time to do something about Mom's drinking," he said. We all shook our heads. Lucy scooted closer to him, head tilted, eyes fixed on Andrew.

Paul turned to me. "Can we, Cath?" he asked.

I held his hand. "I hope so."

"The question is," continued Andrew, "just what exactly *can* we do?"

"Patty's mother went away to learn how to stop drinking," I said. "But her father took her mother there and our father would never do that."

"Well, maybe he would, Cath. One of us should talk to him. How about you?"

"No, I'm too scared," I said, feeling a pit in my stomach. "You do it, Andrew."

He shook his head no. "Let's take a vote," he suggested. "Everyone in favor of Catherine speaking to Dad, raise your hand." Three hands went up; three pairs of eyes stared at me.

"Tonight would be the perfect night, Cath," he continued. "Mom's already in bed, and Dad's been in a very good mood . . . go ahead down to his office. We'll wait here, and you can come back and tell us what happens. If you're not back in a half hour we'll all come down and get you."

I grabbed my rosary beads, put them in the pocket of my shorts, then went straight downstairs. I wanted to get it over with, the sooner the better.

Outside his office, I kissed the crucifix on my rosary, made the sign of the cross and just stood there, waiting for my heart to calm down, which it didn't, so I finally knocked.

"Yes, who's there?" Dad asked.

"It's me, Dad."

"Oh, how delightful; come on in, sweetheart—come sit down, Catherine Girl."

Dad sat behind his large mahogany desk, piled high with medical journals, textbooks, prescription pads, and samples of drugs. He was still wearing his suit and tie. On the floor on either side of him were more journals and books—some closed, some open, with sheets of paper strewn about.

"What can I do for you, Catherine?" he asked. His blue green eyes were a soft color, more blue than green, welcoming.

I had a lump in my throat and my chest hurt, but I could still speak.

"The four of us had a meeting and we decided I should come talk to you about something important."

"By all means, sweetheart." He smiled. "What is it?" His voice was soft. It sounded caring, like he must sound with his patients.

"Well, Mom has been getting drunk a lot lately, and we thought you should know, because you can do something about it."

"Is that so, sweetheart? And what do you think I can do?"

"Well, Patty's father took her mother to a place called a sanitarium, and they're teaching her how to stop drinking."

"Is that so, Catherine?" His eyes were losing their softness.

"Yes, Dad. It's a wonderful place. It would be so good for Mom."

The kindness in his face disappeared. He tilted his head, took off his glasses, chewed on a temple. "And what about people who really want to drink, who really need it to get through the day?" he asked, eyes squinting and hard, like marbles.

"Yes, that's what this place is for. It's for people who really need it to get through the day. They teach them how to not need it anymore."

"Is that so, dear?" His tone was hostile; his eyes, turned icy.

I shook my head yes.

"Well, isn't this just like you, Catherine, selfish girl that you are?" he asked, grimacing. My heart raced. My face froze, eyes focused on him. "Are you thinking of your mother? Of what *she* wants? No . . . you have your own agenda, and it's a totally self-serving one. You're a very selfish young lady. . . . Get *out* of my office and don't come back down. . . . Do you hear me? And the same goes for those brothers and that sister of yours. . . . Out! . . . And I forbid any of you to ever discuss this again. Is that clear?"

"Yes, Father," I said through my tears, turning to leave.

The next night he came home from making rounds at the hospital with gifts for Mom: a bouquet of red roses, a bottle of gin, a six-pack of beer, and a pack of cigarettes.

Ammy rocks back and forth, staring into space. My eyes rest on her swollen ankles, her legs, which are much thinner this summer, her face. How can I tell her anything true about Mom? I want to cheer her up, not break her heart. And I'm worried about her. Mom and Dad gave her a carton of nutrition drinks when they dropped me off. Dad told her to take two cans a day in addition to her regular meals, but she hardly ever opens them and when she does, she throws them away while they're still half-full. She's been weak a lot while I've been here, and she's all humped over.

"Ever since she came home from the hospital after that pneumonia," Ammy continues, "your mother hasn't been herself. She tells me everything's fine, but I don't believe her."

"I don't know what to say, Ammy," I jump in.

"I know you don't, dear. It wasn't fair to ask you. Your grandmother is just a worrier sometimes." She pats my leg and smiles at me, then coughs and pulls away to reach for a handkerchief.

"Why are you coughing so much, Ammy?" I ask, voice quivering. "This morning you had a long coughing spell, and then during lunch you had one, too."

"I'm sorry, dear. The emphysema is a bit worse. I feel very old today," she says, eyes turning from me to the Goodyear blimp flying overhead. "And I just keep getting thinner. . . . I don't understand why."

I turn away, trying to swallow my tears.

That afternoon, while Ammy plays solitaire in the card room, I write a letter to Mom and tell her I think Ammy might be dying. I don't know what else to do. Maybe Mom can help.

Within weeks Ammy's in the hospital in a coma, and not expected to live. She has cancer in her lungs, even though she never smoked a cigarette.

Mom, Dad, Andrew, Lucy, Paul, and I all stay at her house, and one evening when Mom comes home from visiting hours she asks us to kneel in the living room and pray the rosary together. I'm relieved, because we've never done this before and it's a very good idea. Ammy needs our prayers, and the nuns always say that "the family that prays together stays together." Maybe if we pray hard enough Ammy won't die.

Ammy's living room is pretty. The walls are light, and there are flowered drapes in soft colors: green, lilac, pale yellow. We kneel by the wall opposite her baby grand piano. We gather in a circle, and Mom begins with the first Sorrowful Mystery, the Agony in the Garden, when the phone rings. She hesitates, then walks to the phone. "Hello, O'Connor residence," she says, looking straight ahead. Her hand covers the receiver. "It's the hospital," she whispers. "Mother's nurse is getting on." Andrew, Lucy, Paul, and I look at each other . . . everything feels spooky.

Mom turns toward Dad. "Mother has passed," she says.

"Yes, dear," he replies, nodding, looking blank.

Mom returns to the circle and adjusts her rosary beads. "The first Glorious Mystery, the Resurrection," she says.

"Did you hear that?" I exclaim. "Did you hear what you just said? We were saying the Sorrowful Mysteries but you just went to the Glorious. I think that means Ammy is in heaven now!" I'm jubilant, but it doesn't last. Later, huddled under the covers, I cry myself to sleep. Everyone else cries too, except Dad. Andrew says Dad's happy because he hated Ammy. He heard Dad screaming about it one night while I was gone.

Today is my first day back in the neighborhood since Ammy's funeral. It's a hot summer and we don't have air-conditioning,

so I take a bath when I get up to wash all the sweat off. I put on my favorite summer play outfit, blue and white plaid Bermuda shorts with
a matching blue and white plaid sleeveless blouse, white bobby socks,
and navy blue Keds. My hair is light brown from the sun and short,
cut in layers, held back off my face with a white grosgrain-ribbon hair
band I made. I sprinkle a few drops of Jean Nate cologne behind my
ears before I leave the house, just in case Peter McCall is around.

I run down the steps of our stoop, turn to look up the street, and
there he is, walking toward me, smiling. I feel different since Ammy
died. Older. I wonder if he'll notice.

"Hi, Catherine! Where you been? Haven't seen you 'round lately."

"Oh, didn't you know? I've been out of town." My voice sounds
happy. Why? I didn't mean for it to sound that way. My stomach feels
all twisted. I can't talk. I stare at Peter.

"You been visiting relatives or somethin'? Have a good time?"
He's throwing his baseball in and out of his glove. I think about how
he might have liked Ammy, and she would have liked him. "Stick to
wholesome boys," she used to say, "with good manners." Peter's usually too shy for good manners, but his shyness around girls feels like
manners to me.

"No, we didn't have fun. My grandmother died. I've been in
Princeton for her funeral." My heart is in my throat.

"Oh, sorry," he says, looking bewildered, and continuing down
the street. "See ya later."

I don't reply. My feelings are too hurt that he didn't stay and talk
to me. I burst into tears instead, and with my head hanging down,
walk toward the park, hoping that the fresh air and exercise will make
me feel better. I am so lonely.

There's a curved granite wall around a white sandstone mansion
on the corner of Montgomery Place and Prospect Park West. My eyes
follow the edge of the wall while I'm walking, and suddenly I notice
the words *Peter McCall loves Catherine Graham* written in green chalk
in his cursive handwriting. My heart leaps. I run all the way home
to tell Mom. But I hesitate at the top of the stairs near the kitchen.

I smell beer and cigarettes and Mom's talking to herself, slurring her words. I tiptoe by the kitchen, hoping the floor doesn't creak, and sneak upstairs to my room, closing the door tight, without making noise. I grab my rosary beads, kneel in front of my statue of the Blessed Mother, and, sobbing, pray the Five Sorrowful Mysteries.

Chapter 9

I'm fourteen and it's the middle of the night. I'm still awake, because I can't stop thinking about the wonderful day I had. My parents let me go to Breezy Point with my friends today, and I didn't have to be back until ten. Peter was there with his friends, too. It was perfect.

We all had a barbeque at Charlie's parents' bungalow, and afterward Peter asked me if I wanted to go for a walk on the beach with him and watch the sunset. It was windy and cold and he took off his windbreaker and wrapped it around my shoulders. I thanked him and asked if he'd be cold. "Are you kidding, Cath?" he replied, blushing. "No way. I'm with you." He smiled and reached for my hand. My heart skipped a beat and I hesitated; I could hardly believe my ears, and wondered if he was really reaching for my hand or if I'd imagined it, but then he paused and spoke again.

"Would you mind if I held your hand? I hope you don't think it's too forward of me. I really like you."

I smiled. "I really like you, too," I said, extending my hand. Peter squeezed my fingers and smiled back. There was a bounce in his step as we walked toward the ocean. The surf was rough, but my heart was calm. His hand felt strong, and as I lie on my bed, staring at the ceiling, the memory of his skin touching mine feels as good as any kiss could ever be.

What's that? My heart flips into racing gear. Something horrible is happening. I hear my father yelling at my mother, but I don't know what he's yelling. "Oh no, George, stop! Please, stop!" It sounds like he's pulling her from the kitchen . . . into the dining room . . . into the TV room, the room right next to mine. They sound drunk. He's yelling at her but I can't discern the words. I'm staring at the ceiling, crying. I'm thinking about how it's too bad I didn't move up to the third floor in time. Tomorrow the men are coming to move my furniture so Lucy and I can share a room. My room will become part of the living room on the second floor, because they're expanding it since Dad moved his office back home, into the first floor.

My door is thrown open, and the hallway light spills into my room. I'm trying to pretend I'm asleep, but he's yelling.

"Catherine will do what I want! You get in here and sit down, and I'll show you. Catherine will do anything I ask her to. She knows who's boss in this house."

I'm like petrified wood, but I'm not that lucky.

He's pushing Mom into the chair by my bed. I peek. She's hanging over the side, drooling. She has a beer in one hand and a martini in the other. The martini is spilling onto the Oriental rug Ammy bought me when we decorated my room.

"You sit right here, Cate," he says to Mom. His voice is gentle now. He's bending, adjusting her in the chair, patting her. I can hardly catch my breath, my heart is beating so fast. She looks disgusting. She's wearing her negligee and he's wearing only his boxers. "Everything's fine. I have to go downstairs and get something, and then I'll be right back," he says to her.

I want to escape, but my legs won't move. My body won't move. The only moving thing is my heart. It's working hard to keep me alive, since the rest of me can't. I hope Lucy and Paul are okay. I start crying.

A few minutes later he comes back into my room. He's giving me a shot, in my left leg. Or is it the left side of my bottom? It stings. He has no right. But he's doing it anyway, just like a devil sticking in a pitchfork, and he's pulling my pajama pants and underwear down, all the way off. I'm squirming, turning my head back and forth.

"No. No. Stop it. Get off of me." My voice is shaking.

He puts his hand over my mouth. "Now just be quiet, Catherine Girl. Everything's fine. There's nothing to worry about."

Liar.

He smells disgusting. Like martinis. Mom smells like martinis too. The whole room smells like martinis. Even me.

He's throwing up on me. Or am I the one throwing up? I can't tell. All I know is that I'm lying in this disgusting throw-up and I feel sick to my stomach, and he's lying next to me, in the vomit. And all I can think about is a picture of a painting of a drooping clock by a man named Salvador Dalí that my teacher showed us during art class one day.

He's getting up. Running back and forth with towels and washcloths. Mom's yelling at him.

"You know you shouldn't have given her that! You *knew* it would make her sick."

Is she talking about the shot? Is she talking about his thing?

Now they're talking about washing my sheets and making my bed so that when the others get up in the morning no one will be able to tell anything happened. They turn on the overhead light. It hurts my eyes, but it doesn't matter. Everything hurts already anyway. Dad unbuttons my pajama top, takes it off, gives it to Mom, gets another one out of my drawer, and throws it across my breasts. Then he tells her to go downstairs with him.

The laundry room is downstairs, off his office, in the old butler's pantry. It sounds like they're laughing and partying while they go down. They must think it's very funny, what they did to me.

I'm freezing. My shoulders, arms, hands and feet feel like ice. And I'm thinking about the crazy people I see on my way to school. I'm wondering how they got that way. Probably something like this could do it to a fourteen-year-old.

Ammy always said to trust Jesus. I need to find Him. *Now.* I want my crucifix, but I'm having a hard time remembering where it is. I wonder if forgetting such an important thing is the first sign of going crazy. *Think hard,* I tell myself.

I remember it's hanging over my bed, but when I stretch my arms up I can't reach it. It doesn't occur to me to stand on the bed and get it.

"So, you want Jesus, do you?" Daddy's standing over me again, sneering. He's pale and sweaty and he has dark circles under his eyes. "Well, *here's* your crucifix." He rips it off the wall and throws it at me. How did he know I wanted it? Can he read my mind?

I grab Jesus. I hold on for dear life. I'm shaking.

Chapter 10

I keep going to Mass every morning, but I don't have nice chats with Mom when I come home for breakfast anymore. She hardly ever gets out of bed before I leave for school, and when she does, she has alcohol for breakfast. She keeps a can of Pabst Blue Ribbon beer and a bottle of Gilbey's gin with a glass beside it in the kitchen cupboard above the sink, and she drinks right in front of us. Usually she starts out drinking beer from the glass. She tells us it's just ginger ale, but she's lying. I know because I smell the glass every chance I get whenever she leaves the kitchen. By the time we get home from school, she's sipping straight gin, like it's water. I've checked that one out, too. She thinks we don't know. But all of us do, even Paul.

Dad gets up early and helps Lucy and Paul get ready for school. He has office hours Monday through Friday, and he performs surgery on Wednesday afternoons. Most days I think he's the good parent and Mom's nothing but a miserable failure. I feel sorry for Dad. He can't rely on his wife for anything and we can rely on him for at least some of the basics, but he often drinks two or three martinis before dinner and one or two after, and though his eyes aren't bloodshot, his words don't slur, he's not sloppy or passing out, drinking makes him get verbally hostile. He goes on and on critiquing every move we make and he's cruel to Mom. Some nights, Mom's so drunk that her head falls in her plate during dinner, but Dad keeps talking to her anyway, mocking her over and over. Andrew and Lucy and Paul and I don't say a word. We stare at each other—we can communicate volumes of anguish with just our eyes. Dad finally stops talking when he carries her off to bed. She's collapsed on the floor a few times on their way up. During these episodes I hate them both. I hate their guts. And I wish they'd die, so I could raise Lucy and Paul myself. But that'll never happen.

I'm fifteen, a freshman in high school, and failing Biology. If I fail the final, the New York State Biology Regents exam, which is in only three weeks, I'll have to go to summer school. And of course it affects my grade point average, so I'll never make it into the honor roll, not even second honors. I haven't told my parents yet. I hate Biology. Every time I try to study I get a splitting headache. I know that headaches can be caused by astigmatism, so on a rare day that Mom and Dad are both in good moods, I finally tell them and Dad examines my eyes, but I don't need new glasses.

"What you need is a private tutor," he says, as we leave his office and walk upstairs.

"Come into the living room, Cate!" Dad calls to Mom as we approach the second floor. "Catherine has a problem that we need to help her with."

Mom exits the kitchen, one hand wiping her apron, the other holding a Coke and a lit cigarette. The three of us go into the living room, Dad and Mom sit in their chairs opposite the TV, and I sit on the piano bench, facing them.

"Cate," Dad starts, "Catherine's glasses are fine. The lens prescription hasn't changed one bit. I think the problem is that she must have a mental block of some sort, which is quite extraordinary, given what a highly intelligent girl Catherine is. The Biology teacher over at St. Saviour's must be very, very poor."

His assessment of my teacher sickens me, but I'm not about to tell him that I rarely even do the assignments.

"She needs a private tutor and I can't think of anyone better suited to do the job than me, can you, Cate, dear?"

"Oh, what a marvelous idea, sweetheart," Mom says, turning to me. "Catherine, you are so fortunate. . . . Dad is such a wonderful, patient teacher. . . . How marvelous for you, Cath." Ashes from her cigarette fall on the gold carpeting but she doesn't notice.

Dad sets up a card table and chairs in the corner of their bedroom and creates a tutoring syllabus and time schedule for the next three weeks, which includes what time Mom is to bring us our meals. He drills me morning, noon, and night on the weekends and evenings during the week. It's hard work, and the setup of Dad and me in their bedroom with Mom waiting on us feels bizarre, but it's also fun. He is a good teacher. I'm learning and gaining confidence. Mom and Dad are staying sober and acting like they're on the same team. I feel supported by both of them for the first time in a long time, and I pass the exam, though with the lowest passing grade, a 65. The joy of that accomplishment is short-lived, however.

Within days Dad comes home with an expensive new tape recorder and upgraded microphone, and Mom is furious. I'm watching TV when I hear them fighting in the kitchen with the door closed during their cocktail hour.

"Three *thousand* dollars? How *dare* you spend so much money?" Mom yells. "We have four children in parochial schools and Andrew will be in *college* next year. How *dare* you, George!"

"Now, Cate dear, calm down," Dad retorts in a placating tone. "This tape recorder is far superior to the one we had. It's just the thing we need for Catherine's rehearsing . . . her voice will sound so true, so pure!"

"Oh, for Catherine is it?"

I run into the bathroom next to the kitchen, and hide, not wanting them to know I'm around and can hear them.

"Catherine, Catherine, Catherine . . . you and Catherine! . . . Is it? Is it for Catherine, George, or is it just another toy for you?"

The kitchen door slams, I hear Mom grunting, stairs creak, and finally, Mom and Dad's bedroom door slams.

Andrew's out with friends, Lucy and Paul are home, each in their rooms doing homework. I listen for a while to see if anyone is preparing dinner for us, but nothing happens, so I go in the kitchen. Dad's there pouring himself a cocktail, and he shows me five plates on the counter, each with cold servings of mixed vegetables and lamb chops on them, so I gather Lucy and Paul, bring all of our dishes to the table, and pour my sister and brother some milk.

When Dad joins us he goes around the table in silence, kissing the backs of each of our heads, and then sits and begins eating. None of us speak until I make the mistake of thinking that I might be able to start a stimulating discussion and preempt Dad's entering another dark mood.

"So, Dad," I say. "What do you think about psychology as a subject to study in college? The sister of a friend of mine is actually majoring in it. She's a nun, and she says that there is a natural connection between psychology and theology." I'm trying to appeal to the part of him that cares about God, the part that wanted to name our new baby after St. Paul, but I'm hardly able to make it to the end of the sentence because my heart is pounding so hard, it's clogging my throat. His ivory complexion is turning pink and the blue-green color of his eyes, icy. He moves his martini glass to the side and leans toward me, pointing.

"Let me tell you something, young lady." His voice is deep now, with a bitter inflection. "You'll be a lot better off in this life if you leave some things unexplored. And don't *ever* go near a psychiatrist or anyone connected to psychiatry in any way, if you know what's good for you. *Ever, ever, ever,* do you hear me?"

"Yes, Father," I respond automatically, frozen stiff in my chair, and confused. Most of his friends are physicians. While he was tutoring me for the Biology exam he even explained who Carl Jung and Alfred Adler were, how he had trained under them during his psychiatry rounds in medical school, how he had found their work so fascinating. Why is he against psychiatry now?

He excuses my brother to go back to his homework, sends my sister and me into the kitchen to do the dishes, and returns downstairs to his office. Lucy and I don't speak, there's no point in making any noise. We just get the job done, without attracting any attention.

We're lying in our beds later when I hear Dad come in our room. I keep under the covers, pretending I'm asleep. He's over by my sister's bed, whispering.

"Lucy, dear, I want you to get up now and go camp out in Paul's room for the night, sweetheart."

I peek. He's wearing his undershirt and boxers and he's holding a hammer over her.

"Paul's crying for you, Lucy. Now do what you're told, and there won't be any trouble. Go sleep in his room with him."

She gets up and scurries across the hall. Dad closes the door, and blocks it by putting my desk chair up against the doorknob.

"It's all right, Cath; we can be alone now," he says to me.

I'm afraid he's going to smash my head.

"You can take off your nightgown now, sweetheart. Do as you're told."

I take my nightgown off and lie there, staring at the ceiling. My hair is in rollers with a bonnet over it, and the rollers make my scalp hurt. He leans over me and starts sucking my nipples. I have my panties on and they're getting wet.

He's standing up again. "How are your Latin studies coming along, Catherine?" he asks. I don't answer him. His penis is sticking out of his boxers, and his eyes are getting a wild look. I reach over to my desk and grab my statue of the Blessed Virgin; I had put it there while I was studying. He smirks, but doesn't take it away.

He's in bed next to me now. Naked. Whispering in my ear.

"I love you very, very much, Catherine, dear. You know, we could get married someday, sweetheart, and make babies together."

I'm shivering, staring at the ceiling in the dark.

He's getting on top. He's sticking it in. I hate my hole. It must be a mortal sin.

I can hear Lucy and Paul at the door. Paul's crying and Lucy is telling him to shut up. She doesn't want to hurt his feelings. She just wants to save his life. She knows about the hammer.

"It's okay, Lucy, dear," Dad calls to her. "Everything's fine. Catherine and I are just having a little talk. Reviewing her studies for school. Tell Paul I'll be there in just a minute, dear heart."

Mom and Andrew must be asleep. I'm wishing Mom would climb through all the crap she lives in and kill him.

He's gone. My hole hurts, raw, like terrible. Shut up, I tell it. Just shut up and go to sleep. But he's going into Paul's room. What if he kills them? They didn't mean to make noise. They're only kids. They don't know any better. I want to protect them, but I can't move.

I hear a creak in the floor. He's headed downstairs. I tiptoe across the hall. Paul's bedroom door is cracked. That's good. Dad won't hear me open it. I tiptoe in. Paul and Lucy are huddled on the floor, with their arms around each other. They tell me how scared they are. They say Dad was very mad.

"I'm scared, too," I say. I'm terrified.

I remember Dad was angry at Lucy and that he came to our room with a hammer, but I don't remember anything else. "Let's all sleep in our room."

Lucy agrees.

"Lucy, you sleep in your bed, I'll sleep in mine, and Paul, you can sleep on some blankets on the floor between us. It'll be like camping out. If Daddy comes in, then we'll all scream together. That way we'll be safe." I don't really believe a word about the safety, but we need each other.

They like the idea. They have that look in their eyes like it's all up to me and they trust me. We go into the room and they lie down.

I pick up my clock. It says 3:30. Only two hours left until morning. I set my alarm for 5:30. I want to make myself look pretty before I go to Mass. They say my alarm won't disturb them. They ask me to pray for Mommy and Daddy.

I lie down.

"Not all mothers get drunk a lot," I tell them. "Some mothers never ever get drunk. And some fathers never ever get mean."

"Are you sure?" Lucy asks.

"Absolutely, positively," I reply. Children are a big responsibility.

I listen to their breathing until I know they are asleep.

Chapter 11

I'm sixteen years old, five foot five, 163 pounds, and I wear a size 15/16. Most of my friends wear small sizes. Mom says I'm just big boned like her. But I think she's wrong. I think I eat so much because I'm mad that she drinks too much. I feel ashamed, guilty of the sin of gluttony, and disgusting . . . except when I'm around Peter McCall.

We're dating now. We went to the movie *It's a Mad, Mad, Mad, Mad World* on our first date, and then to Junior's Restaurant for hamburgers and Cokes. Peter talked a lot about how lonely he is. He has a married sister in her twenties and three brothers in their thirties. One is a Jesuit brother, but the other two are married and have children. He loves being an uncle, but he feels like an only child at home, and his dad has been sickly and irritable.

I take voice lessons from an opera singer on President Street. Peter often meets me afterward to walk me home. We sit on the stoop for hours before I go inside, talking about the baseball, basketball, and football teams he's on at Brooklyn Prep, and the activities I'm involved with at St. Saviour's. Peter loves to tell me stories about his little nieces and nephews. I'm afraid to talk about my family, though he knows them all, and they're friendly to him when they see him outside—even Mom and Dad. But I don't want him to know about Mom getting drunk a lot, or about Dad's dark moods and how much he likes to drink martinis. Besides, why spoil the good time we're having?

One of our favorite dates is to take the subway into Manhattan and hang out at The Plaza Hotel. We order Cokes, watch the people, and make up stories about who they are and what they're doing there. Then we walk along Fifth Avenue for a while before heading back to Park Slope.

Andrew is away at college now. Lucy is in eighth grade, and Paul is in fifth grade. Lucy gets into trouble all the time and her grades are poor. Mom's theory is that third children, especially when they're second daughters, are always problem children. One minute she yells at Lucy for being defiant, and the next she's too drunk to care what any of us are doing. Dad accuses Lucy of hanging out with daughters of Mafia members and sneers that she's just like Nana, his mother, whom he hates. What is Lucy supposed to do? She can't win.

I feel guilty because I'm sure I helped to construct her rebellion. It was my responsibility to walk her to school when she started first grade. Neighbors used to call Mom and report that I was yelling at my sister at each corner, and then when she was a bit older, Andrew and I made up a song to criticize her. First he would sing "You ain't nothin' but a great big beautiful doll," and then, in unison, we'd add "bum!" and laugh. Sometimes even Paul joined in. How must that have felt to Lucy? And how does she feel now? She doesn't tell me; we pretty much avoid each other these days, even though we share a room, and even though I'm worried about her.

I'm worried about Paul, too. Dad keeps longer office hours, but he and Mom continue with their cocktail hour each evening, which now extends into the night. Mom is usually drunk by dark, and Dad has had enough martinis to become hostile and dictatorial. Lucy, Paul, and I are required to wait for dinner, which is sparse, burned, or undercooked, and Paul has lost his appetite by then. He's getting taller and skinnier by the week. The only solace I can offer him is sneaking in the kitchen late at night to make him sandwiches and root beer floats or letting him hang out with me sometimes. He also loves listening to me sing. Broadway music and ballads are my favorites. "Somewhere Over the Rainbow" is still his.

I'm seventeen, a senior in high school. I'm wearing a bra and half slip and hanging up my uniform in my bedroom closet. My Barbra Streisand album is blaring. I like to set it at full volume, because it helps me stake claim to my own territory, especially when the rest of the family is downstairs watching TV. I can see in the mirror on the closet door that Andrew is right, I *am* fat. But I'm also sort of pretty. Sister Cornelia, my glee club director, told me today that "People" will be my solo in the spring concert. Maybe I'll go to Juilliard and then sing on Broadway when I grow up. I love singing, and everyone says I have the talent.

Oh, God, Dad's tiptoeing in, and closing my bedroom door. His trousers are unzipped; his penis is sticking out of his zipper. I freeze, stare at him, heart pounding.

He pushes me onto Lucy's bed. My legs hang off the side. He presses against me, grabs my mouth with one hand, yanks at my slip with the other. His penis rubs against my thighs. I'm trembling. I want to scream, but I can't. Nobody would hear me anyway; the music's too loud. Barbra's singing "He Touched Me." *No, No, Stop, Stop. I want Peter to touch me, not YOU!* The orchestra, Barbra's voice, crescendo; the lyrics . . . "he knew it; it wasn't accidental, no, he knew it" . . . pierce my mind like a laser. I pry his hands from my mouth. "*I hate your guts!*" I spit at him.

He grabs my wrists, pinning me back down, squeezing the power out of me. I surrender. He groans, shoves his penis into me, humps on my body, not me. I'm on the wall on the side of my room.

He wipes me off with my slip, snickers, leaves, closing the door gently behind him.

I'm shivering, but I'm not cold. My legs hurt. My hole hurts. My brain is swollen.

I hate my slip. I get up, take it off, wrap it in notebook paper, and stick it in my wastebasket. I'll buy a new one with babysitting money. Mom will never know.

I put on panties and my long, quilted bathrobe.

I grab my purse, pull out a Kent and a pack of matches, and open the window as high as it will go. I sit on the radiator and light up, inhale tar and nicotine into my lungs, and exhale memory of the awful truth. In a stupor, tears pouring down my cheeks, I blow smoke out the window in the direction of our magnolia tree, so nobody in the house will smell it.

There's a knock at the door. It's Paul.

"What are you doing? Can I come in?"

"Just a minute!" I make myself stop crying, put out my cigarette on the window ledge, open the screen, and throw the butt into the backyard. I sit on the matches, pull a wad of Kleenex out of my pocket.

"Okay, Paul, you can come in." I blow my nose and stuff the Kleenex back in my robe.

"Why have you been crying?" he asks.

"Because of Mom," I lie, knowing he's been upset about her lately.

"Mom's drunk every day when I get home from school," he confides. "I want to ask you a favor, Cath," he says, head cocked, voice quivering.

"Sure, Paul, what is it?"

"Could you stop staying at school so late, Cath?" He bursts into tears. *"Please?"*

I put my arms around him and give him a squeeze. Then, still sobbing, he sits opposite me on the radiator and we both stare at the sky. I'm concentrating on swallowing my tears so he won't see how upset I am, and I'm praying: *God,* please *help me with my brother. He really needs a sober mother. Our life here is horrible. We need your help more than ever. Amen.*

Chapter 12

I love St. Saviour's High School. I'm in glee club, booster club, and sodality, and on an intramural basketball team and the backstage crew of the drama club. I'm a class officer, a glee club officer, and a student council representative. I have many friends, and I get along well with my teachers. I love school and I hate home. I know Paul is scared and lonely, but I can't be there for him, and I feel guilty about it.

I binge on junk food when I'm home, anything in sight. And there is always plenty around; my mother buys it because my brothers are so skinny. Sometimes I eat an entire coffee cake or pound cake, and follow it with a pint of ice cream, pretzels, a few cookies. Afterward, feeling frightened that I might have stretched my stomach too far, I stick my finger down my throat and make myself throw up. I feel disgusting at home, normal at school, and even pretty when I'm with Peter.

Peter's on varsity teams at Brooklyn Prep now, so I go to games with my girlfriends and cheer him on, and then meet him later at parties. His buddies still call me "Pete's girl" and I love that. I also love kissing him. Some of our friends like to neck in front of everyone, but Peter and I always find a private time and a private place, and it's never anywhere near my house, except when we linger over goodnight kisses in the vestibule. I run upstairs to my room afterward, to do calisthenic exercises. Lucy wants to know why I'm worried about being fat, and I just tell her to shut up; she couldn't understand how scared I am of losing Peter.

It's two o'clock in the morning, and I can't sleep. I'm worried about the solo I have to sing at dress rehearsal after school. I leave my room in my nightgown and robe and head downstairs. I hear Daddy watching TV. We've had so much fun at the piano together lately. He's been helping me practice for weeks. I enter the living room and see him eating a piece of cake. My heart sinks. His martini glass is on the floor next to his chair, and he smells like gin the way Peter McCall smells like Canoe cologne.

"Yes, Catherine Girl, what can I do for you, sweetheart?" His tone is sinister.

"I couldn't sleep. I was worried about my glee club solo, and I heard you up. I thought maybe we could go over my song a bit, but you look really tired. I think I'll go back up to bed." I'm a goner. He's in a terrible mood. I stepped into a trap, and I never should have opened my big fat mouth.

"Oh, no you don't, young lady. You're not getting away as easy as that. Come over here, and sit right down." My heart races. My stomach feels tight and it hurts.

He pulls my arm and plops me down on the piano bench, then pushes me onto the floor and grabs between my legs.

"Help me get this robe off you," he says. "Help me raise your nightie and get your underpants off." He's already pulled his stupid penis out of his boxer shorts.

I'll kill you first, I think, and don't help him one bit. I make my body stiff, but he gets my underpants off anyway. Then he tries to stick his penis in, but I twist and squirm, and smack him across the face as hard as I can. He gets madder. Presses his fingers around my throat and neck and pounds my head on the floor. I see black spots and pain thuds through me, and I can hardly breathe. I'm gonna die if I don't get him off. My arm keeps reaching up and down, trying to find *something* to save me.

His fork. Where *is* it? I'm trying to scream. I get my mouth open, but my voice won't work. He spits. Right into my mouth. And I gag and then realize my fingers have found the fork. I grab it and stab him in the back.

He jerks backward, just a bit off me, enough so I can push myself out from under him and run upstairs. I think I hurt him. I think I saw blood, but I don't care. And anyway, he's so drunk he probably won't remember in the morning. He probably can't even remember now.

I lie in bed, spread my arms out, and sigh. But soon I'm crying and rocking, and sucking my thumb, which I haven't done since I was a little girl.

I remember none of it in the morning, but I'm embarrassed and ashamed of being my father's daughter. He's contacted Sister Cornelia to arrange setting up his Roberts tape recorder on the stage with his microphone positioned right in front of where I'll be standing for my solo.

The next day I'm nervous about the performance. "People" is Barbra Streisand's song and my voice is nothing like hers. Mine's more toward the Julie Andrews side of things, though nowhere near as amazing. Mom and Dad stay sober all day and into the evening and they and my brother and sister are totally supportive.

That night, with the dark auditorium packed with people, when the piano starts to play I begin to relax. Though the stage lights are blinding, I can see that there's standing room only in our school auditorium, and I begin to sing, projecting my voice with feeling, just as my Dad and my voice teacher had spent hours coaching me to do.

It is so much fun, I don't want it to end, but when it does there is a wonderful gush of applause, a standing ovation that seems to last for ten minutes or more. It doesn't matter that I'm not Barbra Streisand or Julie Andrews. It doesn't matter that I'm fat. It doesn't matter that my father had embarrassed me with his tape recorder or that my family has so many problems. What matters is that what I like best about my relationship with my father . . . the music . . . has become a part of me, a part that I hoped was beautiful and now I know it really is.

Afterward, Peter pushes through the crowd to congratulate me. He's beaming, and all dressed up in his loden green sports jacket and madras plaid tie. I smell that Canoe cologne he wears. "Cath, that was so cool," he says, placing his hands on my shoulders, his brown eyes looking into mine. "Beautiful! . . . You were amazing! . . . Everybody loved it. You got a standing ovation, Cath, could you see? I was standing in the back, in the corner. I could hear you perfectly . . . and I could see the audience's reaction. . . It brought tears to my eyes. I am so proud of you."

I glow with joy. What more can a girl ask for?

It's the night after my senior prom. Half-asleep, I'm dreaming about making love with Peter. But then I wake up. I'm naked, and Daddy's in bed beside me again, with nothing on either.

"That's it. Atta girl. Let it out. Let it out, Cath Girl," he's saying.

"What are you *doing?* Why are you in here? What did you *do?*"

"What's that, dear? Oh, nothing. You must have been dreaming."

"I'm naked! And *you're* naked! What did you do?"

"Why, you must be imagining things, sweetheart. I'm not naked. I have my drawers on. I thought I'd just stop in and kiss you goodnight. Did you have a nice date with Peter?"

"Get out of here! Get out of my room!"

"Yes, dear, whatever you say. But I really didn't do anything, sweetheart."

He walks out the door.

I stare at the crucifix on my wall. Then I get up, put my nightgown on, take the crucifix down, and wrap it in my pillowcase. I can't look at Jesus with his clothes off anymore. He looks too much like Dad and I know they're nothing alike. I stuff the pillowcase into my schoolbag, planning to leave it on the floor in the back of the auditorium in the morning. I know the janitor will give it to the nuns. They are the brides of Christ. They'll take good care of it.

Chapter 13

We've just finished dinner. Mom is drunk. She smells like beer, cigarettes, and underwear that hasn't been washed in days. She's wearing a pale blue cotton shirtwaist dress that's soiled from spilling dinner on herself. Her dress is so tight that the buttons from her collar to her waist won't stay closed, so her bra has been exposed all throughout dinner, and I hate that Lucy and Paul have to see this. My sister is fourteen and her body is developing. She's been getting in trouble—refusing to help out around the house, talking back to my parents, being accused of having a surly attitude—even more than she used to. I think it's because she's so scared of becoming like Mom. And Paul is only eleven. He's very sensitive.

Dad's excusing Lucy and Paul to go upstairs and do their homework. Mom, tipsy, is getting up to clear the table, and Andrew, who's transferred to Manhattan College and is living with us again, has been instructed to help her. "You stay here with me, young lady," Dad says to me. "We're going to have a little talk and get a few things straight." He chuckles. "According to the will of God." He leans forward, lifts his martini glass and turns it a few times, watching the olive swirl in the remaining ounce of gin.

83

Bubbles of anxiety in my stomach come to a rapid boil of fear. I know what the talk will be about. Last night I finally got up the nerve to tell Mom and Dad I think I have a religious vocation. I said I've been talking to one of the nuns at school about it, and I decided I don't want to apply to any colleges. I want to enter the convent—the order of nuns who had taught me at St. Saviour's, the School Sisters of Notre Dame. I want to live out the gospel message by educating children, without the distractions of marriage.

"Lovely, sweetheart," Dad had said sarcastically. "Isn't that lovely, Cate?" He turned to Mom.

"Oh, yes, George, certainly," she said, like a robot. I knew there'd be hell to pay, but I'm on fire with love for Christ.

Dad's leaning toward me now, speaking in a tone like I imagine Satan's voice to have been when he spoke to Christ in the Garden of Gethsemane. "So . . . you want to become a bride of Christ, do you? And what about that Peter McCall? Have you told him about this?"

"No, I haven't. I like Peter a lot, but he's one of the sacrifices I'll have to make, because I believe God is calling me."

"Oh, you believe God is calling you, do you? And just why in the world would God call *you?*"

"I don't know why. I just know it's happening."

"Oh, is that so, dear heart? And just *how* do you know it's happening?"

"I don't know how to explain it to you. It's a burning desire. When I imagine the future I always see myself as a nun. I don't know what else to say to you. I just know that it's true . . . that God is calling me into the convent."

"Well, I'll explain it to *you* then. What's happening is that you've been brainwashed. What's happening is that I never should have agreed when your mother insisted that you children go to parochial schools. . . . Fuck Christ, for all I care . . . I am the abbot of this household, and you will be obedient to my commands. You will *not* enter the convent. You will go to college. . . . Bride of Christ? . . . *Fuck* Christ!"

I'm bawling. I get up from the table to find Mom, to beg her to come to my aid even though she's drunk. But she's locked herself in the kitchen. I bang on the kitchen door, pleading with her to open it, while Andrew stands on the stair landing above, watching me.

"Open the door for your daughter, dear!" Dad commands from behind me, having followed me out of the dining room. "She has something to say."

Mom unlocks the door and I burst in. She's sitting at the table with a half-empty bottle of Gilbey's gin in front of her. Her head is in her hands, and she's whimpering, *"Where* have I gone wrong? *Where* have I gone wrong?"

"Where have you gone wrong? *This* is where you've gone wrong!" I yell at her, grabbing her gin bottle and pouring the remaining contents down the sink. "How could you *do* this to me? How could you let him treat me this way? You're the one who used to thank me for praying for the family! How could you do this to me? Don't you love me at all? . . . Don't you love any of us at all?"

I run out of the room and up the stairs, passing my brother, who smirks and says under his breath, "Goodnight, Sister Mary Flowerpot." I hate him! He's always criticizing me, and he's no help with anything. I slam my bedroom door shut behind me. I can't wait to graduate and get away from this place!

Chapter 14

I surrender to the impossibility of entering the convent, apply to colleges, and spend more and more time with Peter. In late spring, I am accepted to Georgian Court, a Catholic women's college in Lakewood, New Jersey—Mom's alma mater and the only school that would accept a combined score of 750 on my SATs, mediocre grades, and a long list of extracurricular activities. Mom had connections. An old friend was now president of the college.

Peter and I graduate from high school, and Mom and Dad insist on scheduling our family's summer vacation for the week before Peter leaves for West Point. We figure it's because they're afraid we'll have sex, but Peter and I are more disciplined than that. "It's not that I wouldn't want to do more," he says one night while we're making out. "It's that I really do love you and I hope our love will last a lifetime. If we do other things now it might spoil it. I wouldn't want that to happen."

I trust his words, and I love the way he treats me with respect. He's always gentle, hesitant, sincere. He asks permission to hold my hand, to put his arm around me in the movie theater, to kiss me good-night. I feel love and desire in his lips, but he never tries to go too far. I feel safe with him, and cherished, and I'm terrified of losing him. The first few days of our vacation, I cannot stop crying. I'm sure that once Peter gets away from home, he'll realize I'm unlovable.

"Good morning, Cath," Dad says as he opens the door to the cabin bedroom my sister and I share. The rest of the family is at the beach. I'm under the covers crying and have no intention of getting up. "Your mother is very concerned about you, Cath, dear. She knows you're upset about Peter. She asked me to come in and talk to you about it, but I'll tell you what I'm going to do instead. I'm going to fix things so that Peter McCall can never have you. Do you hear me, sweetheart? I'm going to *fuck your insides out.*" He unbuckles his belt, drops his shorts, and yanks the covers off me. I'm still in the same clothes I wore the day I said goodbye to Peter.

"Take your shorts off," he says, leaning over me, yanking a hand-ful of my hair.

"Stop, Daddy. Please. Stop pulling my hair. It hurts." My voice is so weak I wonder why I bother. I might as well be dead. I'd rather be dead.

"I'll pull your hair out of your head if I want to!" he says. "I've seen the way Peter looks at your hair. I'll show him! I'll yank it right out of you."

Now he's raping me. I hang on the bed like a wet rag doll clipped to a clothesline on a hot, humid day.

"*Fuck* you! *Fuck* you, dear! *I'll show you.* I'll teach you a lesson once and for all. You must *never* leave me. Do you understand?"

I don't understand a thing. I'm an automaton.

"Yes, Daddy, I do. I do understand."

Finally, he gets up and pulls on his clothes. Black-and-white plaid shorts. White sports shirt. Black alligator belt. White athletic socks. White tennis shoes. Looks like something right out of his Abercrom-bie & Fitch catalog. Snickering at me, he slicks his hair with my hair-brush and leans over so his face is one foot in front of mine.

"Your mother is very concerned about you, Cath. You might as well forget what just happened. She'd think you've really gone over the edge, and we'd have no recourse but to commit you to a sanitarium. So my advice to you is to snap out of it right now and enjoy this vacation . . . or at least *pretend* you're enjoying it, sweetheart. As far as your mother is concerned, we've just had a little talk, that's all. A little talk to help you recover from your hysteria about Peter."

He smacks me across the face. I'm stunned.

"That's a girl. That one snapped you out of it," he says, and turns to leave.

The smack blasts my memory into a locked vault. For so very long, all I remember is that I was heartsick about Peter, and Daddy helped me to feel better. This is the last time my father abuses me.

I survive the family vacation and I survive summer. When Mom and Dad drop me off for my first year at Georgian Court, I feel as if I've been emancipated from hell. I make friends quickly and become president of my freshman and sophomore classes. I continue attending daily Mass, either early in the morning with the nuns in their chapel, or at noon in the student chapel, where I'm a lector. I do volunteer work in town with a disabled child. I'm a representative from my school to the National Federation of Catholic College Students. I'm in glee club and in the Court Notes, a small group of singers who sing madrigals during glee club concerts. But I organize my life around starving myself. I ration out morsels of food and weigh myself three times a day until I achieve my goal of weighing less than 110 pounds and wearing a size 5 dress. I want to make sure I don't look anything like my mother. I want to be petite.

I take advantage of every opportunity to spend weekends at West Point, and I avoid trips home. Andrew is excelling at Manhattan College, and he immerses himself in his studies. Meanwhile Lucy and Paul are miserable at home. They tell me that Mom is drunk most of the time and Dad, when not seeing patients or nursing martinis, is often too depressed to get out of bed.

Peter is the joy of my life and the promise of normalcy, though dating a cadet bound by West Point's restrictions is an adjustment. Getting to West Point is the first problem, requiring me to take a bus from Lakewood to New York's Port Authority and then transfer to Newburgh. Five hours later, when I arrive in front of Grant Hall and greet Peter, his smile is warm and his eyes gleam with infatuation. But we can't kiss, and can't even hold hands for the entire weekend because there is no PDA, public display of affection, allowed at West Point. Also, the cadets' regimented schedule, which includes taps at ten, doesn't allow significant time for privacy of any kind until after the cadets' first year, called Plebe year, during the summer at Camp Buckner. Camp Buckner is designed to immerse cadets in modified airborne and ranger training for two months. They endure field exercises like hiking in the woods in full gear through mud and pouring rain for five days without a shower and latrine, so cadets live for weekend visits from girlfriends.

Our letters to each other during those weeks are filled with expressions of longing for quality time together, and Flirtation Walk is the one place where a couple's need for privacy is protected. We're both embarrassed the first time we stroll into the heat of its wooded terrain: Cadet uniforms rest, neatly folded, on large rocks; bras and panties adorn tree branches; bushes rustle, accompanied by erotic moans. Neither of us considers turning back, however. We're determined to find our own spot in this garden of eden, and continue walking hand-in-hand while hormones and our affection for each other fuel our curiosity and desire until Peter spreads a blanket and we make out. There is nothing to intrude upon our time together here and there is nothing to fear; there is only the music of our generation—like "We Gotta Get Out of This Place"—blaring from transistor radios across Lake Popolopen. I am with my soldier, my protector. And he is with his OAO, his one and only.

Our relationship matures. Peter confides in me about his struggles at West Point. He didn't come from a family of military lineage like many of his classmates had, and he's not so sure that he wants to dedicate himself to the military career for which he's being trained. Meanwhile, I turn to him for support in dealing with my family. I open up to him about Mom's alcoholism, and Dad's depressions. My family seems to be dissolving. Andrew is now a conscientious objector to the Vietnam War, and lives in Canada. According to Paul, Lucy's usually out with her high school crowd, and when she's home, she sits in her room burning incense and listening to Janis Joplin and Jimi Hendrix. Paul calls me frequently, worried about her, and I worry about him being subjected to life at home alone with my parents so much of the time.

Peter joins the Portuguese Club, the Culture Club, the Pistol Team, anything that might grant him a leave to go into New York City so we can be together away from the West Point military reservation. Sometimes there's time enough to go into Brooklyn and visit with his parents. Peter's mother has a special affection for Paul, so he's often invited along with us.

I'm pinned to Peter by sophomore year, and we get engaged junior year, planning to marry right after graduation. All traces of longing to become a nun have faded away. Though Peter and I are trying to hold off on making love until we get married, I've made out with him enough to know that I don't want to live without sex, and I'm sure God wants us to love each other for the rest of our lives.

We have big dreams about having children and traveling all over the world. We expect that military life will have its difficulties, but we feel prepared to meet whatever challenges await us. West Point takes us through many steps, from buying that first car, to requesting our first assignment, and Peter's brothers and sister have become our primary role models for marriage and rearing a family. Our expectation is that our life together will be an adventure, and our love will propel us through it. When he's issued his USMA class ring with the class of 1970 motto engraved on it—Serve with Integrity—we promise to serve God and each other with integrity throughout our married life.

Chapter 15

Peter was born to Elizabeth and Jack McCall when Elizabeth was forty-two and Jack, forty-seven. As family members tell the story, Jack, a shy, modest man, was embarrassed to be seen in the neighborhood once Elizabeth was showing. They already had four children—the twins, John and Frank, were eighteen, David was fourteen, and Jenny, ten. His brothers call Peter the afterthought, but I like to think of him as the grand finale. Elizabeth told me she spent the entire pregnancy angry at God about the situation, but once Peter was born, she realized God had sent her exactly what she needed most.

He weighed in at five pounds on October 3, 1948, and because of complications in Elizabeth's recovery, they had to stay in the hospital for an extended period. Thus when I came into this world eight days later, Peter's newborn soul welcomed mine in the nursery of St. Mary's Hospital in Brooklyn. His father remembers seeing me in the bassinet next to Peter's the day I was born.

I still remember Peter telling me that when he went home after the first day of school in seventh grade, he told his mom he sat next to the girl he wanted to marry.

It's June 1969, the summer before our last year of college.
Soon after Peter and I became engaged, we're in a restaurant with
his family, celebrating his parents' fortieth wedding anniversary. Peter's oldest brother, John, whom Peter has asked to be best man in
our wedding, jokes about our having been in the nursery together.
"Yeah," John says, "we knew Cathy was there when we heard all the
commotion—she'd rolled over on her pacifier and yelled 'Rape!'"

His brothers laugh, but I feel like I'm going to throw up. I excuse
myself and rush to the ladies' room. Once in the privacy of the stall,
the nausea dissipates and I sit on the toilet seat sobbing, wondering
what is the matter with me. I don't realize that my autonomic nervous
system is activated by the truth of the word "rape." Though I remember Mom's alcoholic binges and Dad's violent outbursts and bizarre
moods, every memory of having been sexually abused is repressed, and
is encoded deep within the cells of my body.

June 7, 1970. We're at our wedding reception in the
Officers' Club. Word is getting around that Lucy's been saying that
as soon as the reception is over, she's running away to live with her
boyfriend. I'm not surprised. She asked for my advice last night while
we were packing, and after hearing about how kind he is to her and
how much they love each other, I said, "There's nothing good for
you here. Get out while you can. If you love each other, you should
be together."

I believe that, but he's black, and the nation is in racial turmoil;
I'm afraid for her. Meanwhile, in sharp contrast, Peter's mother is elated about our relationship. She stands to the side of the dance floor,
dressed in the royal blue silk shantung dress she made for the occasion.
Her dark hair, only beginning to gray, is pulled into a French twist
under the matching pillbox hat she ordered from Mom's milliner. She
smiles with exuberance, looking younger than her sixty-three years
today. "Oh, yes, we're *so* happy," she exclaims to one of our guests.
"This is a marriage made in heaven."

Our marriage begins with a weeklong honeymoon in Bermuda. The first time we make love is extremely painful for me. My vagina throbs, an unrelenting raw ache. And yet, the pain feels more than physical, deeper somehow, layered, as if were I able to peel away the physical pain, I would enter into a world of intolerable emotional agony. Why do I feel so alone, so abandoned, so betrayed? I imagine my traumatized vagina as a cave I'm walking through. Images of my sisters-in-law surrounded by their children, children they conceived through this devastating act, bounce off the walls; conversations I've had with them about sex echo through my mind. Why didn't they tell me how excruciating intercourse would be? And why didn't Peter's brothers tell him?

We talk about it. This is Peter's first time also, and he is as confused as I, though not feeling any physical pain. Finally, he nestles my head on his chest and says, "Let's remember, Cath, there are years of tenderness between us, and years of tenderness ahead of us. It's our honeymoon. We'll figure it out." Miles from our families, I soon realize that I'm in a place of complete emotional safety with the man I love.

After our honeymoon we travel to Seaside, New Jersey, where we live near my college friends for a few weeks, and then move on to a summer camp in the Catskills for a month, where Peter is employed as a baseball coach for the remainder of his sixty-day post–West Point leave from military service.

I love him more and more each day, and I have a voracious appetite for his body. We sleep naked every night, and in the morning, fascinated by his large, athletic build—so different from my father, who is not muscular at all, and my brothers, who are both thin—I can't take my eyes off him while he dresses. Marriage is a feast of sex and we're not using birth control, because we're eager to have children. The next month, I miss a period.

I drive to Wayne County Memorial Hospital in Honesdale, Pennsylvania, for a pregnancy test one morning while Peter's still in bed, and he's waiting on the porch of our little cabin when I return. He's so excited when I tell him I'm pregnant that he hops into our sky blue Chevy Nova and takes off to buy cigars for all the staff at the camp, without even giving me a kiss or asking me how I feel about the news.

I'm terrified. I want a baby. We tried to get me pregnant, and I thought I'd be ecstatic when I found out I was, but I'm crazy with fear.

Peter's gone for a long time, even though he said he'd be right back. All I can do is cry, and I don't want him to see me like this. I walk into the woods, hoping the fresh air will help me get myself together, but it doesn't. I come to an open meadow far from the main buildings of the camp, trip on a thicket and fall to the ground, sobbing into the grass and weeds, perspiration dripping from my face, insects buzzing in my ears. I roll on my back, look up to the sky, and scream to God, "How could you do this? I'm not fit to be a mother! Don't you understand?"

The drama of my reaction frightens me. My feelings are so intense, so strange. Hadn't I played with baby dolls as a child, long after my friends had lost interest in them? And I've always been very responsible and capable. Why do I feel that I'm unfit to be a mother? When I'm sure enough time has elapsed for Peter to have returned and then left for work, I head back to the cabin, as full of shame as I am with pregnancy, and find a cigar on the bed with a note: *Everyone's excited for us. I love ya, Cath, and you'll make a great mother!*

His confidence in me ignites my resilience. I might be scared, but I'm also determined. I place my hands on my abdomen and look down. *I'll take good care of you, Baby, I promise.*

Our first military assignment is in Indianapolis, Indiana, where Peter attends Adjutant General School at Fort Benjamin Harrison for five months, and I do substitute teaching in the public schools. I read everything I can get my hands on about pregnancy, childbirth, and nutrition. Remembering college bouts with anorexia, I'm committed to learning healthy eating habits and sticking to them. The days when I have a prenatal doctor's appointment are the toughest. I don't purge, but I do come home after being weighed and eat everything in sight—cereal, bread, cookies—and then I feel a tremendous amount of shame, and worry that I may have hurt our baby. It's a monthly struggle until we leave Indianapolis and I'm able to leave those dynamics behind.

We depart for our three-year tour of duty in Heidelberg on New Year's Eve, 1970. There, Peter is responsible for making enlisted personnel assignments in Europe and the Middle East, deciding which specific cities and units soldiers should go to at any given time. We are blessed with the arrivals of Claire, Beth, and Annie, in 1971, 1972, and 1973 respectively. We travel with the children during vacations: throughout Germany, Holland, Belgium, Switzerland, and Luxemburg. We make good friends, get homesick for our families and our country, and lay a strong foundation for our marriage, talking at length with each other as we had during our courtship, sharing in the work and the fun of being parents, setting goals for ourselves, while depending on support from each other in achieving them.

When we receive orders for Fort Rucker, Alabama, a place neither of us has ever heard of, we're both surprised. We had hoped to be assigned somewhere in the Northeast, and we know nothing about life in the Deep South. But our spirit of adventure and the prospect of better housing, with a yard for the children, inspire our resolve to make the most of our new location. Before traveling to Alabama, we take two weeks' leave to spend time with my family in Brooklyn, and Peter's, who have moved to the Eastern Shore of Maryland.

After our miserable experience with my parents, we drive to Lucy's apartment to visit with her, her two children, and Paul, who is living with Lucy and her husband. During the visit I'm preoccupied with terrifying fantasies of Dad following us with a gun, determined to kill me. Paul and Lucy, though lovingly empathic, assure me that

I have nothing to fear in that regard, but I can't relax until we leave Park Slope.

We make arrangements to spend the night at the Fort Hamilton transient billets in the Sheepshead Bay area of Brooklyn, and contact the McCalls to see if we can come several days earlier than originally planned.

"Oh, we would be so happy to see you and the children tomorrow," Peter's mother tells me after Peter hands me the phone. "You are always welcome here, Cathy. I hope you know that, and I'm so sorry to learn of your trouble visiting your parents. I had suspected that they were not doing well, but, dear God, I'm so sorry about what happened."

"Thank you for your support and for your caring," I reply. "You can't imagine how much it means to me to be able to rely on you two." I hand Peter the phone and sigh in relief.

Elizabeth and Jack live in a two-story cedar-sided house at the end of a gravel road in a wooded area on one of the small rivers off the eastern coast of the Chesapeake Bay, in Maryland. David and his wife had built it as a vacation home for their family and a permanent home for Peter's folks. They're waiting outside in their winter coats and hats when we arrive.

"Look, girls!" I proclaim. "Grandma and Grandpa McCall!"

Peter opens the car door so that the girls can pile out, while I embrace his parents, inhaling a whiff of his mom's favorite perfume.

"Mmm, there's nothing like being welcomed home to the scent of White Linen by Estée Lauder," I chuckle. She grins and squeezes my arm, escorting me to the porch door. "Oh, it's so great to see you, Cath," she says, "and the children . . . I have been counting the days."

She opens the door, motioning for the girls to come into the family room and get warm. Once inside, Beth nudges me to bend over, then whispers in my ear, "Grandma's house smells like chocolate chip cookies!"

"It certainly does," I agree, removing her hat and snowsuit jacket. "I think I smell traces of apple pie, too!" I smile at Peter, while Beth and Claire follow Grandma into the kitchen.

Grandpa is sitting in a chair by the fireplace holding Annie on his lap, and making silly faces, so she laughs. "Cathy, Mother and I love you very much," he says. "You've always felt like a daughter to us. We don't want to intrude where it's not our business, but we hope we can be of some help."

"That's right, Cath," Elizabeth adds, entering with two glasses of milk she sets on the table for the girls to have with their cookies. "Why don't you go in and throw yourself down on the bed for a while and take a nap? You must be exhausted. Peter and Jack and I can watch the children. Give yourself a break."

When I wake up the next day, I'm shocked that I've slept that long and I cannot imagine ever contacting my parents again. As time elapses, I feel wildly conflicted whenever I think about talking to either of them. What would I say? Not that I would have a chance to say anything. Paul and Lucy tell me that Dad had all the locks on the door changed the day after we left, and my name is never mentioned. It's as if I'm dead and their grandchildren don't exist. I don't know what to do with that, but I do know that my first responsibility is to Peter and the girls. I resolve to protect them from the craziness.

In Fort Rucker, we make a sweet life for our family. We buy a swing set and a puppy, a little West Highland terrier–poodle mix we name Buddy. We grow vegetables and flowers. I teach three mornings a week at the preschool on post that the girls attend. We enjoy the pool at the Officers' Club with the children. I take a painting class at the post's crafts shop and work out at the health club; Peter enjoys the woodworking shop, and we make good friends.

In 1975, when Peter's post–West Point five-year military commitment expires, we decide to leave the Army, concerned about stresses inherent in military life. We'd heard far too many stories about the damage hardship tours—military assignments into combat zones—did to soldiers, their marriages, and their families. Instead, we opt for the freedom of civilian life, unaware of a different brand of hardship tour lodged deep within the recesses of our unconscious minds. In the coming years my body would become a line of fire, our marriage, a combat zone, and our sex life, a hazardous tour of duty through a field of land mines. A long time passes before we're redeemed from the pit and can come home to each other's arms in peace.

PART TWO:

The Geography of Trauma and the
History of Redemption

. . . denying painful feelings is like swallowing a time bomb.
—*Nancy Venable Raine,* After Silence: Rape and My Journey Back

The body keeps the score.
—*Bessel van der Kolk, MD,* Approaches to the Psychobiology of
Posttraumatic Stress Disorder

We carry our wounds and perhaps even worse, our capacity to wound,
forward with us. If we learn not only to tell our stories but also to listen to
what our stories tell us . . . we are doing the work of memory.
—*Patricia Hampl,* I Could Tell You Stories: Sojourns in the Land of Memory

To heal is to touch with love that which we previously touched with fear.
—*Stephen Levine,* Healing into Life and Death

Chapter 16

It's 1976 and I'm twenty-eight years old. When Peter was offered a marketing position with IBM in Montgomery, Alabama, we decided he should take it. We had come to enjoy the slower pace of the Southern lifestyle. We live in a three-bedroom ranch-style house in a small subdivision. I'm considering applying for a teaching job at a local preschool, but for now my job is homemaker and mother.

It's November 2, and I'm sitting on the brick-style linoleum floor of our kitchen, playing house with Claire and Beth, when the phone rings. I hand the doll that Claire and I just wrapped in a receiving blanket to Beth, along with a plastic baby bottle filled with water we were pretending was formula.

"Would you please feed the baby for me while I answer the phone?" I ask, smiling.

"I'll change *my* baby's diaper so she'll stop crying, Mommy," Claire says, full of enthusiasm. She reaches for her own doll and a newborn-size Pamper while I scurry to the phone, hoping to catch it before the third ring. Three-year-old Annie is napping, and I don't want her to be awakened.

"Catherine, he took a knife to my throat," the voice on the other end whispers. "I'm afraid he'll kill me. I don't know what to do. Tell me what to do."

I gasp, pull the receiver cord into the laundry room, and close the door. My chest tightens. I'm shocked to hear from her. Mom and I haven't spoken since the day we ran out of their house when we returned from Germany almost three years ago. Heart pounding, I imagine my father coming toward her with a butcher knife.

"Mom?"

"Yes, dear. Please, help me. You're so sane. Tell me what to do." She sounds sober and desperate.

"Is Dad there?"

"No, he just stepped out to the store." Her voice is trembling.

"Leave, Mom, right now. Go stay with one of your friends and call the police."

"No. I can't do that. It has to be someone we don't know. He'd kill me."

My mind flashes back to the piano he destroyed with a hammer.

"Go to the rectory then," I plead, "or the convent, *immediately*. They'll give you shelter and find a counselor for you."

"I already tried that. They can't help . . . Oh, no! . . . I have to go now. I hear him." Her voice is faint. "Don't call. I'll call you." She hangs up.

Dazed with fear, heart still pounding, I stand in the nearly dark room and stare at the pile of dirty clothes on the floor. I pray to my grandmother: *Ammy, if there really is a communion of saints like we were taught in school and you are a part of it, with any power at all,* do something. Please, *your daughter needs help!*

"Who was it, Mommy?" Claire asks when I return to the kitchen, feeling numb. "Why do you look so scared?"

"Are you scared?" Beth chimes in, wide-eyed.

I wish they hadn't noticed. "No, I'm not scared," I lie, stooping to rejoin them. "I just had a serious talk with somebody, and . . . it was a little upsetting."

That night is election night, and I stay up watching the presidential returns, drinking coffee, smoking cigarettes, and eating chocolate candy left over from Halloween while Peter and the children sleep.

The next morning, fueled on candy, tired from lack of sleep, but elated at Jimmy Carter becoming our next president, I pull out of the driveway with Annie to pick up her sisters from preschool. By the time we get to the entrance of our subdivision I am in a state of panic: Heart racing out of control, I break into a sweat and feel my body becoming weak. What's happening? Am I having a heart attack? Am I dying? Terror-stricken, I turn the station wagon around and race back through the neighborhood, a thirty-five-mile-an-hour zone, at eighty miles per hour. All I can think about is getting Annie to a place of safety.

I drive straight to my neighbor's house and use the last of my energy to bang on her front door. Susan runs toward the foyer to greet me. "Cathy? . . . Is that you?" She swings open the door. "What happened?" she exclaims. "You're gray!"

"Dial 911," I plead. "I don't know what's wrong with me . . . Get Annie out of the car, and call Peter and tell him to go pick up Claire and Beth. *Please!*"

She hops into action. I lie down on the couch, too weak to stand. Paramedics arrive within minutes, and a frantic scene ensues: sirens blaring, lights flashing, stretcher, oxygen tank. Susan holds Annie in her arms and they watch while paramedics take my vital signs, ask questions, and give me oxygen. Susan calls my doctor to tell him they're bringing me to his office, and the paramedics strap me on a stretcher, wheel me into the ambulance, and depart. Susan and Annie follow in my station wagon.

At the doctor's office, the nurse greets us with news that he has just left for lunch. In the exam room, she apologizes for his absence and tells me my heart rate is well over 200, but she has no idea what's wrong or how to treat it. Meanwhile, Susan holds and comforts Annie, who eventually falls asleep in her arms, while I lie on the exam table, terrified, staring at the ceiling. I keep imagining headlines: 28-YEAR-OLD MOTHER OF THREE DIES OF CARDIAC ARREST ON EXAMINING TABLE WHILE PHYSICIAN LUNCHES AT LOCAL COUNTRY CLUB.

When the doctor finally arrives, he hooks me up to an EKG.

"Your EKG is normal," he says. "You had an anxiety attack."

"An anxiety attack?" I ask. "How could that be? I'm not anxious."

"Well, apparently you're a lot more anxious than you realize. How are things between you and your husband?"

"They're fine . . . great," I reply. "We have a good marriage."

"Here," he says with a patronizing smile, then looks down and scribbles on a pad of paper. "I'm giving you a prescription for Inderal. I want you to take it for a couple of weeks. It will keep your heart rate normal. And here's a prescription for Valium to treat your anxiety."

"I told you, I'm not anxious about anything," I reply, insulted. "I'm happily married. I have great kids and good friends. I like my life, and I don't need pills."

He smiles again, looks down at me, and hands me the prescriptions. "Give us a call if you have any more trouble with your heart," he says, walking out the door.

I clench my jaw, put my clothes back on, and stomp out of the room.

I take the Inderal for two weeks and throw away the Valium prescription. I still don't trust my body, but I'm convinced there are healthier alternatives to pills, things that can help me prevent an episode like that from ever happening again. I research internists in the area and find a doctor highly recommended by a trusted friend.

"I have three children under the age of five," I tell his secretary. "I'm their mommy. I have to stay well for them. Please, find me an appointment as soon as possible."

After extensive tests, including a six-hour glucose tolerance test during which I have another attack, the new doctor diagnoses me as hypoglycemic and explains that my attacks were, in his opinion, not anxiety attacks, but something called PAT—paroxysmal atrial tachycardia. He believes the original attack was probably triggered by hypoglycemia in reaction to sleep deprivation, smoking, caffeine, and all the chocolate I had eaten. He outlines an eating regimen for me to follow and recommends I quit smoking and eliminate caffeine from my diet. I exit his office feeling empowered.

I'm eager to tell Peter about my appointment, but once again, life sends me on an unexpected detour. As I walk in the kitchen door, the phone rings and I answer it.

"Hello?"

"Hi, Cath!" It's Mom. Her voice is loud and cheery. "Things are so much better, Catherine," she spouts, without asking one question about how any of us are. "Your father figured out that he's hypoglycemic, and now that he's on the correct diet, everything's fine."

Energy drains from my body. I feel like I'm being sucked into the quicksand of a mysterious, dangerous land. How can Dad and I have the same thing, diagnosed at the same time? Does it mean I'm becoming like him? But what she's saying just doesn't make sense.

"Everything's fine? Do you really think so, Mom? He was trying to kill you last time you called. How can that kind of behavior be fixed by a diet?"

"Well, dear, we're both so excited. We've always thought something was wrong with him, but we never knew what. This must have been it all along. Now that his moods are more balanced, he's very chipper."

"Chipper? . . . Dad's been chipper before, Mom . . . and then he gets depressed, and then angry and then violent. *Please,* go see a counselor."

"Okay, dear, I will. . . . So, how are things with you and Peter and the girls?"

I know she's lying. She won't see a counselor. She wants to change the subject, and I comply. I tell her Peter and I are fine. I tell her about watching my girls at play . . . how they caravan single file out to the yard carrying blankets, dolls, books, stuffed animals. Claire is the leader, directing every move she wants Beth and Annie and their little neighborhood friends to make, until Beth, tired of being bossed around, comes inside for a while to refuel with me. When she rejoins the group she interjects some of her own ideas. Yesterday she brought along Buddy, our little Westie. She arranged him in her doll carriage, complete with blanket and bottle and strolled him along the sidewalk, to the envy of her sisters and their friends. Mother chuckles and so do I. We're playing our own version of pretend . . . that we're a normal mother and daughter. I do it because I want it to be true.

Peter and I make love that night. I suspect I'm ovulating, and tell him so before we begin. He grins and rolls toward me: "Well, we've never felt our family was complete, Cath," he says. "Maybe it's just the right time, you know what I mean?"

I smile, hoping to enter into the miracle of conception, and we nestle together. I believe that if Peter and I love each other, and keep having babies, it will be a lot of work, but there will always be something to be happy about. Our family won't have time to become morose, like the family I grew up in. And my girls will never feel as lonely and outcast as I often did as a child and adolescent. Also, having babies was something the McCall family was good at. Peter's brother John and his wife have five children. His sister and her husband, six, and David and his wife, whom Peter and I have become closest to, have eight. They are our models; we want to be like them.

Three weeks later, when we learn I'm pregnant, we're ecstatic. But I'm also scared. My body betrayed me that day after the election. I can't trust it as I could when I was pregnant with the other three. Will my baby be safe inside me? I keep the fear to myself, trying to be strong, but soon stoicism turns into loneliness, and I long for my mother. I want her the way she is on the rare occasions when she's sober: kind, loving, fun.

She's an early riser, so I call at 7:30 in the morning, figuring the odds are in my favor that she hasn't started drinking yet.

"The baby's due August 16," I tell her.

"You're kidding, Cath . . . August 16 is our wedding anniversary."

"Yeah, I know. Quite a coincidence, isn't it?"

"Well, it certainly is. A coincidence and a blessing. I'm just thrilled with your news."

Several days later she calls to see how I'm feeling, but quickly shifts the conversation back to Dad's "chipper mood," her joy at becoming a grandmother again, and then her big news: She's tired of living so far away from the girls. She and Dad have sold the house and are moving to Alabama to live near us.

My jaw drops. How did this happen so fast? I stare at Peter, who's sitting in front of me at the kitchen table. I point to the phone while silently wording "It's my mother! They've sold the house! They're moving here!"

He leans back, resting his chair against the wall. "What?" he whispers, and waits until Mom and I say goodbye.

I hang up the phone, and plop myself into the chair opposite him. "Whew!"

"Okay, Cath, what's the story?" he says, tilting his head. "Have they really sold the house on Montgomery Place? They're moving here?"

"That's what she said. . . . "

He eases his chair into position and leans forward, looking into my eyes. "I need to hear the rest of the conversation," he says.

"Okay . . . well . . . " I'm fiddling with a handful of crayons the children left on the table. "First of all, she kept telling me Dad's diet has completely changed him. He's stopped acting so angry and bizarre."

Peter rolls his eyes. "Yeah, right."

"I'm with you. I don't trust it. What if something triggers him later on?" I sigh, tapping the table with a crayon. "I mean, I still think he's capable of murdering her." My stomach tightens at the thought.

"I think you're right," Peter says. "And your mother's not the most reliable person herself. I mean, she *seems* like she's been sober for a while now . . . but she's never seen a counselor that we know of. She's never even gone to an AA meeting." He looks at me with worried eyes. "This just doesn't sound right."

"I know . . . it scares me." My body tenses. "But what if it's an answer to prayer? I even think Ammy might have something to do with it. I've been praying to her ever since that day Mom called begging me to help her."

Peter sighs. "I know. . . . Maybe we should give them the benefit of the doubt. They're getting older. Maybe they *are* trying to amend their lives. Who are we to stand in their way? But shit," he runs his hands through his hair and adjusts his glasses, "we could have some tough times ahead."

Lucy and Paul call the night before movers are due to pick up Mom and Dad's things from the house in Brooklyn, and Lucy speaks first: "Sorry, Cath, but all I can say is good luck, and you can have 'em."

I'm scared, hearing this. Is Peter's prediction already coming true?

"Mom's been smashed for three days," she continues. "When Paul and I left tonight, she was hanging out the kitchen window on the second floor, throwing hundred-dollar bills to people on the street."

The image sickens me as I brace myself for her next words: "Dad's been on a tirade, yelling and cursing at her and at us. He's nothing but a pain in the ass. I feel sorry for you and Peter." My heart races.

Paul is on the extension now. "Yeah, be careful," my baby brother says. "They're horrible."

"Shit, Paul, I hoped this wouldn't happen," I reply. "They ruined our childhoods. They're not going to ruin my children's. I won't let them."

"Sorry, Cath. But we thought we should give you some warning."

"Thanks. It'll help us prepare. Talk to you soon." I slam the receiver down and sigh.

Mom and Dad buy a little cluster home ten minutes away from us and appear happy to begin a new life. In spite of my worries, we get along well with them during the first few months, helping them get settled, showing them around town, having them over for dinner every couple of weeks. They seem happy and sober, and I begin to think a normal relationship with them might be possible. Then my labor begins the morning of their anniversary, and our daughter Rose is born healthy and beautiful the next day, August 17, 1977. We are unable to show my parents as much attention, and within weeks Mom begins drinking again. Drunk, she calls to tell me how concerned she is about Dad's dark moods. When Peter or I try to check on them, they lock their front door and refuse to speak to us. By the time Rose is two months old, I break into a panic attack at the mere thought of having to leave the house on an errand. This time I know the causes of my symptoms are more than physical.

I ask my doctor for a referral to a psychiatrist, who, after hearing the current situation with my parents, says, "Mrs. McCall, your parents are two very sick human beings. You and your husband need to move away from them as soon as possible. I recommend that you cut off ties with them forever, or they will drive you crazy."

I'm relieved.

"I recommend that you see one of the counselors in my practice weekly, until your move can be arranged, and I'm writing you a prescription for Mellaril, for anxiety."

Again, I tear up the prescription. Now that I, too, am the mother of four, I fear that I'm becoming more and more like Mom. I refuse to take a chemical just to get through the day, but I do schedule an appointment with a counselor.

Peter and I sit in front of the TV that evening, after tucking the girls into their beds. "I don't get it, Cath," he says, turning to look me in the eye. "I just don't see where a psychiatrist gets off actually prescribing a cutoff from a person's own mother and father."

My stomach is in knots. "He was very intense while I told him stories about them. His face flushed. I got the feeling that he doesn't hear stories like mine often."

"I just don't know," Peter adds. "Let's not rush into anything. Besides, orchestrating a move would come at great expense."

"I know. That concerns me, too," I reply.

"Let's take it day by day, Cath," Peter concludes, wrapping his arm around me as I rest my head on his shoulder.

Moments later, I hear clicking noises coming from the hallway, just outside the door of our little TV room. I get on my hands and knees, crawl to the door, and peek around into the hallway. There sits three-year-old Annie in her footed pajamas, big brown eyes peering at me below the bangs of her short, straight, freshly shampooed blonde hair. She giggles, arms full of books, hands grasping Fisher-Price figures from Claire's dollhouse. I giggle back and swoop her into my arms.

"So, you want some time alone with your mommy and daddy, do you? Well, I think we can arrange that!"

The next day we're in the front yard playing races with the older three girls, when Mom and Dad swerve into the driveway in what Peter has dubbed their pimp car: a big white 1974 Cadillac with a red vinyl interior. Dad, laughing, gets out of the driver's seat and approaches me. He's wearing a thirty-year-old plaid sports jacket, khaki slacks, brown alligator belt, and Nikes. Greeting me with speech so rapid that spit sprays from his mouth, he gets closer to me. He reeks of alcohol. My chest tightens as he grabs my shoulder and kisses my cheek.

Meanwhile, Mom wobbles toward Annie, a lit cigarette in one hand, open purse in the other, out of which pours lipstick, a compact, an open package of cigarettes, bits of tobacco, Kleenex, wadded up with a few dollar bills. "Come here, dear . . . come see Grandma," she says to Annie, who runs to my side and rests her head against my leg.

"Don't you dare come near her," I say, "and you either, Dad . . . both of you . . . stay away from my kids . . . you shouldn't even be driving . . . you're drunk!"

"We just came by to see the baby, Cath, dear. We won't bother anybody."

"Take the kids inside, Cath," Peter intervenes, extending his arm to block my father. "I'll deal with this."

That night Peter initiates a reconsideration of our move. He is now in 100 percent agreement with the psychiatrist's recommendation. We decide on Auburn, the lovely college town that is both home of Auburn University and central to Peter's east Alabama sales territory. We sell our house, and I decide to wait until moving day to tell my parents we're leaving.

After the movers pack our belongings and head for Auburn, Peter and I herd the girls into the station wagon and drive, unannounced, to Mom and Dad's. Peter waits in the car with the kids while I ring the doorbell. This time, Dad answers the door and invites me in. His gray hair is combed but needs a good shampooing; he's pale, which accentuates the brown aging spots on his face. The squared nails on his stubby fingers have yellowed. Mom slouches over the arm of her soiled wing-back chair in one of his old shirts, sleeves rolled up, smoking a Lark—she had switched brands to mine when I started smoking in college. The squished cigarette-pack wrapper is on her lap. Their trashed home smells like a smoke-filled barroom. There are piles of magazines stacked all over, open and unopened cartons, stacks of pictures and antique tables strewn about. I don't know how they get through the day without tripping over something.

I'm afraid I'll have a full-blown panic attack right in front of them, but I muster the courage to sit on the edge of an armchair near the door while my father, still standing, positions himself behind Mom.

"To what do we owe this glorious occasion, Catherine dear?" he asks in a deep voice, the voice I'd learned to be terrified of as a child—the voice of depression, the voice of anger.

"I've been seeing a psychiatrist," I reply, looking him in the eye. "I had a major panic attack a couple of months ago, and I'm still struggling with anxiety. The psychiatrist recommended that I break ties with you and move away."

My heart skips beats while I speak. I fight images in my mind of paramedics reviving me on their living room floor. Yet I'm able to continue. "Peter and I have sold our house and we're moving with the kids this afternoon to a town about an hour away. They're all outside in the car waiting for me. Please don't contact us."

"Why of course, dear," Dad responds. "By all means, do what's best for *you* and your family. We would *never* interfere. In fact, I have no idea how we've interfered, but I certainly hope you have. That is, if you're not too crazy, sweetheart. After all, you *are* seeing a psychiatrist now."

Mom sways in her seat, repeating the same slobbering words over and over. "Oh, really, Cath? . . . Oh, really, Cath? . . . Oh, really, Cath?" She waves at me and, drooling, smiles, showing her cigarette-stained teeth.

I stand, say goodbye, and walk out the door. A weight lifts from my chest. I take a deep breath, and look up at the sky as once again I leave my parents behind and drive away with my family. But a lingering guilt begins, and haunts me all the way to Auburn. Although I believe we are doing the right thing, I also feel that I am abandoning them.

Chapter 17

Auburn provides us with the first loving church commu-nity we've had since we got married. St. Michael's Catholic Church is attended by four hundred families, including many college students, and is run by three Vincentian priests from New York and two sisters of the Missionary Servants of the Most Blessed Trinity, a rare breed of down-to-earth social activists. Although in the middle of rural Alabama, Auburn University attracts people from all over the country, so there is a cosmopolitan flavor about town that reminds us of our old neighborhood in Park Slope, Brooklyn.

Peter enjoys living closer to his computer sales customers and working out of the house in the mornings, and I relish the freedom his new schedule allows me. I resume my childhood habit of rising early to attend daily Mass and often remain in the pew after Mass, savoring moments of contemplation before returning home to the busy routine.

Over time, these experiences, combined with the environment, become a potent mix, stirring up awareness of conflicts between my spiritual beliefs and my behavior toward my parents. I brood over passages in my Jerusalem Bible, particularly Ecclesiasticus, Chapter 3, verses 12–17:

> *My son, support your father in his old age, do not grieve him during his life. Even if his mind should fail, show him sympathy, do not despise him in your health and strength; for kindness to a father shall not be forgotten but will serve as reparation for your sins.*

And whenever I think about the fourth commandment—"Honor your father and your mother"—I become more and more uncomfortable with the fact that I cut myself off from mine. *What's wrong with me,* I wonder, *that I can't comply with God's wishes—wishes so important to God, they're couched in a promise? Why can't I be around my parents without feeling I'll go crazy?*

"Yahweh acts only out of love, standing close to all who invoke Him," Psalm 145 reads. If I believed that, would I need to continue this cutoff? I feel weak and wounded, like a soldier returning from war, damaged in spirit yet believing love is the only thing that makes sense of life.

Psalm 139 becomes my favorite prayer. I recite part of it each morning when I wake up, and again each night before bed:

> *God, examine me and know my heart, probe me and know my thoughts; make sure I do not follow pernicious ways, and guide me in the way that is everlasting.*

I remain conflicted despite these efforts, however, and before long anxiety creeps back into my body, like a bad case of the flu. I become afraid to leave the house, yet staying home is a luxury the needs of my family won't allow. I try to defy my fears, though errands as simple as running to Winn-Dixie for milk and bread terrify me. My heart races and I start to hyperventilate. I learn to cup my hands around my nose and mouth to stop it. Peter is losing patience with me. "Come on, honey," he says often. "Lighten up already!" Then when I take Rose to her pediatrician for a scheduled vaccination and the sight of the needle nearly catapults me out of the room, I know it is time to seek professional help again.

I make an appointment with a professor in the Marriage and Family Therapy program at Auburn University. Out of three names recommended to me, I choose Mary Anne Armour. I like the biblical and protective connotations of her name.

"Good morning, Cathy, and welcome." Her voice is strong yet gentle, and I'm relieved by the sight of her. She is tall, wearing a pale yellow pantsuit, and she has short, thick, healthy-looking gray hair. With a warm smile, she shakes my hand, then leads me to her office, a small windowless room. One wall is papered in metallic gold, covered with branches, leaves, and birds. It reminds me of Ammy's dining room wallpaper.

"My father has always hated shrinks," I say as I sit in the chair opposite hers and notice her eyes are brown like Mom's, her ankles swollen like Ammy's were.

Mary Anne smiles again and tilts her head. "I'm not a shrink," she says. "I'm a marriage and family therapist."

I receive a hint of comfort from her words, but keep talking. "I never understood why he valued everything about the medical field except psychiatry. He hated it. Even preached to us that it was dangerous."

"Is that why you're here? Would you like to find out more about your father?"

"No . . . yes . . . I mean, I don't know. I have a splitting headache all of a sudden. Like my brain doesn't want me to be here. But I've got to be here," my voice quivers, "because I'm afraid of what will happen if I keep everything bottled up. I'm afraid I might die of a brain tumor or something. . . . I hope you can help me."

Mary Anne reaches for the pencil and yellow legal pad on her desk, then asks me what kinds of things are bottled up in my mind. I explain how and why we moved to Auburn, and the guilt I'm feeling. I tell her about Peter and the girls, and how important it is that I be a good wife and mother. She asks me about what it was like growing up in my family.

"I think I had a pretty happy childhood until I was about ten," I tell her.

"Ten?"

"Yes. My mother was drinking pretty heavily by then. . . . Things went consistently downhill after that. But I haven't had to live with my parents since I left for college. Why am I such a mess now, at thirty-one?

"Perhaps your anxiety is inviting you into healing," she replies.

I stare at her. Calm enfolds me like a blanket.

"Your pain travels with you constantly, Cathy. . . . Perhaps it's time for you to get in touch with it and integrate it."

I'm not sure what she means, but I like the reverence in her tone, and her words offer hope. "Do you think you can help me, then?" I ask.

"Yes, Cathy, I do. Of course, there are no guarantees about the outcome, but I can promise I'll do everything in my professional ability to help you." She reaches for her appointment book. "For now, I recommend that you come weekly. In addition, I'd like to meet Peter and the children, so let's schedule a family session soon."

Her suggestion frightens me a bit, but at the same time the thought of all of us spending an hour with an experienced family therapist feels like an opportunity. There is so much at stake. Claire is now nine years old, approaching the age I was when Mother began drinking heavily; Beth is eight; Annie is seven; and Rose, three. We schedule the family session for two weeks later, and toward the end of the session little Rose scoots off her chair, walks over to Mary Anne, and sits on her lap. Mary Anne pats her back, and Rose turns to face her, looks her in the eye, and says "I like you," then rests her head on

Mary Anne's shoulder. Believing that three-year-olds are great judges of character, I feel that Rose has just given me her seal of approval. Mary Anne is trustworthy.

Mary Anne excuses the children into the waiting room and then explains to me and Peter why she feels the girls are each doing well.

I resume individual therapy.

"How long do you think I will need to see you?" I ask Mary Anne.

"I don't know, Cathy. My sense of it is that when the time comes, we'll know."

Seeing a family therapist is a refreshingly different experience from the sessions with the counselor in the psychiatrist's office in Montgomery. For the first time in my life, I feel like I have found someone who hears me accurately, and cares. Whether I talk about my present life or my childhood, Mary Anne's comments, interpretations, and questions reveal a depth of understanding about my family, then and now.

After a year, I'm able to call my parents and tell them I want to reestablish a relationship. Visits with them are sporadic, short, and talked about for hours in therapy. Insurance doesn't cover Mary Anne's fee, so I get a part-time job with Servpro, washing clothes and linens from houses with smoke damage and hanging them outside on the line to dry. I sell *World Book* encyclopedias door-to-door, and begin to think about becoming a therapist myself. I had entertained thoughts of becoming a midwife from the time Rose was born. But now psychological processes are as awe-inspiring to me as childbirth. Besides, in becoming a family therapist I might learn things that could help Peter and me rear our own family. However, I can't imagine how any of us could adjust to my working outside the home.

It's the first day of school. Annie, Beth, and Claire have been delivered to second, third, and fourth grades and Rose, to her first day of preschool. Peter and I have a date in bed. Making love midmorning is a luxury we've been looking forward to. Afterward, he gets up to shower and shave while I throw on a pair of shorts and an old T-shirt and set about the task of cleaning house without distractions. I'm kneeling on the floor of our little hallway bathroom, my hands deep in the toilet bowl, when the volcano begins to erupt inside me. *Is this all there is? He gets to dress up and spend the day meeting people and generating income, while I get to* clean? *What about my intellect? What about my talents?*

"Goodbye, Cath." I hear his voice behind me and look up. He stands at the bathroom door wearing his black wingtip shoes, navy blue pin-striped suit, coordinating navy, gray, and burgundy striped tie, and the white Brooks Brothers button-down oxford cloth shirt that I've washed, starched, and ironed.

"What's so good about it?" I bark, feeling like I might throw up from the stench of mixed Clorox and Lysol vapors. Perspiration drips from my forehead and down the nape of my neck, below my Dorothy Hamill haircut.

"What's the matter?" he asks. "We just made love. . . . I thought you were looking forward to having the morning free."

I jerk my chin down toward the toilet. "Did I refer to this as free? I must be crazy." I start crying.

"What's going on, Cath? I don't get it."

I stand up, grab the Windex and a paper towel, and begin cleaning the mirror over the sink, paying no heed to the fact that tears are blurring my eyesight too much for me to see the mirror, or that snot is running down my face like molten lava.

"Help me here, Cath; why are you crying? . . . It's the first time in years you've had a break. . . . What's the fuckin' problem?"

I put all the cleaning supplies on the floor, sit down, wipe tears and snot from my face with wads of toilet paper, then blow my nose.

"I can't help it. . . . I don't see how I can go to school. Who will do this?" I sob, and then regain my composure. "Everyone in this family relies on me. And I feel guilty every time I try to do anything for myself. I can't even remember the last time I bought a new item of clothing. And I can't imagine us ever having enough income to buy a week's supply of pantyhose, not to mention the cost of childcare, *if* I get a professional job."

Peter's body stiffens. His face pales. "Oh, I see what you mean," he says. "It would be hard. But we can manage . . . at least try. You can always drop out if it doesn't work. And you can count on me. I'll do everything I can to support you." I feel his commitment is sincere, though I fear he is ill-prepared to understand how much might need to change.

I'm accepted into the Marriage and Family Therapy program the following year, with a teaching assistantship to pay for tuition. Graduate school gives me an appreciation for my intellectual brother, Andrew, who is now a university professor. When we moved from Montgomery, I had called Andrew and his wife and told them what was going on. I wanted to make it clear that though I was breaking ties with Mom and Dad, I still wanted contact with him, but I never heard from him again.

Mary Anne suggests that I call and ask if he'd be open to our getting together. But when I muster the courage to do so, he declines, saying, "You seem to think that just because we shared something in childhood, Cath, we should share something in adulthood. If you need a kidney someday, give me a call, but otherwise, I've got a life I'm pretty content with. Give my best to Peter and the girls."

I feel like I've been kicked in the gut. I knew he tended to be distant—when we were growing up Andrew always seemed to find a way to separate himself from the rest of us—but this response feels particularly brutal.

My relationship with my younger brother, Paul, stands in sharp contrast. While Peter and I were living in Montgomery, Paul came out of the closet to the family about his homosexuality. It was a confusing time for everyone, but we kept in touch by phone and in letters. Peter and I included Paul in our visits to the McCalls, and Paul always made the effort to participate in events that were important to me and the children. Six months after we moved to Auburn, after he went through a painful breakup in New York, Paul moved to Montgomery. He had worked his way through college by then, and with a psychology degree from NYU, he was able to get a job in a home for disturbed adolescents. He looks in on our parents frequently—enjoying them when they're sober, caring for them when they're sick, bearing the brunt when they're drunk or acting crazy. Living only an hour away, he spends holidays with us. He even joins me for a therapy session when I ask him.

The most surprising change in my family occurs when Lucy divorces her husband and moves in with Mom and Dad. They are in a sober and sane phase when they hear news of her divorce, and they respond like loving parents, welcoming her into their home. But before long, my parents start drinking again, and Dad becomes cruel to her and her children—mocking and sneering at them, cursing and swearing. She moves into an apartment, where she is harassed by the Ku Klux Klan because of her children's dark brown skin. Finally, she moves back to Brooklyn. Lucy lived in Montgomery for a year, though she tells me it felt like a lifetime.

Meanwhile, I feel that Peter's behavior falls short of the support he had promised. He likes the fact that I'm starting a career, but he seems to want no part of the implications of what I'm studying. He continues to focus on work, leaving me to manage the household almost entirely. At the same time I am learning about the negative effects of a father's absence on children, and the high rate of depression among women with unavailable husbands. I beg him to share in household chores and parenting. More importantly, I plead for more emotional connectedness and understanding. But Peter seems disinterested in giving any of this to me. He says he'll help out and then doesn't follow through. He seems to be married to screens—either the TV or the computer—and I feel ignored by him. How did this happen?

The classes I'm taking give me some insight into the childhood roots of his behavior. Peter grew up in an alcoholic family whose lives revolved around the TV in their living room. His mother would fix his supper and instruct him to watch television, while she took care of his father when he came home from work drunk. Thus, Peter learned how to tune out family chaos. The problem now is that he's not motivated to unlearn those old coping habits. I don't understand how he can be so passive, and it scares me. Have our values become so different? I feel as abandoned in our marriage as I felt growing up in my family, and I don't want to live like this.

When Peter was seven, his mother got fed up with his dad's alcoholism, sat him down, and told him she'd leave him and see to it that he'd never see his children again if he didn't stop drinking. It worked; he never drank again. I don't feel my marriage is to that point, but I wonder what will happen to our relationship.

Chapter 18

I attend noon Mass with Rose the day Father Pat McCormick arrives at St. Michael's, and for me, it is lust at first sight. He is my height, five foot six, with a slight build, black hair, big hazel eyes, and long dark eyelashes, and he has a gentle presence, a keen mind, and a great sense of humor, as evidenced by his sermon. He invites the congregation of fifteen to gather around the altar during the Consecration. I stand with an erotic ache in my belly while Rose fidgets at my side, chewing her peanut butter and jelly sandwich, and Pat pronounces the bread and wine to be the body and blood of Christ. I'm amazed. I've never felt this kind of sexual attraction to anyone other than Peter before.

The next Sunday, as Peter and I are leaving Mass with the children, he stops to hold the door open for me. "Why don't we invite Pat back to the house for lunch today, Cath?" he asks. The girls scoot between us and run off with their friends.

"No, I don't think that's a good idea, Peter," I reply.

"Why not? He seems like a guy we'd have a lot in common with. I'd like to get to know him better," Peter persists, as we turn the bend into the front yard of the church where the children are running around.

I shake my head no. "To be honest, I feel guilty around him, like I'm being unfaithful to you. I feel a strong sexual attraction to him."

"You've got to be kidding, Cath; he's a priest," Peter exclaims.

"No, I'm not kidding. . . . I'm serious."

"That's nonsense, Cath. The guy just moved here. We should be hospitable. . . . I could see where you and he could become good friends . . . all three of us could, really."

I buy into Peter's rationale, feeling both relieved that he's given permission for me to get to know Pat better and intrigued by the danger of it.

Peter, Pat, and I hang out together, going to movies or gathering around the table for a meal at least once a week. When conversation gravitates toward religion or psychology, which it often does, Peter excuses himself to watch television. I feel that he encourages my relationship with Pat so he doesn't have to be bothered with me.

Father Pat and I have a lot in common. He's finishing his doctoral dissertation on medical ethics and moral theology, and I'm working on my master's thesis on family therapy in general hospital settings. The material I'm learning in school about family systems excites us both. These concepts describe the family as a complex, multigenerational, emotional system in which each family member's thoughts, feelings, and actions profoundly affect the others. One person's functioning is predictably followed by reciprocal changes in the functioning of others. These theories, and the notion that anxiety can spread from one family member to another, are useful to Pat in examining the dynamics of the church, and help me in my own therapy, my work as a therapist, and, most importantly, my functioning as a wife and mother.

Pat, who conceptualizes God as loving and inviting us into healing, lends a theological perspective to the issues I'm struggling with in my own therapy. His gentle attentiveness soothes the ache of Dad's religious persecution of me from years before, when I wanted to enter the convent.

Pat struggles with his relationship with the church, which in some ways is his family of origin, since he entered the seminary in the eighth grade. His vision of priest as servant of the people is in sharp contrast to the patriarchal caste system the priesthood has become. Outraged at the oppression of women in the church, and customs such as its celibate men in rectories being waited on by female maids and cooks, Pat begins preparing dinners for parishioners and friends on weekends, providing a comfortable forum for hours of discussion. He's awake and aware, and committed to raising his consciousness and putting his beliefs into action. His energy and priorities are in sharp contrast to Peter's, who often arrives late for our dinner dates with Pat. One night it is after eleven, without even the courtesy of a phone call. "Give me a break, Cath; there was a computer-installation problem at work and I had to stay to resolve it," he says when I confront him.

I'm beginning to think that if it weren't for me, Peter would be content to spend the rest of his non-working life in front of the television set. And I'm afraid I'll die young from carrying the dead weight of him through life. He's not dead at work, though—that's where his passion is—and he's been successful in sales, tripling his income over the past three years. To others he appears to be a responsible family man, a good provider. But this is the early 1980s. I've been reading books and articles by Betty Friedan, Gloria Steinem, and Letty Cottin Pogrebin. I want an egalitarian marriage. It might be tough to create, but I think it would be healthier for all of us, in the long run. What's the value of what we have now? It seems to me that Peter is as addicted to work as Mom was to alcohol, and, like Mom, he's deserting me and the children.

It's not that we don't talk about these issues. We do. But he gives lip service to egalitarian marriages and nonsexist child rearing, and then never changes his behavior. The only intercourse he initiates with me is sex, and it's quick and insensitive. He rolls over into a deep sleep after orgasm while I lie in bed fantasizing about what it would be like to make love with Pat.

Meanwhile, Pat questions the value of celibacy and I yearn to give him what I imagine would be his first sexual experience. But I don't tell him, because I'm afraid if I do it will open a door I'll feel compelled to enter. Too many people might get hurt—especially my girls. I tell Mary Anne instead, and she suggests that I bring Peter in.

Peter has come to therapy with me a couple of times before. But beyond meeting Mary Anne and answering any questions she'd ask him, he's never been interested in the process. I expect to be met with resistance when I ask him to come again, but he is agreeable.

"No problem," he says. "Mary Anne's a nice person, and she's certainly done you a world of good. If she thinks it's time for me to come in with you, I can go along with that . . . as long as we don't talk about sex."

"What? How can you discuss a marriage without talking about sex?" I ask.

"Easy. Just don't do it. I'm a shy person, Cath. I certainly don't want Mary Anne prying into our sex life. It's a special part of our relationship that belongs to you and me only. Promise me you won't talk about it."

"Okay," I respond, hoping I won't regret it.

"How's your sex life?" *Mary* *Anne inquires halfway into* the session, turning toward me.

My heart races as I stare at the floor, pretending not to hear her. If I answer honestly, I risk losing Peter's involvement in therapy. If I keep my promise to him, trying to work on anything is probably a waste of time, energy, and money.

Ironically, we learned about premature ejaculation in my Human Sexuality course last night. Now I know there's a name for what's been driving me up the wall, and I know that I participated in creating it. Wasn't I the one who often suggested he stop home for a quickie while the girls were taking naps or in school? Wasn't I the one to say "Hurry up!" if I'd hear one of the girls whimpering in her crib, or sense the pitter patter of little feet headed to our room in the middle of the night?

My heart pounds as Mary Anne waits for an answer. Suddenly, I'm up from my chair and running out of Mary Anne's office. Like a caged animal cornered for the kill and spotting one window of escape, I take off with a force and speed I didn't know I was capable of. I run all the way home and then propel myself into the back yard, over the little bridge Peter built on the creek, and up the five-foot ladder that leads to the entrance of the tree house he and the girls built the month we moved in. I feel safe here, knowing the children won't be home from school for two hours and sure he'd never think to look for me here.

Perspiration drips through my hair and down my face. The taste of salt sneaks through my lips while I remember our older three carrying supplies, handing Peter hammers and nails, measuring, so eager to help Daddy. It had been a scene right out of *Little House on the Prairie,* with him in the role of Charles Ingalls; Claire as Mary; Beth, Half-Pint; and Annie playing the role of Carrie. The children were full of giggles and anticipation, and I, full of pride, watched out the window with one-year-old Rose in my arms and our dog, Buddy, wagging his tail beside me. Nothing evoked my affection for Peter more than witnessing his patience and attentiveness to the children.

Before long, I hear him pull into the driveway. "Cath! . . . Catherine! . . . Cath!" he calls, but I don't reply. I peruse my surroundings. The little plastic cups and saucers on the floor in the corner seem to plead with me to come to my senses. The heart drawn on the wall with red magic marker, reading "R.M. loves R.D." (Rose McCall loves Ruffin Duncan), is a stabbing reminder that our marriage is a model of what the girls can expect to experience in marriage. The dirty sock wedged in a crack between two planks of wood almost seduces me into believing I can return to the house as if nothing has happened and take refuge in doing laundry, but I start crying, first slowly, and then with the trembling that comes with deep sorrow. My face is buried in my hands when I hear Peter's voice from above me.

"Cath, I've been looking all over for you. Thank God I found you. I was scared. I thought maybe you'd do something foolish, and

I'd lose you forever." His six-foot-two, 230-pound body stands on a thin ledge outside the tree house, his head cocked through the window, looking down at me.

"Lose me forever?" I sniffle. "Me do something foolish? Fat chance! Even when I *want* to do something foolish, I can't. I want to quit my career and make up my mind to spend my whole life being happy and content waiting on you and the girls, but I can't do it. I want to have a passionate affair with Pat McCormick, but I can't do that either."

I hesitate here, hoping Peter will protest. He doesn't even flinch, so I continue. "I *want* to break my promise to you and tell Mary Anne about the problems I have with our sex life, but I can't do it! I *want* to keep my mouth shut in a situation like this, because I feel like I'm working so much harder on this marriage than you are. But can I do *that?* No." The tears start flowing again.

"Cath, I love you so much, and I've been a jerk. I'm sorry."

"If you love me so much, why do you keep rejecting me?" I manage to blurt between the tears.

"Because I've been an asshole. I have no excuses. I take full responsibility for the way I've been, and I'll take full responsibility for changing. I love you, and I don't want to lose you. . . . Mary Anne confronted me after you left today. She kept asking why I was sitting there, why I wasn't running after you. She was amazed. I guess I must look like a real wimp. . . . Cath, I love you."

"Actions speak louder than words." My voice cracks under the weight of fear that he might not figure that out himself.

"Yes, they do. I'll take off from work tomorrow afternoon. I made another appointment for us. I hope that's okay with you."

I nod.

"How did you think to look for me here?" I ask.

"I just had a feeling. You must've felt terrible. I might be a real shithead sometimes, but I know you pretty well, Cath." He smiles. "When I didn't find you in church, I drove around town for a while." He scratches his head. "The tree house was my last hope. I know how much you love to come up here and play with the girls." He's blushing. "Could I come in there with you? *I'd* like to comfort you."

"Okay," I whimper, and he climbs around to the door, ducks to enter, and sits next to me on the floor.

He smiles and reaches out to me. I nestle my head in his lap while he strokes my damp hair and wipes each tear from my face.

Chapter 19

For the next few years, we see my parents infrequently, only for some holidays. We focus on our marriage, continuing therapy, and improvements in our relationship ebb and flow.

The Auburn years approach their ending. Mary Anne moves to Macon, Georgia, where she develops both a marriage and family therapy training program and a curriculum for teaching family therapy to family practice residents at Mercer University School of Medicine. Pat is transferred to a teaching position at Mary Immaculate Seminary in Pennsylvania. I earn my degree and work at a pastoral counseling agency until Peter is offered a promotion and we move to Roswell, Georgia, a suburb of Atlanta, where I join a private practice.

I resume individual therapy with Mary Anne once a week. The round-trip drive from Roswell to Macon takes almost five hours, but I leave home before the children get ready for school and I'm back before they get off the bus. It's worth it. Through the psychodynamics of our therapeutic relationship, I experience Mary Anne's psychological reparenting, and notice how it enriches my competence as a mother. I'm more sensitive, more emotionally available, more attuned to the needs of my girls. Claire is now eleven; Beth, ten; Annie, nine; and Rose, five—the age range of my siblings and me when our family dynamics began their sharp decline and Mother's alcoholism advanced.

December 1985. Mary Anne is diagnosed with breast cancer, and both Mom and Dad are admitted to the hospital, all within forty-eight hours. Paul has moved to Orlando, pursuing a childhood dream of becoming an actor. Andrew is overseas on sabbatical. Lucy's still in Brooklyn. I'm called as next of kin to respond to my parents' health crises, and I decide not to tell them I'm coming.

"Hi! How's my mother doing?" I ask, peeking into her hospital room. She's pale and thin, gray hair disheveled. Much to my surprise, she starts crying.

"Oh . . . Catherine!" she exclaims, reaching out her hand. I walk over and bend to kiss her, cupping my warm hands around her shaking fingers.

"I don't want to be rude, Cath, but the doctor just gave me a sedative and I might doze off," she says in a weak voice, as if she's never been rude to me before. "They're putting a pacemaker in this afternoon."

"Yes, Ma, I know. I'll just keep you company until the nurse comes to get you."

I pull up a chair and sit down, stroking her hand on my lap while she sleeps, grateful she's allowing it. But I'm confused. Thus far, our relationship conflicts have been the primary focus of my individual therapy. Is the love I feel for her—and the absence of anger, panic, fears of going crazy—a sign that I've worked things through? Or, with Mary Anne ill, am I transferring my affection for her onto Mom? My heart tells me to stop questioning. This moment has been hard-earned.

I think back to five months ago when Peter and I had taken the girls to visit my parents at their house for the first time in more than two years. Mom and Dad had become increasingly reclusive, sabotaging every effort we'd made to connect, either by declining at the outset or canceling at the last minute. So it was hard to believe they were finally agreeing to our visit. But the plans were confirmed, and we departed with optimism on a hot, humid summer morning. And then the air conditioner in our station wagon died just south of Atlanta.

"Do we have to go to Grandma and Grandpa's?" Claire had whined. "I want to stay with my friends."

"I sure hope Grandma and Grandpa have air-conditioning," Beth added only a moment later.

"Yeah," Annie said.

I knew their reactions were typical for their ages, then fourteen, thirteen, and twelve. And they had every reason not to care about visiting grandparents who'd never even sent them birthday cards. But Peter and I were in agreement about the importance of making the trip; it had been the only thing we'd agreed upon lately. The progress we'd made in marital therapy back in Auburn seemed to backslide after we moved to Roswell. Again, I felt a missing connection between us, and it seemed like I hardly ever saw him. When he wasn't at work or coaching the girls' ball teams—an activity that was good for them and one that I supported—he was glued to the TV or computer. On the rare nights he was home for supper, he'd finish his meal before I even had a chance to sit down at the table, and he never seemed to want to be bothered with disciplining the children. The kids decided he was the fun one, and I was an old bitch because I held them to their responsibilities. At thirty-seven, I felt trapped in my prime, and I wondered if Mom had felt the same when I was a teenager. I remembered her walking around the house holding a beer, singing Peggy Lee's song "Is That All There Is?"

When we arrived at Mom and Dad's, nobody answered the door-bell. I rang again and again, my heart sinking with each attempt. "Go away—we're not up to seeing you," Dad finally shouted through the door. "Your mother is not well!"

"Mom not being well isn't a reason to keep us apart, Dad! Let me in. We've driven all the way down here in a car without air-conditioning. At least let us get a glass of water."

Still there was no response, and I burst into tears as I returned to the car.

We checked into a motel. There was a pool, and we thought we might be able to salvage a good time for our family, but I couldn't stop crying.

Peter kept prodding me to forget my parents and get busy having fun. "Just leave me alone, Peter. You and the kids go swim. I'll be out later," I said. I was so sick of his "keeping busy" philosophy of life, I wanted to scream. Part of me hated him; part of me wished he would just hold me.

"This is the last fucking time we're coming to see these assholes," he said. "All they ever do is hurt you, and they don't give a shit about their grandchildren." He slammed the door on his way out.

I dialed the phone and Mom answered. "Mom, I want to talk to you," I said.

"No, not now. Goodbye." She hung up.

For years, I'd been convinced that she drank because she didn't care about anybody. Now, I realized what power that way of thinking gave to her alcoholism and their craziness—it kept us away. And it kept me believing that she didn't love me. Well, not this time. I grabbed the little pencil and pad near the phone and began writing:

Mother,

You hung up before I could tell you I love you, like the phone was a hot object you had to get out of your hands before you burned. Sometimes I miss you so much. I just yearn to sit in your presence for five minutes. The older I get and the older the girls get, the more I have glimpses of who you might really be, and I see similarities to myself. Andrew and Lucy and Paul's lives are so different from mine, and mine is so similar to yours.

Who would know better than you about the struggles of being in a marriage with the responsibilities and anxieties of rearing and launching four children? Who would know better than you about how disappointing a husband can be? Who would understand how trapped a woman can feel more than you would?

Lately, I keep wishing you and I could talk together, about who we are and how it's been for us. But you never let me see you, and it grieves me. I've been crying ever since Dad sent me away.

I'm not going to give up. My therapist keeps commenting on the good early mothering I must have had. She says I couldn't have become the strong person I am without it, and she sees it reflected in the way I've mothered my girls. Her interpretation resonates to something deep inside me. I do have some happy memories of you and me together when I was a child, you know.

If I could have things the way I want, you and I would sit together like friends, seeing each other as we really are, and loving each other. That would be heaven to me. Why do you keep refusing to see me?

Love always,
Catherine XO

"Mrs. McCall, it's just about time for your mother's surgery. You'll have to leave in a moment."

The nurse's gentle voice interrupts my thoughts, inviting me back into the present. While waiting to be ushered out of her room, I recall Mom's note, which arrived after I had given up hope of a response. Her handwriting was a barely legible scribble. I wondered whether it was caused by the pain and stiffness of arthritis or the tremor of alcoholism, but her words assured me that there was still a chance for us.

Dear Cath,

Sorry am so late in answering your "heart" note. I have read it over and over with love. I sounded like I did on the phone because I wasn't so well that morning and to have to say no to visits was more than I could take. I promise to write in detail on a day when the fingers work better. I often plan a nice walk with you as we talk friend to friend.

'Til later,
Love, of course
Mom

"Take good care of her!" I call to the nurses as they wheel her out of the room. *Keep her alive. We need more time.*

Dad is roaming around his room in a hospital gown when I arrive.

"Cath! Cath! So good to see you, sweetheart! Thank you for coming, Catherine Girl," he says, sounding as if it were always great to see me, as if he had never in his life refused to see me.

His genitals are vaguely visible, flapping under the cotton of his hospital gown, as he walks in front of the sunlit window and approaches me. He pats me on the shoulder and plants an old-man-smelling kiss on my cheek, his unshaven stubble rubbing against my face like sandpaper.

"Hi, Dad. Good to see ya," I respond automatically, reaching for a tissue on the nightstand so that I can wipe his saliva from my face. I feel nauseated. My heart pounds, and I wonder if I'm going to hyperventilate, but as I hear him rambling on, I'm swept away from my feelings and into my childhood role of trying to understand Daddy.

"Your mother has a prolapsed uterus, you know, Cath. *Your* birth caused it. You had a very large head, sweetheart." He walks over to his bed and lies on top of the covers while I approach the window, looking at the outside view so I can avoid the sight of him. "I've been catheterized, Catherine Girl. *Cath*eterized. Isn't that a coincidence?"

I imagine his legs are spread apart, exposed, for me to see his penis with the tube in it. I'm angry.

"Why aren't you looking at me, Cath, dear? Why do you keep looking out that window?"

"I'm waiting for you to put the covers on yourself." My voice is calm, firm, like a mother taking charge of her two-year-old's unruly behavior. But inside I feel tense, the pit of my stomach tight with fear.

"Oh, I see, dear. Okay, if that's the way you want it."

"That's the way I want it, Dad."

I hear him adjust the covers.

"The covers are on, dear. Everything's okay now."

I turn around as if I'm rewarding a toddler for socially acceptable behavior.

"I've been terribly depressed since 1970, you know, Cath. Or maybe you don't know. How could you know? There's been a tremendous lull in my life since then. Fifteen years, Cath." He laughs and begins singing: "There has been a lull in my life . . . "

Nineteen seventy was the year I got married and my sister left home. Listening to him is like taking a journey through never-never land. I feel as if I'm in a trance state, able to see this scene, him and me alone in a hospital room in detail, but my feelings are locked in another compartment. As his monologue continues, I tune out, thinking about how ironic it is that Peter and I are having sexual problems again, and here I am, standing only feet away from Dad's penis, which I think has something to do with our problems, but I'm not sure exactly what. I remember Dad prancing around the house nude on many occasions during my childhood, and have talked to Mary Anne about it, but I've never been able to come up with anything more.

As I tune back in to his rambling, I realize he's been recapping every physical illness and accident in his life. "Well, Dad," I say, "it sounds like you're scared about the surgery the doctor wants you to have so he can resolve the pains you've been having."

He laughs. "That's the most ridiculous thing I've ever heard. Utter nonsense. There's nothing to be afraid of. Who do you think you are, putting a damper on my day like that, young lady?"

I'm jealous of the strength of his denial, and I feel sorry for myself. *My* fears—of going to the doctor, of shots and medication, and more recently, of flying—are conscious. And they sometimes make my life hell.

Mary Anne, Mom, and Dad all recover from their surgeries, but only months later Mary Anne's cancer recurs. She undergoes another mastectomy, but this time there's lymph node involvement, and she needs chemotherapy. Mary Anne is hopeful about her prognosis, but I'm terrified to lose her. Over the years, she often assured me she wouldn't abandon me as Mom had done, and I developed the childish notion that Mary Anne was superhuman. Now I know she's no more immune from catastrophe than any of the rest of us. She will suffer, and there will be nothing I can do about it. Worse yet, she might die.

Around the same time I find a lump in my own breast and also have to face a breast biopsy, which is scheduled for just before Christmas. I'm sure the anesthesia will kill me. While shopping for presents for the girls, I'm plagued with tragic fantasies of their trying to maneuver adolescence without me. But despite my fears, I survive the procedure and don't have cancer. Relief is short-lived; Peter's doctor finds a growth in his lungs after a routine chest x-ray for a physical, so we have another surgery to face. Again, no cancer is found, but his recovery is long and difficult.

As he begins to get his strength back, we struggle to pry ourselves out of the emotional debris accumulated over those terror-stricken months. We are convinced the worst is over, but we're wrong. Our sex life, still troubled by Peter's premature ejaculation problem, has developed a malignancy of its own: Intercourse now launches me into a pit of weeping despair each time we make love.

For the first few weeks of this crying, Peter is oblivious. After orgasm, he rolls over into a deep sleep, snoring, and I cannot bear it. I retreat to the bathroom and curl up on the floor, crying, then write in my journal, and then crawl back into bed. The steps in our sexual dance become even more anguishing after I tell him what's happening.

. "Well, that's no big deal, Cath," he says. "It's just a tension-relieving thing."

"No, Peter. This is different," I say. "I'm trying to tell you it's *horrible.*"

That night, he covers my mouth when I cry, and I just lie there, struggling to breathe through my nose and swallowing my tears at the same time, feeling as if he's trying to murder me. And I hate me. Every bit of me. How can I even *think* that this basically kind—though passive, and often dense—person whom I've known my whole life and who *loves* me would want to murder me? And why, while teaching my daughters to assert themselves in relationships, am I paralyzed in bed with their father? I am miserable.

Mary Anne refers us to a sex therapist. "During orgasm, we have emotional access to all our life experiences," he says when we see him. "And I think it's significant that this symptom didn't start until your therapist, your parents, you, and your husband had all been in the hospital."

The sex therapist teaches Peter how to tune in more, to his own feelings, and to mine. I listen as Peter describes how he never meant to hurt me. He wanted to help me *not* cry, so I could enjoy myself. He asks me to believe that he has only good intentions, but I can't. I knew he was single-minded when I married him, and I liked that quality at the time. I trusted the whatcha-see-is-whatcha-get aspect of him; it was so unlike Dad. But we were only twenty-one then. Now, we're thirty-eight, and I feel violated. Does he really think he has the right to try to manipulate my feelings? Will he ever outgrow his commitment to a simplistic "good guy" perception of himself?

The sex therapist feels that Peter's premature ejaculation problem evolved gradually. As our household became busier, it was harder to find time for sex, and as Peter's work life became more stressful, he lost touch with his feelings. The therapist recommends books for us to read and teaches us more about the nuances of male and female sexuality, and our sex life revolves around the sex therapy exercises he prescribes. Initially, Peter and I enjoy these interludes, and our sex life feels as tender, passionate, and playful as it had been during the first seven years of our marriage. But their frequency soon decreases, and old problems resurface.

"Where have you *been?* It's five thirty in the morning!" I meet Peter at the door, bombarding him with questions. "I was worried sick about you. I called the police to see if there were any accidents involving a blue Maxima wagon, and then I called three hospitals to see if you'd been admitted to any of them!"

"Whatcha do that for, Cath? You knew I was at work." He stands before me, his body hanging in his suit, collar unbuttoned, tie off, pale, eyes bloodshot.

"How would I *know* you were at work?" I pace the family room in my bare feet and nightgown, as relieved that he's home safe as I am furious at his lack of consideration. "Did you call and tell me?"

"Yeah. Yeah, I did. I called you at seven o'clock. I distinctly remember, because I was staring at the clock when Rose answered."

"And do you recall what you said?" My arms are on my hips now.

"Yeah. I said things weren't going well with that presentation I had to prepare and I'd have to work late." He rests his briefcase on a chair.

"No. You said you'd have to work a *little* late."

"I don't remember it verbatim, Cath." He takes his jacket off and holds it in his lap as he sits on the couch. "But I remember what I meant. I meant *late.*"

I close my eyes, sigh, pull my hair back, and then look him in the eyes. "Do you have any idea how many nights the kids ask what time you're coming home, or why you don't eat dinner with us, and all I can say is *I don't know?*"

"I'm sorry, Cath." He leans forward. "I don't mean to hurt you or the kids. Next time I'll call. I promise. But if you were so upset, why didn't *you* call?"

"I did, many times. It just rang and rang. I figured you weren't there, or some psychopath had gotten into the building and sliced your throat with a knife!"

His face stills. "Shit, Cath. I was at the office the whole time, but I was in the copier room making foils. *Damn.* There isn't a phone in there."

I sense he's telling the truth, but I'm disgusted. I don't want to live like this anymore, and I tell him I'm going to divorce him unless he works on whatever it is that drives his workaholism, and then changes. He agrees to join me for another round of marital therapy with Mary

Anne, who has recovered well from the cancer. Mary Anne's husband, Rollin, joins the work as cotherapist.

Rollin is six feet five inches tall and wears the largest shoes I've ever seen. He is slim except for a small paunch around his waist, with gray hair, a beard, and glasses. Now a professor in the Religion Department at Mercer, he counseled couples as an Army chaplain years before. Mary Anne suggested that his inclusion would enhance the therapy, but I wonder if he's equipped for a couple like us.

Peter talks about his childhood, and we begin to understand some of the forces driving his behavior. His father was a stockbroker in New York in the 1930s, and lost everything he had during the Depression. I learn for the first time that Peter's mother had often told him his father's whole attitude about life changed at that point, that she lost the optimistic, ambitious man she had married.

Peter earned his appointment to the United States Military Academy because he knew his parents couldn't afford to send him to college. He wanted to ensure he wouldn't be a burden to them—they were in their sixties by that time, and cadets received a salary. Now, with our own children preparing for college, Peter wants to provide them the opportunities for success his parents couldn't provide him. Working with a passion has kept his fear of not being an adequate provider at bay, while preserving the sense of personal competence he couldn't find in our sex life. No wonder our discussions about women's and men's changing roles had never penetrated his motivations. My attitude softens, and I begin to hope we can strengthen our relationship.

"Pat McCormick's coming this weekend," Peter tells Mary Anne and Rollin while we sit in her office one warm July evening. "That's why she's crying. She doesn't want him to come. It's ridiculous. He's a good friend. He ought to come."

Mary Anne's face flushes; she adjusts her bifocals and squints, looking at me. "What's this about from your perspective, Cathy?"

"I . . . I hate him for the use of that word, 'ridiculous,'" I say. "I've been fantasizing about Pat. I think I'm still in love with him—"

"She is not," Peter blurts. "This is nonsense."

"Peter, I think you had best sit tight and listen to what Cathy has to say," Mary Anne retorts in a firm voice.

"I want to cancel Pat's visit, because I want to seduce him . . . and I will, at the first opportunity. I just know it."

Mary Anne straightens in her seat, not taking her eyes off me.

"I'm scared," I continue, my voice cracking. I begin crying again, but keep talking through my tears. "It feels dangerous, Mary Anne."

"Why do you call this ridiculous, Peter?" she asks, turning to look at him. "Don't you feel threatened?"

Rollin leans back in his chair, tilting his head, watching Mary Anne out of the corner of his eye. His presence is a comfort. I have learned that he is kind, gentle-spirited, and insightful, different from both my husband and my father. And I trust that he cares about me.

"Do I feel threatened? Hell, no," Peter says. "First of all, Pat loves Cathy as a friend. He's not interested in her as a romantic or sex partner. I can just tell. And secondly, even if he were, Pat and Cathy both have a lot of integrity. They just wouldn't do something like that. I'm sure of it. I don't feel threatened one bit."

Mary Anne stands in front of Peter. "*What* is the *matter* with you, Peter?" she asks. "Why aren't you protecting your family?" She seems to be losing her composure. I've never seen her react this way before.

"I appreciate your concern, Mary Anne, but I just got finished telling you, Pat McCormick is no threat."

Arrogant, narcissistic idiot, I think. But I cannot say a word. My throat hurts; head aches.

I take the driver's seat for the trip home, though I'm still crying.

"Are you sure you should be driving? You're so upset." Peter's voice has a judgmental tone. *Far be it for him to get upset, Mister High and Mighty.*

"Yes, I'm sure. I'm fine," I say. I need to take control of *something.*

I turn the radio on and drive toward Atlanta, regaining my composure. My eyes are on the road while my mind wanders, reviewing the session. I hear Peter snoring. *Fuck this. Why am I asking him to support me in canceling Pat's visit? Why have I allowed myself to become so dependent? I'm calling Pat myself, the minute I get home! I'm tired of feeling fucked. No more!*

When we arrive home, I slam the car door and stomp inside. Peter awakens and follows me.

"Why are you storming off like this?" he asks.

"None of your business!" I blurt, stomping through the kitchen.

"What's the matter with you?"

"You *dare* to ask me that question?" I turn to face him. "You fell asleep and *snored* all the way home. What kind of husband are you? . . . Are you going to protect your family from your wife having an affair? Hell, no! Are you even going to really give a shit? Hell, no! . . . You're gonna sleep through the whole thing. I could have an affair in our bed and you wouldn't even notice. I can't believe I've just spent two hours listening to you *snore!*"

"Cath, I'm sor—"

"I don't *care* if you're sorry. I've heard 'sorry' from you more times than I want to remember. I'll protect *myself* from seducing Pat. I'm going upstairs to call him right now. *I* feel too vulnerable, and *I'm* going to cancel his visit!"

Peter walks in front of me. "Cath, don't, please." His eyes tear up. "I'm disgusted with myself for letting you down again. Please, let me call. I want to make it up to you. Let me take this burden away. It's a beautiful night. Come out on the deck. Look at the moon. Listen to the crickets. It'll be good for you." Tears roll down his face as he pleads with me.

"Okay," I reply, softening.

"Wait here for me, Cath." He holds the door to the deck open for me, and then goes upstairs.

Minutes later, he returns and sits on the bench opposite me. Crickets click their evening song while an awkward silence grows between us. And then Peter speaks.

"I told Pat we were having some problems here in the family, and it wasn't a good time to visit. I love you, Cath. Could we put all this aside and go up to bed and make love? I want to begin to repair the damage. I love you deeply, and I want to communicate it with my body."

"I love you too, Peter." I know it's true. "Let's go check on the girls on our way upstairs."

The girls, now eighteen, seventeen, sixteen, and twelve, are watching TV in the rec room in the basement. We visit with them for a little while, and then send everyone off to bed. When the house is quiet, we go in our bedroom, close the door, light candles, turn out the lights, and take our clothes off. We hold each other's nakedness, lingering in a tender embrace as we gently fall onto the sheets and make love. Premature ejaculation problems become history. The thrusting of his penis is hard and strong, penetrating deeper and deeper into the depth of my being.

"Oh, Peter, this is wonderful. It feels so good. Oh, Peter, it feels so new."

No. No, it doesn't. Oh, no! It's just like the rape. What rape?

I'll show you, *Catherine! I'll show* you! *And you'll keep your mouth* shut!

Oh, Daddy, no. Oh, no. I see his face and his brown hair and his shoulders. And he's mad . . . so mad.

And this *is for your mother!*—pound, pound.

And this *is for your grandmother!*—pound, pound.

And this *is for your older brother!*—pound, pound.

And this *is for that sister of yours!*—pound, pound.

And this *is for your baby brother!*—pound . . .

The child in my mind whimpers like a ten-year-old girl in the terror of rape, yet my body is my forty-year-old self, feeling erotic pleasure, sweating, and climaxing, ignoring the instant replay of horror as if it were irrelevant. Suddenly, I realize where I am in my mind. I notice the picture of the Sacred Heart behind Daddy. I'm in Mommy's bed. Another part of me turns to look for Mary Anne, while a gentle and loving voice inside me says, *It's all right to remember now, Cath-*

erine. Mary Anne and Rollin and Peter are standing by. It's safe now. It's safe to remember.

Peter falls to my side, spent with pleasure, unaware that his cure has placed him in the role of perpetrator to a ten-year-old, while I stare at the candlelit ceiling, shocked into a stupor. Peter, legally blind without his glasses, grabs them and rolls over to look at me with a grin on his face, until his eyes adjust to what they're looking at and the sparkle of joy in them clouds with worry. He strokes my cheek. "You look like something's the matter. What's happening?"

I explain. He says nothing.

"It's true," I say. "I know it's true. But I can't believe it. I can't." And then the dam breaks. I cry and he holds me.

"Gosh, Cath," he whispers. "I always wondered why you were in such extreme pain the first time we made love . . . this must be why. . . . But we got through it. We'll get through this, Cath . . . we'll get through it." He strokes my head.

I had studied about flashbacks, had worked with clients who'd accessed long-repressed memories through the trigger of a sight or a sound or a feeling. I had been intrigued and respectful of the psyche's power. But now, in the wake of my own flashback, I am awed, and flooded with insights and questions. So *that's* why I was so hysterical about Peter not supporting me in canceling Pat's visit. My unconscious had been pleading, *Please don't let me have sex with Father!* The memory of my father raping me was beginning to emerge. And was it a coincidence that I was ten years old in the memory, and that I've also been in therapy with Mary Anne for ten years? On some deep level where the marriage of spirits abides, could Peter have sensed what had happened to me all this time, and could his sexual dysfunction have been a way of protecting me from it?

What about Dad? Did his behavior occur in the mania of psychosis, was he drunk, or did he just plain hate me and the rest of the family? What happened before he raped me? How did we live together afterward? Did anyone else in the family know?

Answers to these questions have to wait. Mom calls the next morning, asking for help. Dad has been admitted to the hospital with severe pains in his prostate. Though the timing of his symptoms—pain so near his genitals—seems to be in some psychosomatic way an affirmation of what I remembered, his trip to the hospital ushers in a series of medical and financial crises that make it clear that my parents are no longer capable of living by themselves and managing the little amount of money they have left. Life demands that we deal with the present.

Chapter 20

Peter and I continue seeing Mary Anne *and* Rollin, receiving emotional support and assistance with decision making. Mom injures herself in a bad fall during a drunken binge and becomes chronically ill with back pain. Dad, unable to tend to her, gambles away their limited financial resources through various mail-order get-rich-quick scams geared to the elderly. I remain distraught about the rape, but I still love my parents, and I worry about them. I don't want them to die in the gutter, though Mary Anne suggests there might be a part of them that believes that's all they deserve. After an extended heat spell of over one hundred degrees when, unable to afford air-conditioning, they become too weak to buy and prepare food, Peter and I decide to intervene and call my brothers and sister for help.

"Take them to Peachtree Street and give them paper bags," Andrew says in a fit of exasperation. "They've done nothing but put us all through hell for as long as I can remember."

My oldest brother's advice isn't a surprise, but the phone call with my sister is, and it hurts. "You must be as crazy as they are," Lucy says. "You're just trying to make sure your girls take care of you when you're old."

Paul sounds saddened by my request. "I feel like I've already spent too much of my life trying to take care of them," he says. "Besides, I live too far away. There isn't much I *can* do. But if you need any financial help, call Uncle Sean. He loves Mom, and Dad has made sure he couldn't get anywhere near her for years. I know he'd jump at the chance to help."

Paul is right. Uncle Sean's response is affectionate and supportive, and he offers to help in any way possible. Uncle Sean actually becomes a sounding board for exploring options for my parents' living and medical care, while the intimacy of our sessions with Mary Anne and Rollin enables Peter and me to compartmentalize our painful feelings and look at the situation objectively. We move Mom and Dad to Atherton Place, an assisted-living apartment complex for seniors that is about a twenty-five-minute drive from our house. We have concerns about their living so close to us, but the frequency of their crises is sure to increase, and it's obvious the burden of their care will fall on our shoulders. At the same time, our responsibilities for our immediate family are immense. Claire and Beth are in college, Annie and Rose in high school. Peter and I both work full-time. We hope Atherton will minimize disruption in our lives and accommodate my parents' shifting needs.

We tell Mom and Dad that the move comes with our commitment to oversee their care until they die, but our pledge is contingent upon two factors: They must give us power of attorney over their financial and medical affairs, and they must promise to stay away from alcohol. They agree. Paul and Andrew help with the move, and Andrew, Uncle Sean, Peter, and I pool financial resources to subsidize their Social Security and Dad's medical disability from the Army, thus making Atherton affordable.

The community atmosphere of Atherton is as powerful an influence on my parents as any AA group could be. Their physical health improves almost overnight, and their mental health stabilizes. Dad maintains a "jolly old man" mood and begins entertaining folks for hours a day on the baby grand piano in the foyer, while Mom enjoys having girlfriends to pal around with. They go on planned outings and join our family for holidays. With coaching from Mary Anne and Rollin, we keep visits brief, infrequent, and controlled, honoring the delicate balance between my need for contact and my need for distance. Though getting to know my parents as sweet, sober, elderly people is pleasant, the memory of Dad raping me thirty years before continues to haunt me, as does my distrust of their ability to maintain their apparent improved health.

Their first year at Atherton is a period of genuine happiness for Mom. She tells me she knows she's been emancipated from a hell on earth, and she's determined to make good of the time she has left. She appreciates the opportunity to see Peter and me under enjoyable circumstances, and she cherishes getting to know her granddaughters. She's also proud of her sobriety.

"You know, Cath, I don't even miss it," she tells me over lunch one day. "I only hope the way I've wasted my life hasn't made God so angry that I'll be deprived of the sight of Him forever."

Only two weeks later, she shows symptoms of a stroke, and is diagnosed with Binswanger's disease. "This is a terminal brain disease," the doctor tells us. "She'll have millions of tiny strokes daily, until—if something else doesn't kill her in the meantime—she'll most likely die within twelve to eighteen months."

I feel a mixture of relief and dread. An end to the burden of being her daughter is in sight. But how to orchestrate her care from hospital to rehab center to nursing home—a series of events the doctor outlines as likely—remains a Medicare/Medicaid maze of insurance papers, application forms, waiting lists, and the hoped-for grace of available beds.

Dad, a bit hunched over, starts crying, and Peter escorts him to the lounge while I remain with Mom, anxious to hear her reaction to the news. Her blue-and-green plaid blouse and khaki elastic-waisted polyester slacks have been replaced by a hospital gown, and she looks frail, sinking into the sheets of the emergency room bed, railings up. She stares at me. I can't tell whether she's deep in thought or in a daze.

"Cath," she says, pulling at the two-carat engagement ring and platinum diamond-embedded wedding band on her hand. "Help me get these off, will you please?"

I reach for her hand, certain this interaction wouldn't be happening if Dad were still in the room. Images of the day she told me Dad was going to sell her mother's and grandmother's Lenox china to an antiques dealer flash through my mind. I couldn't stand the thought of Ammy's china being sold to someone outside the family, so I begged Dad to let me buy it. He fought the idea, accusing me of being self-serving and greedy, and then agreed to a price of $400. The girls were twelve, eleven, ten, and six at the time, and Peter and I had been saving for their college funds. Buying fine china was the last thing on our minds. But we never regretted the investment, and I've often felt comforted by the sight of our dining room table set with Ammy's finery.

"Take good care of them, will you, Cath?" Mom asks, and I secure her rings on one of my own fingers. "And this one too, dear," she adds, pointing to the diamond-encircled sapphire on her right ring finger. Her father had bought it in Ireland, and gave it to her on her eighteenth birthday. "I always loved it, but you should have it now, Cath."

I smile at her, though a tear forms in each of my eyes. "Thanks, Mom. I've always loved it too. I can remember being a little girl sitting next to you during Sunday Mass, watching it sparkle."

She turns from me, stares at the ceiling, and sighs. "Who would have ever thought this would be my way out? Thank God you and Peter are here. Where would I be without you?"

One year later, she is dying in a nursing home. "Catherine, I love you," she says. "You know, if we had more time together, I think we could have some very, very good conversations. . . . But we don't have more time. I have to go . . . soon."

Her words come in a slow, hoarse whisper, requiring so much of her that she naps between sentences. She turns her frail body closer to me, reaches out her hand, and blows me a kiss.

"This means I love you," she says.

"I love you too, Mom. Very, very much," I respond.

Then the trembling begins, accompanied by "Lord! . . . Lord! . . . Oh, my Lord! . . . It's okay, Cath . . . I'll be okay . . . Lord!"

She seems to be experiencing agonizing pain, but she is going with it, accepting it. And she appears to have complete faith in God. I sit in her wheelchair beside the bed, with my cheek next to her mouth, so I can hear.

"I'll have to go soon, Cath. Will you let your father look up to you instead of looking down on me?" She weakly grasps the fingers of my left hand, which had been holding hers. My heart sinks at her request. *Charity begins at home,* I remember the nuns teaching.

"Peter and I will look after him, Mom," I respond. "I promise." I suspect that keeping this promise might cost us more than we can imagine, but I've watched her suffer and deteriorate for months. How can I say no?

"He's very nice, you know, Cath," she says.

"Sometimes he's nice, Mom. Sometimes he's not nice at all. He's the furthest away from nice a person can be." I can't let that one go, deathbed or not.

"Oh, I know! . . . I know exactly what you mean," she says, and then pats me on the head. Her voice, spoken from the circuitry of a demented brain, sounds innocent, childlike.

She falls into sleep and I stroke her face, feeling the structure of her skull. Only skin covers her bones. No muscle. No fat. The body that had worn sizes 16 through 20 during my lifetime now weighs a frail ninety pounds. I think about all the ages and stages in which I remember her face. *This is my favorite. Here, she is closest to God.*

She jolts and turns toward the door, eyes wide open.

"Oh . . . the fathers are having sex with the daughters and the daughters are having sex with the fathers, and there is nothing I can do about it," she wails in a surge of energy and strengthened voice. "Somebody, help!"

I'm startled, awed. Is she trying to tell me that she knows Daddy raped me? Is she saying he raped Lucy too, or that Grandfather O'Connor raped her?"

"*What*, Ma? What are you talking about? Tell me," I plead, but she jolts again and falls back into sleep, showing no signs of having heard me. She dozes for twenty minutes, then awakens with her eyes on me.

"I love you so, Cath," she whispers. "You are such a *fine, fine* person. I love you so much. . . . Not just because you're nice. Because you are *you.*"

"Thanks, Ma," I reply, feeling all the years I thought she hated me melt like snow in the warmth of her love.

"I want to put on my new spring dress later, Catherine . . . later . . . my pretty blue dress . . . when I go. . . . You know what I mean?"

"Yes, Mom. I know what you mean." She means that for her wake and funeral she wants to wear the blue dress I'd bought her at Kmart last spring—a far cry from the fashion finery she wore for many years of her life. But it was all the budget allowed. She carried on and on with words of appreciation the day I gave it to her. You would've thought I bought it from Saks.

"It hurts again, Cath," she whispers.

"I see that, Mom," I say, watching the trembling resume.

"Lord! . . . Lord! . . . I don't have words for it, Cath."

"It looks like labor pains to me, Ma. You look like you're giving birth. I think you're trying to birth your spirit into eternal life."

"You have the right idea," she whispers, while in the background I hear Dad's and Peter's voices in the hall.

"What, George? No kiss for me?" she teases as Dad enters the room; responding, he bends to kiss her.

"I really must go soon, George. I tried a couple of times, but it was just too much. I just couldn't do it. But I need to."

Dad, looking startled, lifts and readjusts her in the bed.

"No, George! Stop!" she exclaims with surprising strength. "You're hurting me too much! I don't want to be moved!" He persists, regardless of her feelings. Some things never change.

"You people, I have to go now. I *have* to go upstairs," she says.

Dad's face turns red and his eyes fill with tears. Peter walks to a chair at the foot of the bed and sits, looking uncomfortable. I lean over Mom.

"I hear you, Mom," I say. "We know you're tired. We know you want to go. Dad will be okay. Won't you, Dad?"

"Yes, yes, dear. It's okay," he replies. "We can go somewhere together . . . somewhere that we can be happy together."

I hate him for not letting go, for implying, in the guise of agreeing with me, that they must stay together . . . that only *if* they stay together there will be happiness. *Selfish to the end.*

"No, George. I have to go *alone.* I have to . . . separate. Don't you understand? I have to get my things together. Things you people can't even know about. I have to go *myself.* None of you *can* go with me."

I'm stunned. She has actually told him, for the first time in their married life that I'm aware of, that she has to take care of herself; that even though he's not letting go, she is separating. She has her own journey, with its own timing and its own tasks.

When we arrive at *Mom's* *hospital room ten days later,* she's lying in a fetal position, dehydrated and unconscious, hooked up to an IV and a heart monitor. Dad, pale, unshaven, and smelling as if he hasn't bathed in days, paces the floor, giving the nurses instructions as if he's chief physician on call and Mom can yet revive herself and manage to live a little longer. The nurses ask Dad to leave, and Peter escorts him to the visitor's lounge. They ask me to help them prepare Mom for an enema, which she needs before diagnostic tests her doctor has ordered to determine if she has cancer of the rectum or bowel.

"You have got to be kidding!" I exclaim to the nurses. "Does someone expect to *treat* her if they find out she has cancer? Mercy sakes!"

They look at me pleadingly.

"Mrs. McCall," one of them says, "those are our sentiments exactly. We're so glad you're here. Your father is hard to deal with. He's beside himself with fear. But your mother *is* at death's door. We hate to do one more procedure—it breaks our hearts—but we have to follow orders. The only way this can be stopped is for you—you have power of attorney—to file a 'no code' with the doctor. We can give you a number where he can be reached."

"So be it," I reply. "Don't do one more thing until I return."

The head nurse gives me the number. I rush to the waiting room and motion to Peter that I need to talk with him in the hallway. He agrees to keep Dad entertained as long as possible, and I run downstairs to another phone; I don't want Dad within earshot.

Mom's doctor and I cover the relevant issues about the decision, and she's placed on no-code status, with instructions for the nurses to keep her as comfortable as possible. There will be no more diagnostic tests. Nothing will be done if she suddenly stops breathing or her heart stops beating. She will be allowed to die a natural death.

I run upstairs to tell Mom's nurses the news. As I say the words "no code," I hear footsteps at the door followed by Dad's voice: "Just what do you think is going on here, dear?" I feel an icy chill go through me.

Lucy is twelve, I'm fifteen, and it's late. Mom and Dad were both drunk at dinner, Dad was cruel to Mom all evening, and then they went to bed. Assuming they've passed out, Lucy and I lie in bed talking to each other about how scared we are of Daddy and how much we hate him. Then I hear the floor creak, and I look toward our bedroom door. There he is, in his boxers, holding a hammer in his hand. "Just what do you think is going on here, dears?" I'm terror stricken.

I stomp one foot on the floor—a technique Mary Anne taught me, to ground myself in the reality of the here and now. I remind myself that night was twenty-five years ago. This night is different.

There's no need to become paralyzed. I love Mom, and I've pursued what is right. I have all the power I need. I must proceed with doing what has to be done.

Peter grabs Dad and leads him out of the room. I turn and look at Mom, who remains in a fetal position. One of her veins collapsed from a needle given to her earlier in the evening, and her entire arm is purple. I close the door—if Dad returns, I want to hear him enter first, before I have to stomach the sight of him.

I touch Mom's hand gently and stare at her, yearning to connect, but her consciousness seems so far away, there's no point in trying to talk. Knowing its words hold urgent meaning for me now, I pray aloud the first prayer she taught me as a child.

"Hail Mary, full of grace; the Lord is with thee; blessed art thou among women, and blessed is the fruit of thy womb, Jesus."

Suddenly, Mom's frail, thin, ethereal voice continues the prayer: "Holy Mary, Mother of God, pray for us sinners now, and at the hour of our death. Amen."

Amazed, I start crying, but continue praying aloud. After several Hail Marys, Mom says, as if ending a decade of the rosary, "Glory be to the Father, and to the Son, and to the Holy Spirit. Amen."

"Oh, Mom, I'm going to miss you *so* much," I say, heaving with emotion.

Her body responds to my sobs with a jerk. Her glassy eyes seem to search for the sight of me, though I know she can't see me. She's in a place between here and the other side, a place where only love can connect—I feel it. And then Our Lady appears, looking down upon Mom. Her veil is draped in a loving embrace around us both. *This must be a vision, like the saints used to report seeing,* I think, and in an instant the image disappears. Or is it my ability to see her that disappears? I only know my certain assurance that Mom is in God's hands.

She passes away two days later, just before the rainy dawn of May 13, 1990: Mother's Day. She expires while Dad's at the nurses' station calling to ask me to come to the hospital, and when Peter and I arrive, we agree that her body looks as if she fled from it.

At her funeral, I read a poem she wrote as a college student over fifty years ago, entitled "Sunrise," which describes her passing as I like to imagine it:

> . . . *Through threads of silver rain*
> *She gently moves,*
> *Pushing aside the clouds*
> *Of misty veil enfolding her—*
> *Then waits.*
>
> *Birds sing their nuptial song,*
> *And she*
> *With measured step*
> *Glides slowly*
> *Down the golden aisle.*

Chapter 21

At home after the burial, Paul and I retreat to the dock behind my house. Mallards squawk and play on the lake, while an occasional carp pops out of the water near us, and then dives in again. Cottontails hop through the woods. Blue jays, cardinals, and finches play musical chairs on the budding tree branches above us. Paul sits on a bench while I walk toward the hammock under an umbrella of wild magnolia leaves and climb into it.

"This place is a sanctuary for me," I tell him. "I don't know how I would've made it through the last few years without being able to escape down here from time to time."

"Yeah, I can imagine," Paul replies. "I'm glad you and Peter have this. It must be really good for the kids, too. A far cry from Brooklyn, huh, Cath?"

"Yes." I'm staring at the lake. "Mom only made it down here once. When we were getting ready to move them. Dozens of big turtles were sunbathing on the water's surface. She said it reminded her of a Walt Disney movie."

"Sounds just like her." He chuckles. "I loved your eulogy, Cath," he adds. I turn my head to look at him, and notice tears in his eyes as he continues.

"When you were talking, I started crying so hard I could hardly breathe." He smiles, then sobs. "Oh, Cath, I can't stand it! I loved her *so much* . . . more than she loved herself!"

I want to get up and hug him, but I hesitate, thinking he might not want it.

"Fuck! Fuck, Cath! Fuck! Fuck! Fuck!"

I notice his pulse beating through veins protruding in his long, extended neck. "Interesting choice of words," I say, smiling. My heart rate picks up speed. I've been talking to Mary Anne for months about how frightened I am that Paul will get AIDS. It's the early '90s, and AIDS is known as the gay man's disease. I promised myself that next time Paul and I were together, I would talk to him about it. *Fuck.*

"Forget I said anything about Mom's funeral," he says, straightening his body and wiping the tears away. "Let's just change the subject. Let's have an hour when Mom's death is not talked about."

I nod. "Well . . . what would you like to talk about?"

He laughs. "I don't really know!"

"How about *your* life? How's it going? Are you happy?"

"Sometimes . . . about some things. . . . Like, one big one is I decided two years ago to live a celibate lifestyle. I was scared, constantly, of AIDS, so I made a commitment to myself."

"I've been worrying about you, Paul." Tears threaten to pour; I force them back. Now is the time to say it, though I hate doing so. "I don't want you to get sick. I don't want you to die."

"I probably *am* sick, Cath," he says, looking at me intently.

My heart pounds. "What are you saying?" I ask, feeling tears again.

"I'm sure I'm HIV positive. . . . There's no way I couldn't be. . . . That's why I'm celibate. I don't want to give it to anyone else. I don't want to hurt anyone in the name of loving. There's been enough of that."

"Have you been tested?" I'm groping for escape from his certainty.

"No. And I don't want to be. I don't want to know for sure." His voice quivers as he speaks. "It would terrify me even more."

I stare at the lake, letting the tears come, too distraught to stop them.

"Is it difficult for you . . . the celibacy part?" I manage.

"Sometimes, yeah. But for the most part, no, not anymore. I pray . . . meditate. I—"

"It's difficult for me," I say.

"What? . . . *My* celibacy?"

"No." I'm crying harder, sitting up on the side of the hammock, rubbing my eyes. "I can't bear the thought of your getting AIDS. I worry about it a lot . . . and if it happens, God forbid, I want to be near you, to care for you. I'd want Peter around, the kids. People who love you."

I look up. He's crying.

"I wouldn't want that," he says. "I know you've been burdened with Mom and Dad, and I feel guilty about it. I just have no resources to help carry the load. If I got AIDS, I'd go off in a forest somewhere and die by myself."

"What? . . . Why?"

"Because I've decided to. Simple as that. I have my own ideas about living and dying," his eyes fix on mine, "and I hope you can respect them."

"I can . . . I will . . . I do."

I get out of the hammock and reach for him. He stands and we embrace; then he eases away from my arms and returns to the bench, while I sit on a chair near him.

"Remember when I was living near Mom and Dad, in Montgomery?" he inquires, "and I asked you for a referral to a therapist?"

"Yes, I do. In fact, the guy whose name I gave you was a friend of Mary Anne's, someone she thought highly of."

My six-foot-four, 145-pound brother stands and approaches the edge of the dock, looking like a tree himself: long, thin, gentle, carrying a weathered and weary soul within. "Well, I really appreciated the referral," he says as he looks out over the water, then turns to face me. "Things were going great, until one day, I went in very upset about some images that kept haunting me. And he put me under hypnosis. . . . I've been wanting to tell you about this for a long time, Cath, but I haven't been able to."

"What, Paul?"

"Well, I remembered Dad giving you an abortion."

My skin crawls; my head feels like it's swelling.

"I couldn't go back after that. I was angry. I didn't want any more therapy. I swore I'd never set foot in a therapist's office again . . . and I haven't."

I'm stunned. Confused. I can't speak.

"A couple of months ago, when you told me about the flashback you had of Dad raping you, it blew me away. I started having a lot more images, about me and Lucy being threatened by Daddy—that if we ever told anyone, he'd murder us." He shakes as he speaks; sweat beads appear on his forehead and face. He turns toward the water, pulls another chair over, and sits down again. Now his back is toward me.

"I just wanted you to know. Thought you *should* know. And I don't want to talk about it ever again. It's too painful. Can I have your agreement on that?"

"Yes." My voice is weak. I feel as if I've just been kicked in the gut. *An abortion? . . . Paul and Lucy threatened with murder? . . . Never speak of this again?*

We both stare at the water. I remind myself to keep breathing.

Two months later, the director of Dad's senior-living apartment complex calls Peter to say that Dad has been misbehaving with Dorothy, one of the women living near him. Dorothy's son reported that Dad had been courting Dorothy for several weeks, spending the night in her apartment, giving her and two of her friends internal examinations, interfering with her diabetes treatment regimen by bringing her cake and candy. And according to the director, he also accompanied her on several visits to the bank. Just this morning, Dorothy tried to withdraw $1,000. Dad was beside her, smiling. The bank teller got suspicious, so only gave them $300 and then contacted Dorothy's son, who paid his mother a surprise visit and asked about the money. Dorothy denied having it, and her son suspected Dad had helped himself. The director wants us to look into the matter immediately and Peter assures her we will.

That night, the staff make certain Dorothy and Dad stay at the bingo game while we search Dad's belongings. As we open the door to his apartment, we're assaulted by George Gershwin's "Rhapsody in Blue," full blast.

"Classic," Peter comments. "The guy's got his old stereo rigged up. Your dad is *absolutely* classic."

The humor of the moment is short-lived. Forty glasses, thirty-three plates, thirty napkins, two hundred brand-new disposable razors—I count them—are strewn in a foot-deep layer all over the floors of his living room and bedroom areas. An empty grocery store cart lies on its side in a corner. Mom's old prescription drugs are scattered on tables and on the couch. Dorothy's personal papers—including bank statements and last will and testament—are on the coffee table, with a ham-and-cheese sandwich of indeterminate age smashed into the tabletop beside them. By the phone I find an original letter he'd written six months ago, in late 1989, accusing us and Uncle Sean of abandoning Mom and moving her into a nursing home against her doctor's recommendation. Several pairs of underwear with dried-up defecation on them are in the bathtub. Photographs of Mom's family are on the floor, frames broken, glass smashed.

"What the fuck *is* all this?" Peter exclaims, glancing around the room.

"*This* is rage. *This* is greed." I swing my arm. "*This* is lunacy. *This* is my father."

The scene before me creates a rolling series of shocks that don't seem to want to end. There are three opened boxes of plastic gloves on Dad's bed, the kind a physician uses for vaginal or rectal examinations.

Folders and envelopes are strewn about. I'm numb, but keep diving into the debris, as if I can find buried treasure somewhere in the rubble if only my emotional stamina holds out long enough.

I sit on Dad's bed, peeling through layers of paper: a report on exercise I did in fourth grade; letters from Sister Almira, my elementary school principal, and Sister Claude, my high school English literature teacher, thanking me for the Mass cards I sent them when their fathers died; a letter from Sister Cornelia, thanking me for doing such a good job as glee club president and class treasurer; several programs from glee club performances in which I was soloist; photographs of me ages twelve to seventeen; and a thank-you note I'd written Mom and Dad and mailed for them to receive the day after our wedding. My stomach is literally in knots. I feel as if I'm looking at a shrine to me, and all I can think about is Paul's story of abortion.

Peter and I decide to admit Dad to Wesley Woods Geri-atric Hospital Psychiatric Ward near Emory University in Atlanta. "You may choose one of two options," I tell him. "Either you can be in the lobby at eight in the morning, dressed and ready to go voluntarily, or I will commit you, and the police will deliver you."

"You can't be serious, Cath, dear."

"I can be and I am. I'll see you at eight."

When we arrive the next morning, Dad's in the lobby wearing his three-piece navy pin-striped suit and black wingtip shoes. He has shaved and shampooed his thick, white, wavy hair; it's fluffy from being blow-dried. He looks like a distinguished elderly medical school professor.

Delivering him to Wesley Woods is the flight from Egypt for me. He will finally be evaluated and cared for by the appropriate people.

"Your suspicions were accurate, Cathy," the psychiatrist tells me during a consultation when their evaluation is complete. "Your father is bipolar, and we'd like to keep him here for about two months. Get him stabilized. Make sure he's got the right meds regimen. Then when it's time for discharge, he'll need to be moved into a personal care facility. We'll help you with finding one."

Tears of relief roll down my cheeks.

The social worker leans forward, handing me a box of tissues, and waits while I pat my face. "Cathy, in all the years we have been doing clinical work, we have never met a man quite like your father," she says. "We want you to know that. Your dad has zero ability to empathize. Zero."

"Thank God . . . finally . . . you can't imagine . . . manna in the desert . . . this is manna in the desert for me." I stand to leave. "Thank you both so much."

*Peter and I, weary and in need of rest, take a week's vaca*tion at home that month, and one night during that time I dream about Mom for the first time since her death. In the dream, I'm standing at the kitchen sink, cutting up fresh vegetables for salad. Rose comes running into the house.

"Look, Mom!" she calls. "You got a letter from Grandma."

Sure enough, there's an envelope with no stamp on it, in Mom's handwriting, and addressed to me.

"How could it get here without postage?" I ask.

Rose and I smile at each other and then, in unison, say, "You don't need stamps to mail things from heaven!"

I open the letter and read it:

Dear Catherine,

I want you to know that I am so, so very happy here. It is absolutely wonderful, beyond anything you could possibly imagine. I don't know how to tell you, except to say that when fish die they become the ocean. It's marvelous, Cath. I know you can't understand what I'm saying, but I know you know it. Like you knew what was going on inside me when I was dying, even though I couldn't use the correct words. You understood like no one else did.

I want you to know how totally happy I am. It is wonderful beyond anything I ever hoped for.

Love,
Mom

Mom's astrological sign was Pisces.

Chapter 22

May 1992. I open a small gray box containing the new pair of southwestern-style earrings I bought in anticipation of this day. They're oval, outlined in silver, embedded with red and black stones. Black for power; red for anger. It has been two years since Mom's death, and there is so much to be angry about.

I am still crying gut-wrenching tears after orgasm, and I've been plagued with flashbacks. I tell Mary Anne I feel like I'm living with time bombs inside my head; we discuss the option of including hypnosis in my treatment. Thus begins the phase of incest recovery I think of as major surgery, with our relationship as the anesthesia, and hypnosis as the knife. I continue with individual sessions weekly, keeping notes on nightmares, blips of memory, and full-blown flashbacks that intrude into my daily life, so that I can explore them further under hypnosis at intervals Mary Anne and I agree on. I also join a support group for incest survivors that meets weekly in Atlanta.

Peter travels with me to Macon on hypnosis days, and though neither of us has been inclined to pray the rosary as adults, he sits in Mercer Medical School's library and prays with Mom's old rosary beads while Mary Anne takes me to the office of a colleague experienced in hypnotherapy. Knowing that Peter is praying while I'm under trance gives me courage.

Mary Anne and I return to her office for debriefing after hypnosis, before Peter drives me home. The day is long, expensive, and arduous. The process of retrieving repressed memories is like putting together pieces of a jigsaw puzzle. Each piece builds on those around it, but because each piece is laden with feelings—fear, horror, dread, anger, sadness, relief—the emotional fallout is difficult to manage. I've restructured my professional life, reducing my client load to less than half the usual. I've been consulting with a psychiatrist well versed in the nuances of trauma recovery for supervision of my clinical work, and I've developed a consultation group with three colleagues who, like myself, are committed to examining how our personal lives affect our clinical work and vice versa. All of these choices have helped prepare me for this day.

"Hey, Cath!" Peter calls from downstairs. "We don't need to leave for another half hour, but I just want you to know I'm home. Meet you down here when you're ready!"

"Okay. . . . Thanks, Peter!" I call as I open the dresser drawer, pull out a black bra and black T-shirt, and put them on. Next, I need a strong symbol of Christ—something to remind me of the power of good over evil, something to remind Dad of my faith in God.

My faith has grown in ways I could never have predicted. And who would have ever thought that I would leave the Catholic church, where as a child I found strength and hope? But once I learned that incest is most common in patriarchal systems, it became impossible to participate without either feeling guilty about being part of a process that breeds abuse or becoming enraged by the church's oppression of women in the name of God.

I hunt through my jewelry box and find a three-inch-long rustic silver crucifix on a chain of quarter-inch links. Peter and I received it when we gave a talk on commitment at a college student retreat in Auburn years ago. I pull it over the black T-shirt and admire my reflection in the mirror, but my stomach tightens with anxiety. "Stand tall," I tell myself out loud, "even though you're terrified."

Self-talk isn't enough. I dig through a pile of books by my night-stand, looking for *Journeys by Heart: A Christology of Erotic Power* by Rita Nakashima Brock, then flip it open to a favorite line and read aloud: "Anger is a key to both love and nonviolence, and it is pivotal to self-affirmation and liberation. It is the healthy response of a self to violation and a crucial avenue to self-acceptance and acceptance of others."

This passage speaks strongly to me. I've been plagued with self-contempt for as long as I can remember, and I tend to be perfection-istic and judgmental of others. Furthermore, every emerging memory of Dad's abuse seems to feed my dislike of Peter. He joined a partners-of-survivors support group and decided to protect me from having to deal with Dad directly—handling all phone calls and taking him to the doctor when necessary—and gives me his unswerving dedication, driving me to Macon and praying for me. Yet *anything* about him that resembles Dad—his corny sense of humor, lack of awareness about *his* personality flaws, his dependence on me, even his love—fills me with disdain. And there are months when I cannot stand the sight of his pe-nis. In fact, lately, I've been experiencing erotic longings for women.

Why? Is it an unconscious wish to love my own body back, or to find out just what it was that Dad enjoyed so much? Maybe my psyche is work-ing hard to protect me from being promiscuous with men. . . . Part of me wants to fuck them all, use them to act out my rage at Dad.

Our bed is a mess. I lean over, pulling the covers back and smooth-ing the fitted sheet, then pull the top sheet up, shake out the blanket, and tuck it under the mattress at the foot of the bed. *And just because I can't bear having sex with Peter, that doesn't mean I don't get horny.*

Easing the blanket over the top sheet, I run my hands along its surface, until the ripples disappear. *I yearn to have sex with someone, anyone with whom I have no history. . . . Is that why I'm attracted to women now?* Sometimes I imagine going to a lesbian bar, just to find someone to try it with.

I reach for the pillows, fluff them up, and place them beside each other. *Think of the people who could get hurt . . . Peter, our children, the woman I'd be using. Besides, I'm a therapist. . . . I know part of me is regressed to the ages of abuse . . . too young to be having sex. Why reabuse myself?*

I stand back; the bed is made. Rays of sunlight dance across our pillows. *Will we ever get beyond all this sexual pain?*

"You about ready, Cath?" Peter's halfway up the stairs. "It's getting to be time!"

"I'll be down in a few minutes!"

"Okay, I'll wait for you in the car!"

Bending to put my panties on, I remember how often my father took them off. *You will be safe today,* I assure my vagina as I pull on black bikini underwear. Next, I slip into black knee-highs and black jeans, and hunt through clutter on my closet floor for black boot-shoes: the finishing touch to the vestments of my day. I am now a priestess, schooled in the private seminary of prayer, reflection, study, and psychotherapy, and I will go about the business of exorcising demons.

Dad is now out of the psychiatric ward and living back in Atherton, the facility where we originally moved him and Mom, but in the personal care section. I've alerted the director about my plans to meet with him and asked her if she'd keep an eye on him after we leave. I also made an appointment with his psychiatrist, so that I could inform him of the details of my plans in case Dad has some kind of breakdown afterward. I asked for his opinion about the likelihood of Dad becoming violent in response to our visit, but his psychiatrist was positive that wouldn't happen. "Your father is a weak old man, Catherine," he said. "And he's taking medication—he might become upset, but he won't get dangerous. Those days are over. But I suspect he'll deny everything . . . I hope you're prepared for that."

I think I am. I insert the earrings into my pierced ears, admiring their reflection in the mirror, then pause and make the sign of the cross. Today I will meet the source of my heartache. Speak my truth to my father. Look him in the eye and give voice to my agony.

"Come right in, sweetheart," Dad says as he opens the door. He leans forward to kiss me. I flinch.

"I would prefer that you not touch me today," I say, sickened by the stale stench of his flesh. I look for Peter, who had gone to Dad's room first and told him I'd soon be visiting him with my therapist. Mary Anne and I had arrived twenty minutes later. Our plan is that Peter will restrain Dad should his psychiatrist's prediction prove wrong. Peter stands next to the window opposite us, his arms draped over Mom's old crewel-upholstered, wing-back chair.

"Yes, of course, dear," Dad says when I refuse his kiss. I wonder if he suspects our agenda.

"Please, have a seat." He points to the purple-velvet-upholstered Victorian couch that had been in Ammy's living room until she died, the one that Mom inherited.

"Yes, thank you," I say. "We'll sit down. But first I'd like you to meet my therapist of the last thirteen years, Mary Anne Armour."

"Yes, how do?" Dad asks, shaking Mary Anne's hand just as he once greeted patients in his waiting room.

His current home is one bedroom with an adjoining bathroom. To the right of the door, on a wall unit Peter and I bought at Kmart, is Dad's Fisher stereo unit, radio, and turntable, several old records, and some books. Among those, I see the copy of Anne Morrow Lindbergh's *Gifts from the Sea* that I'd given Mom for Mother's Day 1989, plus an ornate leather-bound German Bible that was his great-grandmother's. Beside the wall unit is a framed papal blessing from Pope Pius XI. Next to Dad's twin bed, on Ammy's old night table, are an old lamp and a telephone. But the night table's finish is warped from years of Mom and Dad's spilling drinks they never bothered to clean up.

I wonder if my sensitivity to the details of the room is a form of dissociation, an avenue away from my anxiety. I'm ready to confront Dad, but I'm terrified. Not so much of speaking as of what might happen later. Will a wall in my unconscious come tumbling down? Will a dam break, spilling even more wretched memories into awareness?

Mary Anne and I sit on the couch, which gives forth a musty mixture of alcohol and cigarette smoke. *Though Mom's dead, their history lives on in the upholstery.* I turn to look at Mary Anne.

"This was my grandmother's," I whisper.

"Ammy's?" she whispers back.

"Yes. It's comforting, sitting on it. Feels as if she's with us."

Mary Anne takes my hand and squeezes it. "I know that helps."

"Well, to what do I owe this glorious occasion?" Dad asks, looking at Mary Anne. "Catherine hasn't visited me for such a long time."

"I haven't been to visit you because I've been struggling with some very difficult things," I say, intercepting his detour attempt. Then I try to appeal to his love of medicine. "It's sort of like a person with cancer. Like I have a melanoma threatening to destroy the healthy cells of my body, and so I'm in treatment, to rid my body of the disease."

"Oh, is that so, sweetheart? I'm sorry to hear that, dear." His tone is sarcastic as he leans back in Mom's chair, the same chair Peter is standing behind, and crosses his legs. He wears black penny loafers and black socks, a pair of gray flannel slacks, a white Dacron drip-dry shirt with a soiled red foulard bow tie, and the black, white, and red hound's-tooth check sports jacket he's had for over thirty years. The wool has thinned and the cuffs are frayed, but he's often said he thought he looked dapper in it. I'm struck by the fact that he and I have on the same colors, red and black, and I wonder if he dressed this way after learning from Peter that I was coming, or if it's typical for him to wear these winter clothes in the middle of May. He looks hot and pale, but younger than his eighty-one years.

"I've come to tell you about some events I remember happening when I was a child," I say. Mary Anne's warm fingers squeeze my hand.

"Is that so? Well, carry on then, dear. I imagine this is quite difficult for you, and as your father, of course I would want to help you in any way I could." He says this in a monotone, as if reading something he's not at all interested in.

I speak in the clear, calm voice I had hoped for, listing the incidents I'd reported to his psychiatrist: molesting me by the piano as a child, the first rape at age ten, fondling my breasts in the middle of the night after I got my first bra, and raping me in the guise of teaching the facts of life while holding a knife to my throat. Dad watches me without interrupting.

"I have felt devastated by these events, Dad," I finish. "I am so angry at you, and I am so hurt. *How* could you do those things to me?" My voice quivers and my eyes fill with tears.

He turns away from me, directing his words to Mary Anne. "Obviously, my daughter is crazy. This, I am sure, is very clear to you. Something is seriously wrong with Catherine's mind, and I suspect this has been true for a very long time."

"No," Mary Anne says. "I know Cathy very well. Cathy is *not* crazy. I can assure you of that, Doctor Graham. In fact, she has remarkable psychological strength. And she's talking to you about her pain. I see this is difficult for you to hear, but it's true."

"Oh, I see what you're saying," he says, taking his glasses off and chewing on the end of the earpiece while he glances up and down across the room. "Hmm . . . well, I can tell you that yes, Catherine's mother was in the hospital for a long time when she was ten. And yes, Catherine did everything her mother did not do."

Bingo.

"But she enjoyed it. You enjoyed every minute of it, Catherine Girl," he adds, turning his attention to me.

"What? I did not!"

"Well, you certainly never complained." He shifts his eyes back to Mary Anne. "Catherine was a very capable, very remarkable child. She cooked, did dishes, pots, pans, laundry, kept an eye on the younger ones, and never complained. She was eager to please. I had no idea it bothered her to have so much responsibility. Cate wondered sometimes if we were expecting too much of her, but Catherine always said she *wanted* to help out."

"And what about the rapes? What about the way you touched my breasts?" It is all I can get out. I am turning numb.

"That's out of the question, dear heart," he says. "It never happened. And I'm sorry you're in so much distress that you would dream up such utter nonsense. Obviously some kind of craziness has gotten into your head."

"I have to go now." I stand and motion for Mary Anne to follow me. To Dad I say, "I've had enough. Goodbye, Dad."

I walk toward the door, with Peter and Mary Anne close behind.

"Well, dear, I'm so sorry you have to leave so soon, but I understand, sweetheart. I hope you are well again someday, dear heart." His tone is still sarcastic.

Peter goes to tell the director we're leaving, and I walk Mary Anne to her car. I feel raw, raped again, except for one very important factor. This time I have an advocate: Mary Anne.

Peter and I spend the weekend trying to comfort each other. Meanwhile, the director calls to report that Dad's doing fine. He had told her that the reason I hadn't been visiting was because I had cancer, and that in all likelihood I wouldn't be coming anymore because I was very ill and would be undergoing treatment.

On the evening of Father's Day 1992, Paul calls.

"What did you *do?*" His agitated voice comes over the line without even a "Hi, Cath, how are you?"

"What do you mean? What are you talking about?"

"You know what I mean, Cath. I just got off the phone with Dad, and he sounds so upset. He said you arrived with your therapist and you accused him of sexually abusing you."

"That's true, Paul, I did. But I also alerted his caregivers so they could give him any support he might need. I didn't do it in a cruel way."

"How could you? He's so upset."

"Paul, why are you acting this way? Why are you turning on me?"

"Because you turned on our father!"

I feel spit upon by the one relative I thought I could rely on. I think about the incest survivors in my support group, and the ones I've treated in therapy over the years: This is consistent with their experiences. I remind myself that my family had been organized around keeping these secrets for decades, and we children were brainwashed to believe Dad was entitled to never have to be accountable for inflicting pain on our family. Just because I'm ready to change the family rules doesn't mean I can expect Paul to be ready. I cry, hard, feeling as if I'm in the middle of a nightmare. And then I hear Paul crying, and he speaks.

"I'm sorry, Cath. I'm *so* sorry. Here you are, my sister, and I love you so much. But he's my father, and I love him too. And he's an old man, a widower. And I'm so confused. I can't *imagine* him doing those things. It's just too much. I'm sorry. I want to be supportive. I really do. I just don't have the emotional stamina tonight. I'll call you back in a couple of weeks."

It's difficult to absorb his words. They fracture my trust in him, and stir up tidal waves of grief. Wasn't he the brother who had told me he witnessed our father giving me an abortion? Hadn't he already acknowledged that the incest memories I shared with him had triggered more of his own memories?

I hang up, feeling as if I'm releasing the last of my hopes to ever be understood by the people I grew up with. All of them . . . even Paul . . . are deserting me in recovery, just as they were absent during the most excruciating events of my childhood.

Chapter 23

When I return home from work the next day, I find a letter in the mailbox from Atherton, notifying us that the rates will be going up January 1. I sit down and write a letter to my father:

Dad,

I'm thinking about what an incredible person you are. Every time you sexually abused me, you broke eight of the Ten Commandments, and you continue to deny it all. Even if you had no conscious memory of these events, still, you were able to look me in the eye and not care a thing about what I was going through. I used to excuse your behavior. No more.

We have been notified by Atherton that their rates are going up in January. I'm no longer willing to burden myself by contributing to your finances. Your follies have cost me more than any child should ever have to pay. I'm also no longer willing to participate in a living arrangement for you that requires Peter to be responsible for taking you to the doctor. I hate to think what kind of stress it must be for him to even be in your presence.

I will find you a personal-care home that is completely within your financial means. It will be a downgrade from the life to which you have become accustomed, but I will see to it that your next home situation provides transportation to all doctor appointments and includes adequate psychiatric care, so that your moods, functioning, and medication can be monitored. As soon as an adequate place is found, the family will move you.

Catherine

I put the letter in our mailbox, and as I raise the little red flag, I see myself at age thirteen, naked from the waist down, kneeling beside Ammy's bed, crying. She is in her nightgown, under the covers, dead. The image scares and confuses me. It doesn't fit with my memories of being in my grandmother's house. It doesn't fit with the sense of pride I've always felt about Mom's family.

They lived on the second and third floors of their funeral home in Princeton for most of Mom's childhood, and Ammy continued living there after Mom, Uncle Kevin, and Uncle Sean married. The offices and casket display rooms were on the first floor, and in the basement were the embalming rooms, the freezer, and the tunnel to St. John's Church next door (for rolling caskets through for funerals). Family members and employees counseled the bereaved and collaborated with clergy in ministering to the dying. There was a sense of honor about their business, a sense of being called to do God's work.

Where are these horrible images of my kneeling at Ammy's bedside coming from? Ammy died on July 14, 1962. The day I sat with her on the porch, I didn't understand why she was coughing and so weak. Neither did she. Or perhaps she knew, and didn't want to upset me. Later, I learned that despite a mastectomy in her sixties, her breast cancer had metastasized to her lungs. She died at age seventy-six. I saved a copy of the obituary that appeared in the Princeton paper:

MRS. BRIDGET MCNAMARA O'CONNOR

Our town will miss the gracious presence of Mrs. Bridget McNamara O'Connor. After a busy and fruitful life she is gone. It is safe to say that no Princeton woman was better known. To hundreds of families she was both friend and counselor in the sensitive hour of bitter loss. Blessed with a retentive mind, she was on a first-name basis with most, readily expert in calling off in detail their genealogies.

Widowed in 1939, she carried the management of her funeral home successfully, following in the pattern set by her personable husband, Kevin P. O'Connor.

Her death leaves a wide gap in the civic, charitable, and church activities in which she was a leader.

I remember crying myself to sleep many nights as a teenager, missing Ammy. But I always thought it odd that I couldn't remember her wake, funeral, or burial.

After weeks of more memory blips similar to the one I experienced at the mailbox, and a haunting sense that something important might have locked away other memories, I schedule a hypnosis session. Perhaps that "something important" is a memory I could be free enough to know only after releasing myself further from Dad's power. Most of all, I want to exhume the part of me that was buried with Ammy.

As he did in previous sessions, the hypnotherapist, while guiding me into a trance state, tells me that when I come out of the trance I will remember in detail everything accessed during the session. "Go to the events around Ammy's funeral," he says, once I have reached a deep level of trance. "Anything that seems to be important. . . . Tell Mary Anne and me about it."

"There is an incident with my father."

"Okay, Cathy. We will listen, and if at any time you want to come out of the trance, raise a finger on your right hand, and I'll bring you out. Do you understand?"

"Yes, I do." A scene comes into my mind. "I'm standing around Ammy's bed with my cousins. I'm toward the back, by the window. Uncle Sean is by the door. He's telling us it's okay, we can leave now. Ammy loved us very much and she's in heaven. Even though she died, she still loves us. Her love will never die. He says she wanted us all to be there together, around her bed. She put it in her will, because she didn't want us to be scared seeing her in a casket.

"Uncle Sean's leading my cousins out the door now, toward the living room, but Dad's standing in the hall, looking at me. I'm trying not to have an expression on my face because I don't know what kind of mood he's in. I'm staring straight ahead, following my cousins into the living room. My cousin Brendan's sitting on the piano bench crying, and everyone's trying to help him, especially Aunt Mary. Poor Brendan, he wants Ammy to not be dead.

"Aunt Mary is telling us we're all going back to their house, while Uncle Sean and Mom and Uncle Kevin do important things here at the funeral home. I'm glad we're going to their house. I love it there. 'Catherine and Uncle George will stay behind for a while and help,' she tells us.

"Uh, oh. She's saying we'll join them later. I don't see *why* Dad and I are staying behind to help. Mom's the one who always does all the work. Dad doesn't help at all. He hated Ammy, and he hates everybody in Mom's family. I'd much rather stay and help Mom instead of Dad.

"Aunt Mary and my cousins and Andrew and Lucy and Paul are getting up to leave now, and I'm walking into the guest room. I'm closing the door so I can be by myself and pray. Mom and Uncle Kevin and Uncle Sean are going downstairs. I can hear them."

Silence. Then, "I see Dad dragging me out of the guest room and into Ammy's room. I'm fighting him: 'No! Leave me alone!'

"'Now, Catherine Girl, stop this nonsense,' he says. 'I arranged with Uncle Sean and Mommy that we could go in Ammy's room—just the two of us—so you could have some private time with her body, sweetheart. Because you were so close to her.'

"'No!' I say. 'Ammy didn't want it that way! She had it in her will! You're going against her wishes!'"

Silence. I feel one tear roll down my cheek.

"Watch it like a movie, Cathy." The hypnotherapist's voice is gentle, reassuring. "Put it on the screen, and tell us what you see."

"He's smacking his child across the face now and telling her to shut up or she'll be the next person dead. He's dragging her into her grandmother's bedroom and throwing her on the other bed. He's angry. And talking mean. 'You think all those O'Connors are so great. You think Ammy was so great. Where are they *now*, huh, sweetheart? *Nobody's* helping you now, are they, dear?'

"It doesn't matter that his thing is going in and out of the little girl's hole like a saw, because she's staring at her grandmother's face, and her grandmother looks peaceful. Even though the grandmother is dead, she still loves her granddaughter very much, and the girl knows that."

I stop, unable to speak until the hypnotherapist reminds me that he and Mary Anne are there, and tells me to continue.

"He's leaving the room now. My panties are on the floor and my legs are hanging over the side of the bed. But that's okay, because panties are only clothes, and bodies are only shells. And anyway, I'm sleeping over with Ammy, and she's alive, and my family's still in Brooklyn, and they decided not to come get me for weeks—maybe never. Maybe I can just live with Ammy for the rest of my life.

"I love the wallpaper. It's so pretty. It's a pink background. Mrs. Flynn, Aunt Mary's mother, always said a woman should have soft pink in her bedroom because it gives her complexion a rosy glow. That's why Ammy picked it out. And it has fuzzy white flowers on it. I rub it, and rub it, and rub it. Ammy lets me, as much as I want, 'cause it feels good."

I feel tears in my eyes and dripping down my face.

"The girl is getting up and going over to her grandmother. She's talking, sort of in a whisper but a little bit louder. 'Ammy, I'm sorry. I didn't mean to. I couldn't help it.' She's kneeling down now, next to the bed, and she's touching her grandmother's nightgown, and she's crying very hard. She's trying to pray, but the only words she can think of are *I better get out of here. Fast.* She's standing up, putting on her panties. She's looking in the mirror, adjusting her skirt and her blouse and her hair. She's not thinking anymore, 'cause her mind is bursting with fear and sorrow. She's going out into the hall, automatic-like, and she bumps into her father. He doesn't even get out of the way.

"'Catherine, you must not trouble your mother with *anything*. Is that clear?'

"'Yes, Father.'

"'Is that *perfectly* clear?'

"'Yes, Father.'

"He tells me there's been a change of plans. That I'm to go downstairs and straight down the hall of the funeral home to the back entrance. That one of the men will drive me to Uncle Sean's.

"I'm running downstairs and through the hall now, past the portraits of Grandfather O'Connor and Great-grandfather O'Connor and Great-grandfather McNamara. They're my ancestors, and *they* were strong enough to get over here from Ireland and keep this family going. *I* can be strong, too."

Silence.

"What's happening now, Cathy?"

"I'm hiding in the bathroom at Uncle Sean and Aunt Mary's house, crying. Mad and sad. Trying to wash my bottom with a washcloth and Aunt Mary's sweet-smelling guest soap. I'm afraid. My panties are dirty. I smell horrible. What if they think I never change my underpants? Aunt Mary's calling me: 'Catherine! Catherine! Come down here and help out!'

"I'm running downstairs. Cousin Eileen is bossing her brothers around. She's the oldest and she's very responsible, like me. Little Sean and Brendan are a handful, so she's always helping her mother. Aunt Mary is tending to Baby Margaret. It's getting dark, and I'm worried because the funeral is tomorrow and Mom and Uncle Sean and Uncle Kevin and my father aren't back yet. What if they never get back?

"I miss Mom, but I'm scared to see her. I feel like I'm in a movie about an orphan in a concentration camp . . . like I'm Anne Frank, but I know I'm *not* in a concentration camp and my family isn't like Anne Frank's at all. It's weird.

"They're back. I'm looking into the living room and I can see that Mommy's very tired, but she's glad to be with her brothers. Dad gives me the don't-tell-anything-to-your-mother look. Why? There's nothing to tell.

"Mom's glad to see her nieces and nephews, and she's going over to the bassinet to pick up Baby Margaret. She's talking to her. My mommy loves babies. She wishes she had one. I wish she had one, too."

Silence.

"We just finished dessert. I'm helping Eileen with the dishes and I'm starting to cry, but trying not to. Eileen can tell. 'Catherine, I know you're sad. You loved Ammy so much, and Ammy loved you. And she still loves you.'

"Mommy was watching us. She's coming over and putting her arms around me. Her hug feels so good, but I forgot to close my eyes. I can see Dad over her shoulder. He's staring at me like I'm doing something wrong and I'm gonna get punished if I don't stop. I'm pushing her away now. She doesn't need to worry about me. She has enough to worry about.

"'Come on over here and have your cocktail, Cate!' My father is talking to her. 'For medicinal purposes!' He's smiling. What does he mean, that cocktails are medicine? I hate it when he makes Mom drink.

"I'm going upstairs to check on Lucy and Paul now. Aunt Mary sent them up to take a bath and put their pajamas on. I'm running—accidentally—right into Andrew. "He's on his way back down the stairs. He's been up there playing with our cousin Sean.

"'Isn't this really too much, Cath?' he's asking. He likes it at their house. That's what he means.

"'Sure is,' I'm saying back to him."

Hypnosis amazes me. I remember awful things, yet remain relaxed. However, like Novocaine wearing off after a dental procedure, the anesthetic effect of being in an altered state of consciousness subsides, leaving raw pain. As it had after previous sessions, that process begins the next day, intensifies within forty-eight hours, and then lingers, waiting for integration of my thoughts and feelings. As usual, some are typical of a child at the age of my regression, some typical of my current age. So many thoughts and feelings. To help express them, I write the following poem:

> *I'm in a fucked-up Saturday*
> *feeling all fucked over and over*
>
> *The sun shines and birds sing*
> *but my body is weighted down by lead*
>
> *My heart pines over my vagina—*
> *a cave of destruction and fear*
>
> *It hurts. It hurts. Dear God, it hurts.*
>
> *Your Spirit is willing*
> *my flesh is just aching*
>
> *This temple, he thought it*
> *was his for the taking.*

Several months later, after the hypnosis, I feel compelled to go back to Ammy's house and make arrangements with Uncle Sean and

Aunt Mary. I had told them about the incest after Mom had died, though not the particulars. They'd both reacted with expressions of grief, love, and support. Later, after Uncle Sean had asked me several times over the phone whether the therapy was helping and whether it was good for me to remember horrible events, I sent them a tape of a talk Marilyn van Derber Atler, a former Miss America, gave for the Georgia Council on Child Abuse about her incestuous history with her father, and her therapy. I needed Uncle Sean and Aunt Mary to understand what it was like to grapple with post-traumatic stress, and I had identified with much of what Marilyn had to say. Furthermore, because of her status, I thought the information coming from van Derber Atler would sound more credible to Aunt Mary and Uncle Sean. Too often, people attribute incest to lower socioeconomic classes and uneducated people. I felt that perhaps Uncle Sean and Aunt Mary's understanding might be hampered by this assumption. As it turned out, Marilyn's tape did help. After hearing it, they called and again offered support. Their questions about the value of remembering ceased.

When making arrangements to return to Princeton, I tell Uncle Sean I want to spend a day at the funeral home, that I want some time alone in Ammy's apartment, that I want to go to Mass at St. John's Church, and I want him to take me to the cemetery to visit Ammy's grave. He is eager to grant my wishes.

The funeral home, a two-story, all-brick Georgian-style building with white pillars and a basement, was constructed in 1959, three years after an arsonist's fire destroyed part of the original building, plus the entire original church and rectory next door. I remember Ammy showing Mom blueprints for the building, and I remember her excitement about the wallpapers she'd selected for her bedroom and the guest room, dining room, and kitchen. None of the wallpaper has been changed. Though Uncle Sean has arranged some office furniture in her old bedroom, there are a few remaining pieces of hers: a bed and night table in the guest room, a table in the hallway, a few other odds and ends. Her apartment smells the same, and it looks as if she moved out just yesterday.

"I don't know what exactly you want in here, Cath," Uncle Sean says, standing in the same spot where Dad had stood thirty years before, warning me not to trouble Mother with what he'd done to me. "But I'll leave you alone for as long as you need. If there's anything I can help you with, don't hesitate to tell me. I'll be right downstairs in my office."

"Thank you, Uncle Sean," I say, smiling at him. The six-foot-two, sixty-four-year-old gray-haired man standing before me is, without knowing it, giving me what we therapists call a corrective emotional experience, and I feel blessed.

"I love you, Uncle Sean."

"I love you too, kiddo, and don't you forget it." There's an oomph in his voice that reminds me of Ammy, and though he wears a handsome glen plaid suit and black dress shoes, he resembles Mom in his thick hair, parted on the side and brushed back; his round, droopy chin; his brown eyes slanting at me from behind glasses; and the horizontal lines wrinkling his square forehead like the hint of a musical staff.

He turns to walk down the stairs. At their foot, he closes the door with a brass sign reading PRIVATE on it behind him: His respect for my boundaries is palpable.

I walk from room to room, stroking the walls, the drapes, talking to God and to Ammy. I feel gratitude for the ability to be here, until I enter her bedroom and stand in the spot where the bed that I'd been raped in was. I imagine my thirteen-year-old self, terror stricken and bare bottomed, and a surge of rage ignites inside my stomach. I sit on the floor and write in my journal:

The thing about dead people is that they're gone—no matter how much they loved you or you loved them. Even if you get raped right next to their corpses, there's nothing they can do. Nothing.

Maybe when an uncle says "Your grandmother is in a heavenly sleep," he means like magic—so she really could wake up, for just the moment when you need her the most.

Ammy, wake up, please—just for a minute! I won't tell anybody. I need you. I need you to tell me it's okay. I don't want you to be angry. And . . . please, tell me God won't send me to hell. Come back, Ammy! Come back and talk to me!

It's over. Heavenly sleep means dead, and you know it. She's gone somewhere else. Doing other things. Can't be your grandmother anymore.

I close my journal and put down my pen. Sprawling out on the floor, I cry until I'm exhausted. Then I walk into the guest room I slept in as a child, lie down on the bed, and fall into a peaceful sleep.

I awaken an hour later, when the church chimes, a sound I cherish, strike the hour of three. Time to go to the cemetery. I walk downstairs, wishing I could take Ammy's apartment back to Georgia with me and leave the memory of rape behind.

"Catherine, I want you to follow me down to the basement." Uncle Sean is standing in the lobby with a large set of keys in one hand, directing me down the hall with his other. "There's something I need to show you before we head over to the cemetery. I never knew it existed, until I found it down here a few months ago."

He leads the way down the hall, then the stairs. "Aunt Mary and I have discussed it, and we both agree you're the one—out of all the members of this family—who should have it. There's no doubt about that."

He reaches behind one of the old filing cabinets in a dark corner of the storage room. I am struck by the solemnity of the moment, and my heart races in my chest as he pulls out an eighteen by twenty-two color portrait of Ammy. My eyes fill with tears.

"It's in very good condition, Catherine. Oh, the gold leaf on the frame needs touching up, but that's simple enough." He places it on a nearby table and pulls the chain hanging from a lightbulb overhead. I wipe tears from my face and take a deep breath, thinking, *You have no idea how much this means to me. I haven't told you the real reason why I needed to come back, and I can't. It might hurt you too much, and you'd think I'm crazy.*

"I would say that your grandmother was in her early fifties when this was done. It would've been shortly after your grandfather died and she'd taken over the business. She probably felt it was important to do because of all the other portraits in the hallway upstairs. And then I guess she decided not to hang it. I don't know."

The portrait has a dark brown background. Ammy wears a burgundy dress with a thin gold trim, and a cameo at the bottom of her long V-neck neckline. Though her facial expression is serious, her brown eyes look warm and loving. Her hair is gray and parted on the side, with soft curls on top and along the edges, just below her ears. She wears small pearl earrings.

"Catherine, this was a very difficult stage of life for your grandmother," he continues. "Grandfather O'Connor had been ill for ten years before he died, and she stood by him through it all, even with the pain she must have felt about his affair with his secretary—you knew about that, didn't you?"

I nod, remembering the fights my parents had about my grandfather. Dad would ridicule Mom for continuing to love her father after the affair, and then she'd cry, or head for the liquor cabinet and drink herself numb.

Uncle Sean's voice is somber with his own grief. "And your grandfather was bankrupt when he died, and had never told Ammy about the financial troubles. She must have felt so betrayed. But she was quite a woman, Cath. She took over the business and paid back every penny of debt—and she didn't have to, you know. She believed it was the right thing to do. She gained our reputation back, and she made a success of this business. Your grandmother was a strong woman, and so are you. Aunt Mary and I hope this portrait will be a comfort to you. Find a special spot in your home for it—especially now, during this difficult time in your own life. It will be good for those girls of yours to have it around, too. Family legacies are important."

I throw my arms around him and squeeze, but he keeps talking, so I pull back.

"Your grandmother loved you, Catherine. And she loved the way you loved her." He smiles. "Oh, I can remember how she just ate up those letters you used to write her. She'd read them over and over. And she still loves you. People die, but their love never dies. She's in heaven right now, proud of you, I'm sure."

We embrace. I rest my head against his lapel, tears of gratitude dampening his suit, while he pats the top of my head.

Chapter 24

In an effort to reduce stress and take better care of my body, I schedule weekly massages with a massage therapist who is sensitive to the issues of incest survivors.

One day, as she presses against my neck, I feel intense emotional pain and scream inside my mind: *No, Daddy! No!* Please *don't do it!* Please *don't! No! It's mine and you can't have it!* Stop! Then I see him smack me across the face, roll me over, and stick a needle in my backside, holding my neck down tightly while Mom holds my legs. I tell the therapist I'm having a flashback and ask her to stop.

"I can stop if you want me to, Cathy," she says. "But we could also try something else. You could imagine your body as a big teapot. Your head is the lid, and the flashback and associated emotional pain is the water boiling. You could close your eyes while I massage your scalp, and imagine that you are opening the lid, letting all the steam, all the images of abuse, out of you."

I try her suggestion and, feeling empowered, am able to enjoy the massage. But in the days and weeks following, the torment of similar flashbacks persists in seemingly random contexts. I am able to manage my life despite their intrusion until I experience two ovarian cyst attacks. One occurs when we return from taking Beth to college. After reading on the dock behind our house, I decide to go in and start dinner, but on the way up the hill I suddenly double over in pain. Am I having an attack of appendicitis? I call for help, but no one hears. I crawl into the house, then up the stairs, crying for Peter, but he's fallen asleep in front of the TV on the second floor and doesn't rouse. I lie on the kitchen floor in the fetal position, wondering if I'm dying while praying that I'm not. The pain subsides by the time Peter awakens and comes downstairs, and I'm convinced that my symptoms must have been psychosomatic. Mary Anne told me once that launching children—letting go when they reach that necessary stage of separating in order to pursue their own lives—can feel like emotional labor pains. Hanging on to that metaphor, I conclude I must be having a tough time letting go of Beth.

When the pain returns two months later, I make an appointment with my gynecologist. She gives me several vaginal exams and a vaginal sonogram over a period of a few months. These procedures terrify me, triggering more flashbacks, and after each one I am exhausted. For the first time in my life, I consider suicide.

I'm taking a hot bath before bed. Every cell seems to want to scream itself out of my body. The comfort of the bathwater caressing my skin is soothing, but it's not enough. I want it to caress my head: the place where all the memories are stored, where the psychological work takes place; where the prayers get said, and refuse to be said; where my eagerness to pursue the truth is born, along with fear and a stubborn resistance; where the factory of my dedication to being a sober, sane, and loving mother is housed, along with the will to hold on to a wilting marriage in hopes of change.

Killing myself seems so easy, so benign. I feel like a fish, yearning to go deeper and deeper into the ocean so that returning to the anguish of dry land is no longer an option. Then I recall Mom's words in the dream I had about her after her death: *When fish die, they be-come the ocean.* I start crying—a short cry, just enough to embrace my burning desire to be reunited with Ammy. *There's* so much *I want to talk to you about, Ammy.*

I'm intrigued by how easy it might be to float on my stomach, lay down my head, drink in the water through my eyes, nose, mouth, and ears, and drown. And I'd like to be able to say I choose not to kill myself because it would be wrong, or because I'm thinking about how much it would hurt my children, or Peter, or Mary Anne, or my friends, or my clients. But I don't know for sure why, or how, I control my impulse to self-destruct. It might be that I'm so accustomed to choosing life in the face of death that getting out of the tub and drying off is the natural thing to do.

Yet, I still know something is wrong. Naked, I hang my towel above the tub, walk to the phone, and call Holy Innocents Catholic Retreat House, trying to sound calm. "I need a private retreat," I tell Sister Mary Magdalene when she answers. "Do you have any room for me this weekend? I can be there by noon tomorrow, and I'd like spiritual direction with one of the sisters if that's possible at such late notice." She assures me they have space and that she'll schedule me with Sister Barbara.

That night, Ammy stands before me in a dream. Catherine O'Connor and Catherine McNamara, my maternal great-grandmoth-ers, are behind her. They smile at me and then, in unison, say, "We're all pulling for you, Catherine. Keep at it. We are so proud of you. We're with you every step of the way. Don't give up. *We're* working *with* you."

The weekend at Holy Innocents is nourishing. Daily Mass is scheduled at noon, and the sisters invite me to sit with them during meals, where hearing about their quiet lives tending to the grounds, and meeting for prayer and meditation are a pleasant diversion. I meet with Sister Barbara after breakfast and lunch. She had been a social worker for many years, so she is an ideal fit for me. We talk, pray together, and she suggests Scripture verses to reflect on during the day. In the evenings, one of the nuns stops by to check on me before bed. I depart well rested and refreshed, but when I return home the flashbacks are unrelenting. Mary Anne and I plan another hypnosis session, to help take control of the flashbacks. The day before the session, I wake up with excruciating back pain. I sit with ice packs behind me at work that day, and go straight to bed when I get home. Still phobic about medication, I can't even make myself take a Tylenol.

I'm in bed on my back, knees up and bent, wrapping my arms around my legs, pulling, trying to stretch out the pain, when Peter returns from work and enters the bedroom.

"Why is this happening *now?*" I ask, and then burst into tears. Before he can respond, I blurt, "Maybe it's a body memory. Do you see what this position is? The position in which a woman delivers a baby! I *know* he gave me an abortion. I *know* I need it to hurt, to help me remember."

I'm hysterical with tears for an hour and a half, wanting to scream aloud, "I want my baby! . . . I want my baby! Daddy, what are you *do*ing to me?"

I shake and quiver; Peter stays with me until I'm calm. We're both awed, and we're both frightened. Peter is scared I'm going crazy, and I'm scared I won't make it to Macon for hypnosis the next day. "Don't worry; you'll get there if I have to carry you!" Peter exclaims.

"It's dark. I hear my mother crying." I'm in a deep trance now, and my heart is beating very fast. "I want to reassure her I'm okay, but I can't. Too weak. It's dark and peaceful. Restful. I had died—gone to visit *love.* But my life got launched back into my body.

"Oh, no. Here I am. I hear my father: 'See, Cate! I told you she'd be okay. I know what I'm doing. What do *you* know? You're not a surgeon. *I'm* the one who's the surgeon. I see this kind of thing all the time. People's hearts stop beating, and then they start up again.'"

"What led up to this?" The hypnotherapist's voice is gentle.

"It's so dark. . . . I don't know. . . . I see my mother. She's wearing a striped jacket: blue, yellow, green, red, white. I have ponytails down the sides of my face, but I'm not that young. I'm seventeen. That's what I see. . . . I don't know if it makes any sense. I can't put it together. It's too dark. Too dark and too peaceful. I think it's so dark because this is the worst thing that has ever happened to me in this life."

"Why do you say that, Cathy?"

"Because it's true. But . . . I'm not able to put the light on the wall where it's all written down. Maybe because I feel so peaceful, and if the light went onto the wall, I wouldn't be peaceful. I . . . I just can't do that right now."

"Okay, then go to the pain in your back. Is it hurting?"

I nod.

"Where? And is the pain associated to anything you need to remember? . . . Anything you're ready to remember in order to heal?"

"My back . . . it hurts. Lower right of my spine. Like when Beth was born and the doctor injected an epidural. . . . Had to lie in fetal position while he did. . . . I was having contractions. It was very painful. But that's not what *this* pain's trying to help me remember. That's about another time."

Silence.

"I see a vagina. It's my vagina. Instruments are being put into it. Hands are going into it. They're my father's hands. He's up in my womb, cutting something: something connected by a thread—a nerve, or a muscle—to the muscle in my lower back. It's spasming . . . because it's rebelling. My father is cutting a life from me, and he's sending it back."

"What do you mean by 'a life'?"

"My baby! My father's sending my baby back!" Tears flood my cheeks. I cry from a deep place inside.

"What's happening?"

"I'm being covered in a . . . a blanket of peace. Feels like I felt in the tunnel."

"What tunnel?"

"The one where I moved from death to *love* and from *love* back. Back to alive with my parents. But my baby's okay. Ammy told me she'd take care of my baby forever. I want to tell my mother that I saw Ammy. And she spoke to me. But I better not. It would upset her too much."

"How old are you?"

"Twelve. That's the first age that comes to my mind, but then seventeen comes forward, too . . . bigger."

"Why?"

"I don't know why. I'm just very peaceful. *So* peaceful . . . nice. I like it, but you don't understand how difficult it is for me, for the two babies to be on the other side. Two babies I know physically," I struggle for the right words, "that I had a physical relationship with. My heart's beating fast, and my legs ache, and my hands are warm and clammy, and my vagina has a sharp pain in it. . . . "

Silence. I feel tears on my face.

"What is it, Cathy? What can you tell us now?"

"It's so hard—that they're on the other side. And in a way it shouldn't be hard, because really, I know they're okay. They're in that place I visited. The place where I saw Ammy. They live with her, and with Mary and Jesus."

"Okay," I hear the hypnotherapist say, then, "when I count to five, you'll gradually become awake. But before I do that I want you to imagine a big brick wall, and it stands between you and anything else you might need to remember to heal. I want you to imagine that wall disintegrating. . . . "

I feel joy, because as one section falls away I see Jesus on the other side, and I know that whatever I have to go through, I'll be okay. One day, there will be no barrier between me and Jesus.

I wake up and look at Mary Anne. She's wiping tears from her eyes with tissue that's still in the box. She holds her arm around me all the way to her car, and we sit beside each other in the front seat. Feeling embarrassed and awkward, I laugh about how funny she looked. Her eyes fill with tears again.

"I didn't want to disturb you, Cathy," she says, "and I was so sad, so *grieved*. You looked and acted near death."

The warmth of her love penetrates my body. This moment feels holy.

One month later, the week before Christmas, a package from Dad arrives in the mail. I open it to find a Christmas decoration: a painted-plastic eight-inch-square figurine of Baby Jesus wrapped in a blue blanket, lying in a mound of hay. A Scripture verse is inscribed across the top: *For God so loved the world, that He gave His only begotten son, that whosoever believeth in Him should not perish, but have everlasting life.*—John 3:16.

I sit down and write, no longer able to call him Father:

George,

I received this in the mail today.

I have recently remembered being given two abortions by you, and having a near-death experience during one of them. That you should send me a baby for Christmas is quite timely. That it would symbolize Jesus is what keeps me from throwing it into the garbage. But then, you would be expecting that, wouldn't you?

I am returning it to you. Nothing you say, do, or give me can ever take away the realities of the pain you have inflicted on me.

Catherine

I mail the letter and return to the house to call Peter.

Chapter 25

Two weeks later. New Year's Day, 1993. The table is set with Ammy's china, our sterling silver, and the crystal glasses Uncle Sean and Aunt Mary gave Peter and me as a wedding present. The decadent cheesecake I made this afternoon, with five pounds of cream cheese, five egg yolks, and heavy cream, sits on the hutch. I've prepared Peter's mother's chicken divan recipe for dinner, along with steamed fresh green beans, rice, homemade whole wheat bread, and a large salad. Rose is in the kitchen with me, commenting about how great the holidays have been with her sisters home from college, how much she loved waking up this morning to the honey-wheat scent of bread baking. I instruct her to put the last of the serving dishes on the table, and have just grabbed a pack of matches from the kitchen windowsill to light two candles on the pine-and-holly centerpiece when I have a strong sense that someone is leaving an emergency message with my office answering service. I put down the matches and go to the phone and dial.

"Yes, Mrs. McCall, a message came in for you two minutes ago," the woman's voice responds. "A nurse from St. Peter's Hospital in Olympia, Washington."

My heart races. Paul moved to Washington State a year ago. We mended our relationship after the conflict over my confrontation with Dad, and we had a good visit before Paul moved, but we haven't spoken in three months, and our conversation then felt strained and superficial.

"She left the number," the woman continues, "and asked that you call as soon as possible. Your brother is seriously ill."

Frantic, I dial the number while Rose, sensing my panic, asks, "Mom? . . . Mom? . . . Is something wrong? . . . What's happening?" and Peter, Claire, Beth, and Annie, hearing Rose, flock into the kitchen, asking Rose what's wrong with me.

"Oh, Mrs. McCall, I'm so glad to hear from you," the nurse at the other end of the line exclaims. "Your brother had one of your business cards in his pocket; that's how I got your number. He's so miserable. And he's seriously ill. We're not sure what it is yet. We suspect pneumonia."

I hear Paul groaning in the background. *God, no, please don't let it be AIDS.*

"Cath." Paul's voice is hoarse, weak, barely audible. "This is it, Cath. I'm calling to say goodbye."

"What? What are you talking about? What's happened?"

"I don't know. Been sick for weeks . . . decided to come here . . . maybe they could help." He starts crying. "Oh, Cath, I'm so scared. I'm *dying.*"

I believe him. The frail quality of his voice reminds me of how our mother's sounded as her death neared.

"I'm coming. I'm coming to be with you, Paul."

"Would you? . . . I don't know if I'll be here. . . . I don't know how long it will take. I think I might die tonight."

"I have to tell you something, then. Don't be scared. It's peaceful. It's full of love . . . love like you've never known before. Try not to be afraid."

"Are you sure? How do you know?"

"I went back to that abortion you told me about . . . under hypnosis . . . the one you believed you witnessed. I had a near-death experience when Dad gave me that abortion, and it was all peace and love and rest on the other side."

"Thanks, thanks for telling me. . . . It helps. . . . I love you, Cath . . . so much."

Terrified of the trip, I procrastinate about leaving. I hate flying anyway, and just before the holidays my gynecologist had told me I would need surgery for the ovarian cyst. There's a chance I have cancer, so she recommended I see a gynecologic oncologist to get another opinion about whether I should plan to have a laparoscopy or hysterectomy. My emotional reserves have been depleted with worry. Now, all I can imagine is that the cyst will rupture on the plane and there'll be nothing anyone can do to help me. Tempted to give in to fear and cancel the trip, I turn to Mary Anne for help.

"I know you're frightened, Cathy, and those fears are real," she says, "but the scenario you've built up in your mind is highly unlikely, whereas Paul's life seems to be hanging by a thread. I don't think you realize how terrified you are to face his death. And the only way to do it is to put one foot in front of the other, and take one step at a time."

I'm grateful for her interpretation and for her advice. It helps me move forward. Beth and Annie have returned to college but Claire's home for an extended winter break, so she's able to stay with Rose, who's still in high school. Peter and I arrange for people to cover for us at work, so we can spend up to five days with Paul in Olympia.

Paul recognizes us when we arrive at the hospital, and I feel weak and grief stricken at the sight of him. Emaciated and pale, he looks more like an AIDS patient in a TV documentary than like my brother, and he has that creepy way of staring that reminds me of Mom's dementia. He grabs my hand, looks at Peter, and shouts his name at full volume. Peter and I both burst into tears. Thus begins a grueling reentry into the world of the dying.

Paul's doctor meets with us at his bedside the next day, to tell Paul all the test results are in and that he has AIDS. He lists Paul's infections, including meningitis, and describes the medications they're treating him with. I hold Paul's hand while listening, distracted by how it frightens me to do so. I feel guilty about being scared, but we're both perspiring, and now that the AIDS diagnosis is official, I struggle with doubts about the data I've read about how AIDS is and isn't transmitted. What if the data's wrong? What if ours is the one case where transmission occurs through the union of two sweaty palms?

The same discomfort arises when I lean my ear close to his mouth to hear what he's saying and he suddenly coughs: "It's a pretty nice way to go, really, Catherine." *Cough, cough.* "And it's a good time to go. I'm not ready now, but I will be when the time comes."

The time comes on the morning of January 14. Peter and I had to return to Georgia, and after a period of unresponsiveness Paul dies quietly and alone.

As per his request, we have his body shipped to Roswell. The funeral Mass is held in the Catholic Church of St. Ann, near my house, a site I choose in honor of Paul's Irish setter, Annie, his loyal companion. A priest who's active in the AIDS ministry in Atlanta is the celebrant, and gives a beautiful, gay-sensitive liturgy. We bury Paul next to Mom, in Greenlawn Cemetery in Roswell. Uncle Sean pays for all the expenses, which is a godsend. Andrew and his wife are there, along with Uncle Sean and my cousin Eileen, and Peter, Claire, Rose, and several of my closest friends. Beth and Annie are away at college, in the middle of exams, and Lucy doesn't come; she feels she's already said her goodbyes to our brother.

One week later, I write Paul.

Where are you, Paul? What's it like? Are you happy? Are you at peace? Can you see us? Can you hear me? I feel you saying "yes."

I was a basketcase the last day I saw you. Saying goodbye to you was one of the saddest experiences of my life. I felt like I had a huge mountain to climb. I put my hiking boots on that morning and a rainbow T-shirt.

Were you able to notice? Remember how you loved to hear me sing "Somewhere Over the Rainbow" when we were kids? I wanted to sing it for you that morning, but I didn't think either one of us could handle it.

Peter and I had a hard time checking out of the hotel, we were both crying so hard. We waited outside your room while the priest heard your confession. Then he invited us in for the anointing. I hated the priest— you know how picky I am about those things. And I was surprised when you agreed to him coming by, since you had told me how conflicted you were about religion. But then he invited Peter and me to lay our hands on your body and pray over you, and I knew that was good for all of us. I kept forcing my tears away while we prayed. But when we got to the Lord's Prayer, that did me in right at the start: "Our Father Who art in heaven." I thought of all the pain we had with our father who lives on earth. I felt that if you slipped away to heaven, you'd finally be where you belonged. From the time you were a little guy, all you wanted was for everyone to love one another.

Afterward, I had to write a bunch of information down for the hospital and fill out forms, while Peter balanced your checkbook. We did all this in your room. You watched TV, with that brain-diseased stare. I burst out crying a couple of times and you looked at me with compassion. At one point, you motioned to me to sit on your bed. Do you remember? You asked me what time we'd be leaving, and I—for the first time all weekend—gave an evasive answer. You seemed disappointed in my evasiveness, and I regret it, but I just couldn't bring myself to tell you we'd be leaving in one hour.

You tried to talk to me, but I couldn't understand a word you were saying. You half smiled, as if you were getting a kick out of watching me try so hard. Then you yelled, "No!" and grabbed me into your arms, and we cried so hard. It's amazing, what can be said in one two-letter word.

You patted my back and stroked me. It felt like you were trying to memorize what I felt like, so you could keep me when I left. Or was I trying to memorize your embrace?—the tender affection I felt in your hands (hands I watched grow from infancy to manhood, the hands even AIDS couldn't stop from communicating the strength of your loving heart).

I wanted to bring your Annie home with me, to take care of her while you were in the hospital—she's such a dear dog—but she looked old and tired and I didn't want to put her through the trip—it might have been too hard on her. And besides, I didn't know you'd die so soon. The doctors were saying you could get better and live another year or so. I didn't know you'd stop communicating after we left. I didn't know you'd take such a dramatic turn for the worse.

I hear you speaking to me now: "Yes, you did, Cath. And so did I. I had nothing to live for. I was ready. And now, I want you to live. I know you're frightened about your surgery, but you will do well. It will speed up your recovery. You have a lot to live for and a lot to give to life. I know. You gave to me. Don't let your heart be troubled. Remember me hugging you and you kissing me. Remember the tears we shared that spoke of love. Visit my grave. Let yourself do whatever you need to do. Take heart, and take joy. I am with God, and you are too."

Joy escapes me; I'm consumed with guilt. Nothing anyone says can console me. I feel a constant sense of self-loathing for the way I treated Paul.

"This is just irrational, Cathy," Mary Anne says when I tell her. "You were so caring, so loving, so loyal to him. Maybe we could find out the source of your reaction through another hypnosis session."

Once I'm in a deep trance, the hypnotherapist asks what my guilt concerning Paul is about, and I begin talking:

"It's about the basement."

"What about the basement?" he asks.

"You don't understand. You don't understand how horrible this is."

"Okay, Cathy. Tell us. Watch it like a movie, and tell us what you see."

"I'm following my father down the basement stairs. He's telling me he wants me to come down and look around with him, so I'll see that it's okay—that he's concerned I hadn't gone down there since Dixie went crazy."

"Dixie? Mary Anne and I haven't heard you mention anyone named Dixie before. Who's Dixie?"

"My dog. My parents gave her to me for my birthday when I turned nine."

"What kind of dog was Dixie?"

"A German shepherd. I asked for a cocker spaniel. I loved cocker spaniels. But Daddy said German shepherds are smarter."

"Oh, I see. How did Dixie go crazy?"

"They gave me Dixie as a puppy, and she was really sweet. But they wouldn't let me take her out or play with her. They made me keep her locked up in the basement. One night I went down to feed her and she attacked me. It was horrible. My parents had her put to sleep the next day. They didn't even tell me they were gonna do it. They didn't let me say goodbye. My sister cried a lot about it. I didn't really care, 'cause I was scared of Dixie, and I promised myself I'd *never* go back to the basement."

"Oh, I see, Cathy. Continue with the scene."

"He's taking my hand and being very kind, and he's encouraging me to keep coming farther down, until we get into the large room at the foot of the stairs. This is where Dixie was kept. It looks okay to me. I'm not scared.

"Now he's taking me to the room off that room. A laundry room, where the big sinks are. Back in the corner there's something with a sheet draped over it. I'm not asking what it is. I don't want to know.

"We're leaving that room and he's guiding me down the hall to the coal room. He's telling me about how Andrew and I used to love to roll down the pile of coal when we were little and Mommy would get mad because we'd get all dirty and it wasn't good for us, so he'd make us stop.

"Now he's taking me into the furnace room, where all our bicycles are kept in a bin. We're walking through it, and back down the hall.

"He's squeezing my hand and pulling me into the laundry room again, telling me he wants to show me something. I don't want to see it. I'm scared. He's dragging me over to that sheet thing and showing me that there's an examining table underneath it, with belts hanging off the sides. He's telling me to get on top, and I'm scared stiff and I don't move, like my feet are nailed into the concrete floor. He keeps talking."

"What's he saying?"

"'Since you are such a bright and inquisitive child, Cath, I'm going to let you help me with a science experiment.'"

Silence.

"What's happening now, Cathy? Remember to put it on a screen and watch it like a movie."

"I'm crying, and I'm screaming: 'Momeeee!'. . . Stupid, really. I don't know where she is and even if she's home. Our house is very well constructed. There's no way anyone could hear."

"Why are you crying and screaming?"

I feel tears roll down my face and I sob.

"Why are you crying, Cathy?"

"He tied my wrists and my ankles to the table with the belts, and he left," I say in between sobs. "I heard him lock the basement door and go upstairs. And then I heard nothing, for a very long time. *Hours.* The good thing is, I'm not a little girl. I'm sixteen. And another good thing . . . there are basement windows. So even though it's a very long time, I can see that it's still daylight. But . . . nobody except him knows I'm here. And I think he made a torture chamber on purpose 'cause he wants to kill me!"

I continue sobbing.

"Go forward, Cathy. To the next scene."

"I hear someone come down the stairs and open the door. It's Dad. He's saying, 'It's all right, Cath, everything is fine.' I don't believe him. I keep screaming for my mother. He comes over and looks directly down on my face. He grabs hold of my mouth and holds it open and spits in it. I gag, but it's really no use. He's untying me now, and talking to me: 'Thank you, Cath. The experiment is over and I got all the data I needed. You have just helped me prove that when a human being is isolated and constrained long enough she will eventually go totally insane.'

"He's helping me off the table, saying, 'I'm finished with you now, Cath. You can go outside and do anything you want, but leave through the door on Montgomery Place. Do not go up the stairs to my office, for any reason.'

"He goes up the stairs, and I stay a little while . . . walk around . . . think about using the Kirkman's soap I see on one of the sinks to wash his spit out of my mouth. I try the water faucets. No water comes out. I decide washing my mouth with soap might only make me feel worse. I'm scared Kirkman's soap might turn out to be poison.

"I'm walking outside now, and it is a beautiful fall day, and I am so glad to be outside. I'm sitting on the stoop, thinking about running away from home, trying to figure out where to go. But then I remember Paul is home, alone. I run inside and up the stairs to the second and third floors, looking for him, but I can't find him.

"I listen at the door to Daddy's office and don't hear anything. I'm scared that if I go in there and he catches me, he'll kill both of us. But I'm pretty sure he and Paul are in the basement, so I tiptoe through the office and down the stairs off the butler's pantry . . . terrified, terrified, terrified . . .

"I'm thinking about the cover of a biography I read once, of Mother Catherine McAuley, the foundress of the Sisters of Mercy: *Courageous Catherine.* I always wanted to be like her. This is my chance. But then I hear Daddy's voice, through the basement door. He's saying, 'Paul, because you are such an inquisitive child, I am going to let you partake in an experiment.'

"I peek through a crack in the door. He has Paul tied up like I was, but only worse. I'm peeing in my pants now and it's running down my legs. And I have diarrhea and I can't stop it and I don't even care . . . because I can't. I can't care about anything."

Silence.

"What's happening, Cathy? What do you see?"

"He has Paul's pants pulled down, and he tied up Paul's penis with string. And it looks like his penis is all red, and Paul's shaking.

"I'm running upstairs. I'm too scared to save him. I'm too scared to even tell anybody. What's the good of all that courage, if I'm not courageous *enough?*

"And . . . Paul's penis got him in trouble with his *life*. He *died* because of it. He could still be alive today if I didn't . . . why didn't I go in there? Why didn't I stop Daddy? Because I was afraid Daddy would kill me. That's why. I was afraid he'd kill *me.* "

I cry and cry, and then the hypnotherapist takes me out of the trance, and I look straight at Mary Anne, my safe harbor. Her brown eyes are wet, her cheeks flushed. The pity in her face embraces me with warmth, love, and security.

"Oh, Cathy," she cries. "I wish I could have been there to protect you. And your brother, too."

Chapter 26

The hysterectomy I need will have to wait. The rage stirred up in the aftermath of that session feels like it might erupt into literal self-destruction if I undergo the surgery now.

I know from previous experiences that integrating a session, absorbing into my present personality the impact of the atrocious memories accessed, is best done through a delicate balance between silence and talk. I plan a seven-day retreat at Holy Innocents, and ask if I can see Sister Barbara again for spiritual direction. I pack my Bible, journals, T-shirts, jeans, hiking boots, panties. No bras, no makeup. I stuff a water pistol and plastic slingshot into my purse. Into the trunk of my car I throw the picture of the Sacred Heart, the one that hung on my parents' bedroom wall the night Dad raped me for the first time, and Dad's old hammer, the one he threatened Lucy and me with. I had saved them when we cleaned out my parents' last apartment. Bringing this evidence with me, I perch myself in the driver's seat, pop my Pavarotti CD into the car stereo, and head for the North Georgia mountains, Schubert's "Ave Maria" bellowing through my brain.

I arrive at Holy Innocents in time for noon Mass. The first reading is from the Book of Isaiah 50:4-6:

> *The Lord God opens my ear that I may hear*
> *And I have not rebelled, have not turned my back.*
> *I gave my back to those who beat me,*
> *my cheeks to those who plucked my beard;*
> *my face I did not shield from buffets and spitting.*

After Mass, Sister Barbara leads me down the hall outside the chapel. A musty odor greets us when we enter a conference room with pale yellow cinderblock walls. I notice a field of grass outside the room's corner window, with a statue of St. Francis of Assisi and a birdfeeder in view. The scene comforts me. Sister Barbara smiles and points to a chair upholstered in a brown-and-beige plaid textured, durable fabric, telling me to sit down, while she selects a wooden rocking chair facing me. An oval table next to her holds a Jerusalem Bible. Just above is a statue of the Holy Family attached to a small shelf on the wall behind her.

"Shall we start with a prayer?" she asks. I nod. We make the sign of the cross together, and then I listen while she asks the Holy Spirit to guide our time together.

Sister Barbara, a tall woman in her fifties, wears a white blouse with a small silver crucifix attached. She has short, straight, gray-white hair, a long face with delicate features, and a porcelain complexion. She wears glasses, but they don't distract from her dancing eyes. One of the things I like about her is her sense of humor. I imagine that her faith is a source of joy for her—a state I long for though have no hope of achieving.

"So, Cathy, why have you come at this particular time and for this particular length of time?" she asks in her sweet voice, folding her hands on her navy blue cotton skirt.

"I'm scheduled for a hysterectomy, and I need to prepare. I've been in a rage, and . . . *so* lonely. I feel a deeper sense of God being

with me already though. You just wouldn't believe the timeliness of
the first reading at Mass today."

She tilts her head, and I smile and say, "Or then again, maybe you
would." During the last retreat, we had both been struck by the syn-
chronicity of events in my life. I explain that the first reading stirred
up images of Paul and me being abused in the basement, and I describe what happened to us.

"Mmmm." The sound is deep, pained, and her eyes are closed.
"God is moaning," she says, and I start to cry. She hands me a box of
Kleenex, then says, "The image of you and Paul strapped to the table
reminds me of the Crucifixion."

She moans again; we sit in silence for a moment. And then I
speak, my heart fluttering. "It does me, too. And it also brings my
abortions to mind."

I stare at the floor, remembering a quote I'd read in Matthew
Fox's book *Original Blessing:* "One deep *letting go* that the crucifixion
demands of us is letting go of our projections onto an all-powerful
God. . . . Jesus redefines the power of love—it is not so great as we had
presumed because it is a power of love and not a power of thunder-
bolts and interferences in nature's processes."

I wipe my eyes. "I want to pray about those abortions, Barbara.
And maybe create a ritual honoring them while I'm here."

"And honoring *you,*" she says. "You're their mother."

I flinch. "That is such a disgusting thought."

"No, Cathy, it's not. The fact that your father raped you is disgusting. But their lives, and you as their mother, are not. You know
that I was a social worker, don't you?"

"Yes. Sister Mary Magdalene mentioned that when I scheduled
the last retreat."

She folds her hands in her lap and leans forward. "I spent seventeen of my twenty-four years as a nun working with pregnant
teenagers, and I've delivered many babies . . . babies of teenagers
impregnated by their fathers, Cathy."

My heart skips a beat; I begin to perspire.

"Oh, they were so beautiful. . . . "

I'm in turmoil. Sometimes I try to reach into those memories of the abortions, and carve out a sliver of Dad's intent that I can recognize as loving. It is a difficult thing to do.

She continues. "I think you've been resisting letting yourself be aware of how real those two pregnancies were, Cathy. But they were as real as Claire, Beth, Annie, and Rose, and you've got to accept them before you can mourn."

I blurt, "You're damn right I haven't let myself become aware of how real they were." Then I stare at the floor again. "That would mean my mother and I are *both* the mothers of his children." I stand and pace the floor, putting my hands in my pockets.

"Ask your mother to help you, Cathy," Barbara says, watching me stride back and forth. "You believed she had a holy death. Ask her—and your grandmother—to walk this journey with you. And because the first reading in the Mass today was so close to what happened to you in the basement, imagine walking and talking with Jesus while you're here: processing with each other what your experiences were like. . . . Let's plan to meet after Mass each day, and then again in the evening, after supper."

She stands, and we depart the parlor.

I want to discount everything Barbara said. How dare she suggest I accept those pregnancies as real? Wouldn't that contaminate my other pregnancies?

I rush to my room and throw myself on the bed, crying, remembering how I reacted the day I learned I was pregnant with Claire. How frightened I was. How unworthy I felt.

Now I know what had made me react that way. What has penetrated the atmosphere of my girls' lives with me.

I get out of bed, sit at the desk with pad and pencil in hand, and write a letter that I never mail.

Dear Claire, Beth, Annie, and Rose,

I want to tell you all that I'm sorry. I'm sorry the word incest ever had to come into your lives in a personal way. I know it's not my fault, but I hate it. I wanted your lives to be pure and safe and happy and loving—insulated from horror.

I also want you to know I hate that I have had to invest so much of myself and our time and money on recovery. There have been many times when I would have much preferred to be just plain having fun with you, and couldn't.

Sometimes I try to look at myself through your eyes. I imagine it must be hard to witness the emotional heaviness in your mother and know there's nothing you can do about it.

I wish I could wake up and say to all of you: "Hi! It's all over! I'm healed!" But it takes so long to heal, and I doubt that healing means it's all over.

Love,
Mom

I walk outside, shooting the slingshot I brought with me while singing extemporaneous thoughts to Jesus, warming up for a week of major workout.

I name my two unborn children. The first pregnancy, the one most difficult to comprehend, I name Jesus, after the One I turned to about everything when I was twelve. I also like how the name "Jesus" seals its existence as a child of God. I choose Mary Bridget for the second, after Mary Anne and my grandmother. I write letters to Jesus and Mary Bridget, and bury them in the nuns' cemetery with a stone over each: "1960" written on one, "1965" on the other, in purple marker.

I spend hours walking, singing, meditating, and staring into space. I write free associations and childlike poems in my journal.

"I feel like I've been dancing with grace," I tell *Sister* Barbara toward the end of the week, "and I have an idea of something that might help me integrate the memories. . . . I'll need your help."

She smiles. "Yes, Cathy, what have you come up with?"

"Well, I've been thinking a lot about one of the Scripture verses you gave me to meditate on. The one from Matthew, Chapter 18: 'Anyone who welcomes a little child like this in my name welcomes me. But anyone who is an obstacle to bring down one of these little ones who have faith in me would better drown in the depths of the sea with a great millstone round his neck.'"

She nods, and I continue. "I want to make a model of my father out of paper and tie a bag of stones around his neck, and drown him in the pond. I want to see what it would look like, so I can have a deeper appreciation for what God meant."

"That sounds like a great idea to me," she says, "but it could be disruptive to the other retreatants."

"I know. That's where your help would come in. . . . "

We work out a plan. Since the other retreatants will leave tonight, and the next group isn't due in until tomorrow afternoon, tomorrow morning is the best time.

"I'll explain to the rest of the staff, Cathy," she says when we finish. "And I'll pray for you while you're gone. How much time will you need?"

"Three hours, total. Because I also want to spend time at the grotto. I might want to let out some primal screams or something!"

"Oh, I understand," she says, and I smile, feeling a little devious because I haven't told her all of my plans. She *chose* virginity. I'm not sure she could understand what I might need to do to reclaim mine.

The next morning, I dress in hiking boots, shorts, and my Fight AIDS, Not Gays T-shirt. I follow the trail through the woods to the grotto, singing "Amazing Grace" and carrying a backpack. The grotto is the retreat's cavelike stone structure that holds a life-size statue of Our Lady, modeled after the original Grotto in Lourdes discovered by St. Bernadette. There is a nearby pond and trees.

When I reach the grotto, I place the backpack on the ground beside a bench and pull out the items within it: the hammer, masking tape, two bags—one holding stones, the other nails—paper, a marker, scissors, and the picture of the Sacred Heart. I walk up to Our Lady's statue, kneel, and pray the Hail Mary. My eyes fill with tears, recalling the many times I prayed to her as a child.

"I'm a woman now," I say to her. "I *need* you. Please, help me get the poison out."

I draw a picture of Dad, naked, on large sheets of paper taped together, and leave it on the bench. Next, with bold strokes of the marker, I list all the incidents of abuse on two other large sheets taped together and nail them to a tree—for all the world to see. Then I drag his image to a larger tree nearby. Holding him in place, pounding nails through paper and bark, I'm stung by the similarity I feel to the Romans who nailed Jesus to the tree of his Crucifixion. But then I remind myself that I'm not actually nailing my father. I'm nailing my *anger* at my father.

I shoot stones at him with my slingshot, taking pleasure in the sight of some hitting his penis, and then I spit at him. But it isn't as gratifying as I thought it would be, so I stomp around, screaming to the trees and the birds and the ground and the sky: "Mother Nature, *help* me! *Inspire* me!"

And she does.

There's a massive tree stump behind the pine tree where Dad is hanging. I step onto it and yell as loud as I can, "You will *never, never* see any part of my body naked again!" And then I begin undressing.

"I've taken my shirt off and my beautiful breasts are exposed *and you can't see them!*" I shout. "They're *mine!*" Smiling, I extend my arms and look up to the sky, breathing deeply, smelling the sweet scent of honeysuckle from the bushes surrounding the grotto and feeling the morning chill on my breasts and nipples.

Next, I remove my shorts and panties.

"I'm naked now!" I shout. "Totally naked! And you can't see me. Furthermore, you can't touch me. Only *I* can touch me. Because I am *mine.*" I feel infused with power. "I can touch myself anywhere and any way I want to. And all you can do is hear me, and know the pleasure is mine and God's, *and it doesn't belong to you!*" The last is the loudest yell of my life.

"*Amazing grace, how sweet the sound, that saved a wretch* like me. I once was lost, but now I'm found . . . "

I'm singing this to a rock 'n' roll beat while I put my clothes back on and prepare for the next phase. With hands smelling of sex, I tear the lists of assaults off the tree and roll them and all the supplies into the backpack. I reach up and grab Dad off the other tree, hanging him over my shoulder. While hiking toward the pond carrying my "cross," I chant the Hail Mary. When I come to the clearing, I sit in the gazebo there and hum, drawing in the spirits of my mother and Ammy to assist me. God's creatures rustle in the woods behind me while I retrieve the bag of stones and tape it around Dad's neck.

I walk to the edge of the pond and heave him, swinging while I count: "One, two, three!"

He lands in the center and gurgles as he begins to sink. I watch the water ripple until it's calm. All but two parts sink—his penis and his head—and that makes me mad. So I stomp around the pond over and over, gathering and throwing rocks, stones, chunks of wood, a clay pot, anything I can find. "Fuck you!" I shout at him, and yell about all he did to me, using any street language I can remember. I imagine Mom and Ammy are cheering me on from the sidelines while his penis sinks slowly, but his head lingers, and I decide that's fitting. God will take care of the rest.

Perspiration drips from my face while I gather my belongings once again and then wander to the edge of the woods, where I open my backpack and remove the picture of the Sacred Heart.

"I don't want this anymore, God," I say. "I don't want it anywhere near my house or my family, or any other person. I'm giving it back to you."

I throw it into the woods, kneel, and make the sign of the cross with my eyes closed. With an "Amen," I open my eyes. Two tiny yellow butterflies dance before me, as if messengers of joy and freedom.

When I return to the retreat house, Sister Barbara is waiting by the front door. I am wonderfully filthy with dirt and sweat. She looks me up and down as I approach. "From the looks of you, I'd say you had a productive morning," she says with a smile.

"It was *very* productive. Thank you for assuring me so much privacy. But he didn't sink completely."

"I'm glad. Your father needs to be saved, Cathy. We here at the retreat house will pray for him."

I nod and return to my room, grateful there are people like her in this world.

Chapter 27

March 1993. The morning of my hysterectomy. I drift into sleep and wake up to the good news that surgery has gone well and there was no cancer.

While home recovering, I dream.

I'm in the group-counseling room of a new office, sitting in a circle with women from my neighborhood. They're carefree and socializing, but I'm quiet and nervous; I believe I'm pregnant. Then I laugh. "How silly of me!" I exclaim. "I couldn't be pregnant. I've had a hysterectomy!" They glance at me, then leave the room.

Mary Anne appears as an angel and speaks. "Of course you're pregnant. Not with a baby, but with your integrated, adult self. And yes, you do have more labor, and a delivery to go through. But don't you worry." She smiles. "We have traveled too many miles together for you to get fretful now. I'll be with you for the rest of the labor, and the delivery. We'll watch the placenta come out, and I'll stay with you through the afterbirth pains. Then you will be well, and free, and you'll go about your life joyfully, with much to contribute."

I wake up relaxed, smiling. But within weeks, as the relief of being cancer free gives way to the grief of knowing I will never be incest free, I discern that the labor before me has to do with seeing Dad again, and the delivery is about forgiveness. I work in therapy for three more years before I am ready to forgive.

February 1996. Dad, living in a personal care home forty-five minutes from my house, has been diagnosed with prostate cancer but is doing well. I call his caregiver to arrange a meeting with him, and she suggests the Waffle House near the home.

As I enter the restaurant, I'm hit with the stale, oppressive stench of cigarette smoke. *Just like walking into Mom's kitchen in our house in Brooklyn,* I think. A round clock hanging on the wall behind the counter reads 1:15. Our plan is to meet for coffee at 1:30; I have time to prepare. A perky twentysomething waitress with short brown bangs and a ponytail held by a pink scrunchie greets me with a smile.

"Would ya like a table, ma'am?" she asks with a twang in her voice.

"Yes, please. The most private table you have, as far from smokers as possible. My elderly father will be meeting me here, and we don't get to visit much."

"Oh, how sweet," she says, reaching for two menus. She leads me to a booth in the corner, away from other patrons. "Do ya wanna order now, ma'am, or will ya be waitin'?"

"I'll wait, thank you." The smell of bacon permeates the air. I'm glad I ate lunch before leaving Roswell. The last thing I need is to ingest a layer of grease.

By 1:40, I'm feeling anxious. What if he never shows? I go to the ladies' room, and as I return to my seat, I spot Dad at the restaurant's entrance. He's dressed in the same navy blue pin-striped suit from years before, a white button-down cotton shirt, unironed, and a blue paisley bow tie. He has snow boots on, though it's unseasonably warm. Peter warned me about that. Dad has trouble with corns, and refuses to wear regular shoes though the podiatrist had recommended he do so. His face is red and his hands shake by his side while he speaks with the waitress. She shows him to my booth and pours him a cup of coffee.

Though eighty-four now and humped over, he looks taller than I expected: stronger, healthier. His hair is snow white, freshly shampooed, and blown dry. I feel a knot of anxiety in the pit of my stomach as I approach him.

"Hello, Cath," he says, standing, reaching for the top of my hand to shake it, while he holds his arm stiffly at a distance, just as Mary Anne had told me they teach interns in medical school to do when they greet patients. I kiss him on his cheek, which is splattered with large age spots: some dark, some medium brown, two of them protruding.

"You surprise me, Cath," he says with a flinch. "I never expected a *kiss* from you."

I open my mouth to explain but he keeps talking, though the waitress is standing beside us, ready to take our order.

"First of all, Cath, I want to tell you that I was very happy that you called and that you wanted to see me. I wasn't sure I would be, but more on that later."

I don't want to hear more on that. I suspect he intends to use me as a dumping ground for his anger. Though I'm here with forgiveness in my heart, I've resolved to protect myself. Resuming my role as his victim is not on my agenda.

"Well, Dad, I'd like to tell you why I wanted to see you, but first I'm gonna order myself a cup of decaf. I'm not planning to order food, are you?"

"Oh, no, dear. We always have our dinner at noon at the home. Coffee is fine for me."

The waitress brings my coffee and pours Dad a fresh cup. I tell her to leave the bill and not feel she has to tend to us anymore.

"Oh, yeah," she says while she jots down our total. "I remember. Y'all want privacy." She winks at me and moves on to the next customers.

"Dad, I was in so much anguish last time we saw each other."

He leans forward, smiling, and stares at me.

"I want you to know that I'm beyond that now," I say. "The things you did to me were horrible and they will never be okay, but

I forgive you. I'm moving on. And I found out I love you anyway. I want you to know that.

"There was good in my childhood, I'm aware of that. . . . I remember how you encouraged me to have confidence in school . . . and your interests . . . especially the music and photography . . . added such richness to our lives."

He's still staring at me; I feel calmer than I thought I would, so I continue. "I see that some of your interests are living on in your grandchildren. . . . Rose loves photography. She works for a photographer after school, and he sees natural ability in her. Annie's interested in medicine. Claire majored in economics with a math concentration in college, and all of them have an ear for music. Beth even went back to taking piano lessons." I don't get the sense that he cares about any of this. His demeanor as he listens feels flat.

"Yes, dear." His cheeks are suddenly flushed. "Did you tell the girls about the incest?"

"I did."

"What did you do that for?" His voice is loud and his cheeks are bright red now.

"Because I was going through hell, and I wanted them to know it wasn't because of anything they did. Besides, I needed to find out if you'd hurt any of them."

"I must tell you, Catherine, I have no memory of doing anything to you. All I can think of is how terrible this must have been for Peter. I can't imagine what it must have been like for him."

He seems to care more about Peter's anguish than mine, but that doesn't surprise me. As a man, Peter is an extension of him.

Dad fiddles with his coffee cup and spoon while my mind wanders back to memories of Peter and me in bed: the many nights my tormented cry would begin the moment his penis made contact with my vaginal wall. Then, the night I told Peter about my fear that I was a lesbian. "It's okay," Peter had said with tears in his eyes. "I love you. I'll deal with it. I'll support you no matter what you decide you need to do." Yes, Peter has suffered as well.

Dad's voice interrupts my thoughts. "I can tell you what it was like for *me,*" he says. "Just horrible." His blue-green eyes seem to spit at me: *Take cover.*

"I don't want to get into that now, Dad," I say in a stern voice.

He smiles, playing with his cup and saucer again, but it feels as if he's only mimicking compliance. My stomach tightens. *Don't go there,* I say to myself. *You've worked too long and too hard. Don't allow yourself to get hooked in.*

I look out the window, remembering the hot summer day I told Peter that my attraction to women had disappeared and my yearning for him—every part of him—had returned. We approached each other cautiously that day, savoring the privilege of each glance, each touch, the parched earth of our bodies soothed in each other's arms, and made love. When our wet bodies collapsed beside each other on the sheets, I knew I'd come home again, our marital bed christened into new life.

I feel a tear rolling down my cheek and brush it away before Dad notices. I glance at my hands and adjust my engagement and wedding rings. *Your life is your own,* I say to myself. *Get about what you came to accomplish. Shed all that needs to be shed. Your husband is home waiting for you.*

"There's a second thing I want to talk to you about. Paul's death," I say. "Your caregiver told me you had questions. About how it happened so fast, and where he's buried."

"Yes, dear, go right ahead." His facial expression softens at the mention of my brother's name; a tear appears in each of his eyes. I'm surprised.

"Paul called me on New Year's Day that year. He told me he was very sick, and wanted to say goodbye, because he was dying. As you know, he died of AIDS."

"No, dear, I didn't know that. I knew he had meningitis. Of course there are many ways one can get that. AIDS is only one of them. No, I hadn't known."

He leans back in his seat, lowering his head. I wonder if he's crying. "Oh, I'm sorry," I say. "I thought Andrew had told you."

Dad looks up, tears gone. "No, he only called one day and told me Paul died of meningitis, and he said he'd take me to the funeral. But then he called again the next day and said he wouldn't take me to the funeral."

I'm irritated. At the time, Andrew agreed to deal with Dad for us. I assumed he would at least explain what had happened. Why didn't he follow through?

"Well, Peter and I went out to Olympia, Washington," I continue. "Paul was in St. Peter Hospital out there. He had pneumonia. They kept saying it looked like he had TB, but of course AIDS was the final diagnosis. Paul said he was ready to die . . . and . . . that you were on his mind, but he wondered if he should call you one minute, and knew nothing about anything the next." Tears threaten. I blink them away and take a deep breath.

"Yes, dear, I understand." He seems preoccupied.

"Paul wanted to be buried near Mom, in Roswell," I say. "Uncle Sean took care of the arrangements and paid for all the funeral expenses."

"I see, dear." He pauses, stroking his napkin along the edge of the table, then continues. "Paul was always a sensitive boy—very affectionate, but never happy—and different. Like when he went to the athletic group you and Peter used to go to up in Prospect Park. I'll never forget his reaction when they were teaching him how to play football. He came home upset. He couldn't understand why everyone thought it was fun to hurt each other. He tried so hard, but he just couldn't do it."

Dad stares out the window. "It's terrible to say, but I wanted it to be kept private. No one in society could appreciate such a thing. It was embarrassing to have a son like that." He looks down and fiddles with his cup and spoon again.

The therapist in me knows I'm witnessing a father process news that his son died of AIDS and that he's ashamed that his son was gay. The sister in me is incensed to hear that Dad was embarrassed by Paul's sensitivity. Movie clips of Paul's dying run through my mind;

Kodachrome slides of the insane asylum our "Baby Paul" was born into flash on my mental screen.

Oh, Paul, I think, *how did you do it? How did you survive a day in our family?* I remember when Peter and I visited with Paul the evening of that fateful day we fled from 763 Montgomery Place with the children, after our return from Germany. Paul, nineteen then, shaking and sobbing, said Dad had *urinated* on him one night, told him he wished he'd *flushed him down the toilet* as an infant, that he had thrown a check for $3,000 at him and demanded he get the hell out and never come back.

My heart pounds. Perspiration drips from my forehead and upper lip. *You didn't deserve this, Paul! And neither do I!* I struggle against the seductive power of Dad's evil behavior. I can either allow it to twist me into an angry rage, or I can yank myself back to my power to forgive, the only avenue to liberation and peace.

Dad raises his head, looking at me with an inappropriate twinkle in his eye, reminding me of the way Hannibal Lecter looked at Clarice Starling in the movie *The Silence of the Lambs*—he even resembles Anthony Hopkins. But I don't look a bit like Jodie Foster, and I'm not getting paid a penny for this scene. In fact, I remind myself, I've paid a fortune in therapy bills just to develop the ability to be here.

"I couldn't believe the things you said the day you came by with your therapist, Cath," he says. "But it explained a lot about you as a child. There were days when you would just look at me and burst out crying for no apparent reason. And then sometimes you were so glum. But you always tried to please me. You went out of your way to treat me like a king. It was very special, dear. You were my favorite. You were the one person in the world I felt attached to. I had no reason to get up in the morning for a long time after that day you said those things. And then I finally had to accept things the way they were. I want you to know how horrible those years were for me. I was *so* lonely. I felt like nobody cared about me."

"It was different for me, Dad. I *needed* to detach from you in order to find myself. And loneliness? I felt abandoned by the family every time you abused me. And in these later years . . . Peter and I have cared for you in concrete ways, but I've felt abandoned again. Lucy has washed her hands of the whole situation, and Andrew's help has been minimal. You said you're sorry about what Peter's been through. Peter has been more of a son to you than your own sons, and shouldering so much responsibility has been a lonely burden for both of us."

"I still don't recall doing any of those things to you, Catherine," he says with a smile. I don't believe him. Is his smile a symptom of craziness? A defense against feelings of shame? Is he mocking me? I don't know for sure, just as I'll never know whether his treachery occurred during psychotic episodes, alcohol-induced blackouts, or in the heat of premeditated, conscious choices. But it doesn't matter anymore.

"You don't remember?" I say. "Well, Dad, that presents quite an interesting dilemma."

"What do you mean, dear?"

"How should I relate to you? How *can* I relate to you? The past is the past, that's one thing. But now, in the present, you're denying that incredibly anguishing aspects of our relationship ever existed. And yet, these events are part of what formed me. I can't pretend that a very real part of who I am just isn't there."

"Actually, Cath, I told the psychiatrist I did do it all, and more. How could I deny anything, after all? He was a psychiatrist. He'd think I was crazy!" He laughs. "But I couldn't imagine the things I'd done, without feeling *so* guilty. And when you sent that little manger child back to me with that note about the abortions, I got very depressed—very, very depressed."

He tilts his head and smiles. "I never did anything you accused me of, dear, and that's that." He chuckles. "And now I have you back! Let's have some fun, Catherine Girl. Let's talk about your brother Andrew or your sister Lucy, the ones who are still alive. Tell me what they're doing these days."

"I don't want to talk about your children anymore, Dad." I glance at my watch. His caregiver will arrive any minute. I have no interest in seeing him again, and there are a few more things I want to say.

"I want to thank you for the good things you gave me, Dad," I tell him.

He stares at me.

"First, thank you for my education," I continue, choosing the words with care and working to keep my tone upbeat. "After rearing four children of my own, I appreciate how important St. Saviour Elementary and St. Saviour High were. They gave me a great foundation. I know we never would've gone to parochial schools if Mom hadn't insisted. But you did work to make the money for us to go. As a working parent myself, I want to thank you for that. And for paying for my college. Georgian Court turned out to be an excellent college for me. Being in a women's college gave me leadership opportunities I probably would've never had in a coed college. And the things I learned, especially in theology and education classes, helped guide my adult life. Thanks for paying for that. And thank you for the music. It was a healthy part of our family life."

"I'm so surprised to hear you talk this way, Cath."

"I figured you would be."

His caregiver arrives, and we stand to leave.

"Dad, Peter and I will continue to make sure you have good care until the day you die, but I don't see myself visiting with you again."

"Yes, dear, I realize that. But if I never see you again, it doesn't matter. I'll be happy for the rest of my life, just thinking about today." He squeezes my shoulder. It's okay. It's . . . gentle . . . respectfully affectionate.

I walk him to the door and hold it open for him. "Goodbye, Dad." I lean forward to give him a distant hug.

"Yes, dear," he says as he steps off the curb.

He gets into his caregiver's car and they drive away. I breathe in deeply, a slow, expansive breath, then exhale, and walk to my car. Driving slowly out of the parking lot, I turn toward home, singing a song from an old Barbra Streisand movie, "On a clear day, stop and look around you, and you'll see who you are . . . on a clear day, how it will astound you, that the glow of your being outshines every star!"

Chapter 28

One year later, February 21, 1997. I'm at work. I wave goodbye as my first client of the day exits the office, then reach for the phone to check messages.

"Hi, Cath, this is Peter McCall. Oh, shit! I can't believe I just said that. . . . I'm trying to figure out how I could delete it, but I can't."

I laugh. *This guy's been working at IBM too long.*

"I need to touch base with you today about a couple of items. Don't you finish at the office at two? Give me a call and let me know for sure, and I'll come by and meet you."

The words are familiar enough, but something about their cadence is . . . *off* somehow. I dial Peter's number and reach his voice mail. "Hi, it's me. Yes, I'll be done at two. Is everything okay? Your message sounded a little anxious, and I keep having this creepy feeling something's going on with Dad. If you get a moment, leave another message. Otherwise, I'll just wait here at the office after my one o'clock client until you get here."

I'm able to leave my curiosity with his voice mail and resume the day, eager to step into the diversion of concentrating on the lives of others.

"Hi, what's up?" I say while I lean back in my rocking chair, as if in my routine of opening to whatever my next client will bring into the therapy hour.

Peter stands in the doorway of my office wearing his trench coat, his feet rooted to the floor. His face is pale; his eyes travel from the floor to the window on my left, to the filing cabinet on my right. A hard morning at work? Perhaps. But something under his edginess seems . . . happy. Carefree.

"It's your dad, Cath."

"Yeah . . . what?" I feel a little nervous hearing this. Dad has been suffering for nine months. The prostate cancer spread to his bones, and we were able to move him to Our Lady of Perpetual Help Home in Atlanta, a home for indigent cancer patients, where he could be embraced by the unconditional love and nursing care of the Dominican Sisters and volunteer staff.

"Sister Dolores left me a message that he passed away at 8:10 this morning. He was sleeping and his breathing changed and then he left."

"How amazing," I say, calm. "He's gone—just slipped away quietly, without disrupting the wedding." Claire is due to get married in two months. "What a blessing. For everyone." I feel joy building. "And the morning after Mom's birthday too. I just know she had a hand in it! I feel such peace."

"You do?"

"Well . . . yeah. And a touch of sadness. But mostly peace."

I pull my hair back and scratch my scalp. "You know. . . . It was the oddest thing. I told him I wouldn't be visiting him again, but I had an urge to yesterday, while you were out of town. A strong urge. But then I threw my back out."

Peter leans against the doorframe, nods for me to continue.

"While I was lying on the bed, I sensed Mom's presence. She seemed to be telling me to trust what was going on in my body. That my back going out was a blessing. That I shouldn't visit Dad. It wouldn't be good for me. Then this morning, while I was preparing for my first client, I actually wondered if Dad would die today. Funny . . . he was already dead—just slipped away." I stare at the floor.

"You're really taking this well, Cath."

I look up. His shoulders are relaxed and color is returning to his cheeks. "What did you expect?" I ask.

"I didn't know what to expect. But I've always been scared about how you might react."

"Well, I've wondered, too. But you know, it's a huge relief." I smile.

He nods. "Well, I vote we get all this over with as soon as possible. I'm not up for anything big. We could have him buried tomorrow. Get the guy under the ground without any pomp and circumstance. The funeral home already picked up his body. When Sister Dolores called, she told me they needed it out of there by noon." He shakes his head with a small grin. "She's so businesslike, she cracks me up."

I smile.

"Anyway," he continues, "I'm headed over to the funeral home right now."

"Without me?"

"Aw, c'mon, Cath, let me handle this." He rubs his forehead. "You need to rest your back."

"Absolutely not. First of all, I've told you all along that I need to have a funeral and a burial service." I lean forward and adjust the pillow behind me, needing extra support. "Granted, you've disagreed all along, but I need every step of the ritual, to bring closure."

We schedule the wake for the next evening, and a funeral service in the chapel the morning after, followed by the burial. I consider calling Mary Anne, but it's been four years since I terminated therapy; I decide instead to drop her a note, and I'll call her later, after things have settled down. We contact Andrew, Lucy, the girls, and Uncle Sean. My sister and Uncle Sean decide not to come, and I'm the only one who wants to attend the wake.

Peter pulls a newspaper out of his trench coat pocket and settles himself on a couch in the lobby while the funeral director leads me to a parlor. He opens the parlor door, offering to stay with me, but I assure him I'll be fine; I need privacy. He exits with an understanding nod and closes the door.

I stand for a moment, taking in the silence. I'd often wondered what it would be like to lay eyes on Dad's dead body. I'd been concerned that the sight of him might trigger more flashbacks and launch me into a state of anguish. But now, unafraid, I approach the casket one slow step at a time, and I find the last thing I ever expected there: peace. Profound peace. Utter and complete. I'm fascinated, almost delirious with joy, yet grounded. The storm is over and will be no more. My eyes fill with tears at the freedom of it. Here I am, alone with his body, in absolute safety. I can think and feel and say anything I want.

I look at his face. I had expected it to be contorted, but his features are smooth and in place. He appears to be at peace. And I hope that he is.

I take all the time I need with him. Precious time. And I realize why I'd insisted that Peter run out to Kmart and buy new pajamas for him to be buried in—it was because Dad had always slept in the nude when I was a child. I like the sight of him in the navy blue cotton with red piping. It feels *so safe*. For the first time in my entire life, it's not dangerous to love my father.

"I love you, Daddy. I love you."

I stand in silence for a moment and then sigh. "This is it, Dad," I say aloud. "Eighty-five years of life, and I'm the only one at your wake."

I burst into tears—it's my father and me alone again, with a whole world outside the walls, outside the windows.

I back away from the casket and plop myself down on the couch, a safe distance away. My back hurts. While my body searches for a comfortable posture in the cushions' contours, I realize the couch is the same style as Mary Anne's. Her voice comes up from my heart to comfort me, saying, *I am here for you, Cathy.*

"Thank you, Mary Anne," I say to the silent room.

Weak-kneed, I approach the white lectern in the chapel with a knot of anxiety in my stomach. "I'd like to begin by thanking Father Mike for agreeing to preside over Dad's funeral and burial this morning, on such short notice." I nod at my new pastor, who, until today, knew nothing about my family history. He and I share common ground though. I converted to the Episcopal Church earlier this year because I was disturbed by the increasing fundamentalist population in the Catholic Church and because Episcopalians ordain women priests, allow their clergy to marry, and are considering sanctioning gay marriages. Mike had been a Catholic priest for decades before he became Episcopalian.

My family sits at attention. Peter is straight ahead of me, on the right end of the left front pew, next to Father Mike. The girls, sitting with Claire's fiancé and Beth's boyfriend, are behind them. Andrew and his wife are toward the right. I notice that Annie's head is down and her straight, light brown hair covers her face. She didn't want to come. "I hate Grandpa, and I don't want to give the bastard any of my time and energy," she had said. Her anger felt like a statement of fierce loyalty to my welfare, and in a way, I enjoyed it. But I didn't need her here for him; I needed her here for me. Now, as with the rest of the family, her presence assures me of her love.

I need this reassurance right now. My legs are tingling; my feet hurt; perspiration has dampened my underarms. Yet, it's time to speak.

"First, I'd like to thank God for all the good people in my life who've nurtured my faith over the years." I turn to Father Mike. "You spoke of the story of the good thief at the Crucifixion during your sermon. I don't know if Dad asked for forgiveness before he died, like the good thief did. I don't know if he ever earnestly turned to God. But I hope he did. I do know that he suffered. And I do know that he caused many of us to suffer."

I look at my brother again. Andrew's sitting erect, his large-nosed slim face expressionless; his head is tilted in a way that seems burdened. He turns toward me and nods, eyes hidden by the thick lenses of his glasses.

I face the casket. "The person whose body lies in that coffin today introduced me to some of the most horrific experiences a child—a human being—can live through. And I think the same could be said by my mother, brothers, and sister. Dad emotionally abused everyone in our family, sexually abused me, and I personally witnessed him physically abuse Paul."

Andrew's wife is crying. Andrew is holding her hand and staring at the floor.

I take a deliberate breath. "Having said all that, I must also say that Dad wasn't *all* bad. And my memories of him aren't either. He *was* intelligent, and had a fun sense of humor sometimes. He could even be kind. And his music . . . the piano playing . . . was magnificent."

My voice has sounded calm. My heart is hammering in my chest, though. I look at my index cards: only one paragraph to go . . . the most important one.

"But he was manic-depressive and an alcoholic and rejected treatment for both, leaving a trail of destruction behind him. Each one of us related by blood has a genetic vulnerability to both illnesses. So far, neither has turned up in any of us here. I'm grateful for that, and I hope and pray it continues, but only time will tell."

I raise my head, see Peter and the girls, my soon-to-be son-in-law, and Beth's boyfriend. "Today, as the sickest branch of our family tree falls to the earth and we ritualize the meaningfulness of his passing, let's pledge to call upon every resource we have in the days to come. Let's make life-affirming, healing choices for how we live our lives, for how we respond to one another. We have the opportunity to transform a legacy of pain into a legacy of love. Our choices will determine what new life comes into bloom."

Peter and Father Mike, who've both been looking at me, give supportive nods. I have no idea what my girls' reactions are; their heads have been down the entire time.

I return to my seat next to Peter. "Great job, Cath," he whispers, squeezing my knee. I sigh with relief.

The mild seventy-degree temperature, soft breeze, and sunny sky soothe the weariness of walking from our cars to the gravesite. We file onto folding seats under the burial canopy: Andrew, his wife, Peter, and I in the front row, the rest of the family behind us. Father Mike blesses Dad's coffin with holy water and prayers, then asks if any of us want to add anything. I remove a letter I'd written early this morning, and read it aloud:

Dear Dad,

You are in God's hands completely now. I no longer have to be there for you. As I bury you today, with you I bury my shame and my sense of myself as a victim.
    Goodbye.

Love,
Catherine

I place the letter on the casket, and instruct the undertakers to lower it and close the vault while I watch. They look surprised, but follow my requests. Father Mike, the girls, and their boyfriends are walking toward the cars, chatting quietly. Peter lingers with me for a few minutes, and then joins the others. Andrew nods at me. "Thanks, Cath," he says. He and his wife stay nearby, whispering to each other, looking at Mother's and Paul's grave markers.

The task completed, one of the undertakers shakes my hand and offers his condolences. Peter comes up from behind me, cracking a joke about my making sure Dad is really six feet under. I don't laugh.

"I'm proud of us, Peter," I say, extending my hand, and he joins his to mine.

Chapter 29

I return to the house on Montgomery Place two years later, in May 1999. Rose has graduated from college, and Peter and I decide to celebrate the milestone of having educated our four daughters with a pilgrimage back to our roots. Unlike her sisters, Rose has never been to Brooklyn, so we bring her along.

"Notice how wide this house is, Rose," Peter says while we look from across the street at the Romanesque masterpiece of granite, sandstone, and brick, designed over one hundred years ago by the famous New York architect C. P. H. Gilbert. "It's double the width of most brownstones. Wait until we get inside: fourteen-foot ceilings, beautiful fireplaces in almost every room, ornate detail on the mantelpieces and moldings around the rooms. And the woodwork—solid mahogany banisters, gorgeous walnut paneling—unbelievable! Your mother's parents may have been crazy, but they certainly had an eye for beauty."

I'm halfway across the street by the time he finishes speaking. Feeling anxious, I hope the activity of moving my legs will offset a siege of diarrhea.

"How're you doing, Mom?" Rose calls from behind me. At twenty-one, she's almost six feet tall, with her thick brown hair parted on the side and falling to just below her shoulders. The length of her stride enables her to catch up with me by the time I reach the sidewalk. "Are you okay?" she asks again, tilting her head and squinting her hazel eyes behind small tortoiseshell glasses. She rests her camera on the stoop with one hand while holding a lens in the other. A heavy-looking bag of equipment hangs from a strap around her shoulder.

"I'm okay, Rose. I'm plenty nervous . . . but I'm ready." I take a deep breath and head up the stairs of the stoop, noticing a bronze plaque to the right of the front door, engraved with BERKLEY HOUSE, the last name of the first owner.

"A historic landmark." I turn toward Peter. "I still can't believe it."

"Yeah, I know what you mean, Cath," he adds, coming up the stairs. "Especially when you think of the shithole it had become by the time we returned from Germany."

I turn toward Rose. "This stoop is where your father and I developed our relationship," I say, wanting to shift to a pleasant topic. "We spent hours on these steps, talking."

She rolls her eyes and smiles. Her sisters have often commented that our childhood relationship sounded like a fairy tale, that it made us unable to relate to their problems in the contemporary dating scene. But Rose lived alone with us while the others were away at college and the heart of our marriage was undergoing bypass surgery. She witnessed firsthand the worst of our relationship. A wave of pain moves across my chest, registering the sorrow I feel imagining her struggles and those of her sisters during that time.

I go to the front door and ring the doorbell.

Julie and Brian Murphy, the couple who purchased the house from Mom and Dad, had been active in restoring Park Slope, now one of the most desirable neighborhoods in the metropolitan area. So when I wrote to ask whether they'd be open to giving us a tour, I was hopeful. I wasn't aware that the Historic Society had offered them large sums of money to include 763 Montgomery Place in its annual tour of homes, or that they declined each invitation, placing a higher priority on privacy. So, undaunted when I didn't receive a response to my letter, I followed up with a phone call. When Julie answered, sounding annoyed, I used my best therapist's skills to engage her.

"I know I sound unfriendly, Catherine," she said. "It's nothing personal. Our lives are just more hectic than usual. My mother has Alzheimer's."

I shared that my mother had a form of dementia too, and had passed away nine years ago.

"Oh, I'm sorry," Julie said. "And Paul? I heard your brother Paul died of AIDS."

"He did." I was a bit surprised until she told me she'd known him briefly—they'd hired him to help with renovations after they moved in.

"What about your father, Catherine?"

Without hesitation, I said, "He died two years ago, in Georgia, where we live."

"You're the child that lived far away, then. . . ."

By the time we set up a time for us to visit, we'd made a good connection.

"Hello! Welcome. Please, come in." Smiling, Julie steps backward, motioning to us with her hand. She's prettier than I expected, about my height, five foot six, and slim. Her skin is smooth, with a brush of color in her cheeks. Her gray-brown shoulder-length hair, softly curling at the ends, is held off her face with a hair band.

Thanking her, I reach out to shake her hand, then say, "We're delighted to be here." I introduce her to Peter and Rose.

"I'm happy to meet you," she says. "Come along."

Over the years I had learned that Gilbert's architectural style was known for entry arches that give a sense of being pulled into deep space, but as I step through the front door and onto the vestibule's colorful tile floor, an eeriness comes over me that the architect could never have imagined. I feel a hint of Dad's presence, a heaviness that intensifies as I approach the foyer and glance into the room on the right, only to notice that it's covered by sheets—a reminder of our return from Germany.

Peter and I look at each other.

"Excuse the mess in this room," Julie says, noticing our reaction. "We're in the middle of painting it. This is our dining room, and it'll be quite lovely when it's completed. Shall we go upstairs first?" She raises her arm to lead us in that direction.

Where's Paul? part of me wonders while I gaze at the majestic two-landing mahogany banister, expecting him as an eight-year-old to run down the stairs, eager to help me hang princess pine and green-and-red Christmas balls. I close my eyes for a moment, trying to get my bearings, then turn to Rose and point up.

"Look at this banister. Uncle Paul and I had the job of decorating it for the Christmas holidays when we were kids. Gosh, I loved that job."

In my enthusiasm, I step backward. Julie halts me with the firm extension of her arm and a "Watch out for the dog," referring to the German shepherd nestled on the floor, looking up at us as if we've awakened him from a nap.

"You have a German shepherd?" I ask, eyeing Peter and remembering Dixie, the dog I loved but that had attacked me.

"Yes. Why? Does that mean something to you?" Julie's face holds only curiosity.

"It's just wonderful to see that a full-grown German shepherd lives here," I respond, pretending the scene holds no deeper significance.

Julie nods, appearing preoccupied. "I want to know anything you can tell me about this house, Catherine," she says. "Anything."

"What do you mean? What kind of things?"

"I don't know how to tell you exactly, so I'll just come out with it. There are spirits in this house. I've sensed it from the beginning. I felt compelled to buy the house because of it. Once I moved in, I felt it even more. Maybe *you* can explain what I'm sensing. Can you?"

I feel an odd mixture of fear and relief. "I *can* tell you that some extraordinary things happened here, Julie. But they're private, and I don't know you well. I'm not one to leap into self-disclosure."

With an understanding nod, she replies, "Well, I'll tell *you* a few things then, and maybe you can help me. Some friends—a numerologist and a psychic—came to visit shortly after we moved in. They both sensed spirits too, and a cold spot."

"A cold spot? What's that?"

"An energy variation. I'll show you the spot when we get to it, and then you can tell me if you remember anything about that area."

I glance at Peter and Rose. They're both staring at me. I wonder what's in store for us.

Julie leads us to the second floor in silence; I listen to the stairs creak beneath our feet. Rose breaks the tension.

"Mrs. Murphy, I love what you've done with the old photographs on these walls going up the stairs."

"Yes, Rose. We kept the paint in the same stucco style your grandparents had it—just lightened the color a bit. They had it painted a darker, golden tone. This is more of a sandy, creamy shade, as you can see. It lightens the space, and we thought the matted and framed photographs gave a sense of warmth. A fitting gallery."

As she reaches the head of the stairs, Julie turns to look at me and points. "This is the spot, Catherine, right here. At the head of the stairs and to the left side of the hallway."

I can feel the cold as I follow her into the space. It's as if there's a hollowness in the air, where molecules are unable to hold warmth. I never noticed it before, and it spooks me.

"What do you know?" she asks, urging me on.

I know that this was the threshold to my bedroom.

"You've put a wall here. There used to be a doorway," I say, avoiding her question.

"What do you know? What can you tell me?" She's insistent now.

I know that each time he stepped into this area he had a decision to make. I know that evil won here.

"Well, Julie, I really don't know what to tell you. I'll have to think about it and see what comes." *How do I keep from lying, yet protect myself from becoming too vulnerable?*

"Follow me," Julie continues, not pressuring me. "I want to show you all the changes we've made on this floor." She leads me through a door opposite the stairs. "The back half is our bedroom and dressing room area now."

No wonder you sense spirits. "This was the TV room when I was a child," I say. "The room next door was a nursery first; then it became my room. While I was in high school, my parents converted it into a large living room. I see you've replaced the center wall—they had removed it to open up the space. And now you have a big dressing room here. How delightful."

"Yes. Please, come through and see our bedroom."

"It's beautiful!" I proclaim, standing inside their bedroom door, pretending I'm speaking of the arrangement of their antique furniture, when it's the sky blue fireplace that grabs my attention. I want to hug and kiss its tile facade, the ornate trim on the painted white mantel. *My friend! It's so good to see you!* I want to say. *You saved me! You held me while he raped me. You stood beside me through it all. Thank you.*

Julie's voice beckons me into the room's new reality. "We replaced the windows with these glass doors and added a little verandah," she says, pointing.

"How lovely. You've opened it up to the world." *I was in bed with Daddy opposite the windows you replaced. I was despairing that even when I yelled out of them for help, no one came to my aid.*

I notice pots of red geraniums on the verandah. The view is cheerful; I'm amazed. "Julie, I really can't tell you how much I love what you've done here."

"Let me show you what else." She opens an antique chest to the right of the fireplace. Its shelves are filled with dollhouse furniture.

"Oh, you'll get a kick out of knowing that I spent hours playing with my dollhouse on the floor of this very room when I was a child. My dollhouse was a godsend for me."

"Really? Were you in need of a godsend?"

"Yes." A surge of camaraderie has resurfaced, inspiring my response, and I regret it immediately. I'm conflicted about whether to tell her anything, and if I decide to, how much? "I'll tell you more about that later."

She leads us toward the front of the house. Our old kitchen is now Julie's office, our old dining room her husband's.

"Come upstairs to the third floor," she instructs.

"Now that's a switch!" Peter chimes in. "The whole time I knew Cathy, nobody outside the family was allowed on the third floor. Her parents were ridiculous about it."

"Is that so? I wonder why," Julie muses, looking at me from the corner of her eye.

"Simple, Julie," I respond. "The place was a wreck all the time. It would've been humiliating to let anyone see. And besides, my parents had a lot to hide." Again, I disclose more than I intended. "They were both alcoholics," I remark matter-of-factly, hoping this one sentence will satisfy her curiosity.

"More on that later, I hope," she says.

As we climb the stairs approaching the third floor, I remember my sister at five, running down the hallway, her blond curls bouncing. I want to be able to grab Lucy and rock her in my arms and tell her Daddy's dead and we won't have to experience a nightmare existence, but my thoughts are interrupted by Peter's voice.

"How're you doin', Cath? Everything okay?" He extends his arm and grasps my hand. Rose and Julie are in front of us, headed toward the room Lucy and I shared in high school. I step back and speak in a low voice.

"I'm remembering what a cutie Lucy was when she was little. I want the time back."

"Listen, Cath, we can leave. You don't have to go through this."

"I know. But in the long run I think it'll be good for me."

"Okay, just remember, I'm right here with you."

Rose and Julie are chatting in the room Lucy and I shared.

"See that radiator over there, Rose?" I ask, interrupting them, and step just inside the bedroom door. "I used to sit on it and smoke, exhaling out the window so my family wouldn't know."

My youngest daughter's face shows befuddlement. "Gosh, I find *that* hard to imagine, Mom. You smoking?"

"Yeah, well, I did. And over there," I point to the left of the fireplace, "is where I had a bookshelf with all my athletic awards lined up inside it, and an altar to Our Lady on top, with a pretty statue of her in the center. I used to pick weeds in Prospect Park—when I was old enough to know better, when I knew they weren't flowers—and I'd put them in a glass of water in front of her. Sometimes I'd make her a crown of dandelions woven together."

"I just can't relate, Mom. Your adolescence was so different from mine."

"Count your blessings, Rose," Peter chimes in, putting his arm on her shoulder and looking her straight in the eye for a second.

We walk across the hall and into what had once been Paul's room.

"This is where I keep all my arts and crafts," Julie says, smiling. Boxes of supplies are stacked along one wall, and over a worktable, spools of upholstery thread are attached to a large board affixed to another wall.

"Paul would love this, Julie," I manage. "He'd be so happy to know that his room became a place for artistic creation." *This is where our father urinated on him. This is where he and Lucy hid while Dad raped me across the hall.* I shake the memory away and say, "This is the room where Paul and I sat many a night, sharing our fantasies about growing up and having children of our own. We wanted to own the house one day and turn it into the best orphanage in the city."

"No kidding, Catherine. Sweet fantasy," Julie says, smiling, and I'm relieved that my pain isn't showing.

Next, she leads us to the room that had been Mom and Dad's. "This was my parents' bedroom," I say, stepping in without hesitation, focusing my eyes on the green-painted mantel in front of me. At once I'm paralyzed by a tidal wave of grief. Peter and Rose peek in from behind me, but I can't move to allow them entry; my body has transformed to lead. I push Rose backward with a soft nudge, as if she's a toddler and I'm trying to protect her from danger without letting on that there are real monsters in view. At the same time Peter moves forward, squeezing in front of Rose, and yanks me into the hallway.

"You've had enough of this room," he says, knowing it was the room where I was raped the first time. "And I've had enough of sensing the pain you're swallowing." I'm grateful that Julie doesn't hear him.

"Hey, Rose, come on over here. I want to show you something," he says, pulling me with him into Andrew's old room and motioning to Rose while he approaches the windows. "This is where your Uncle Paul and Aunt Lucy used to hang out the window to see whether I was going to kiss your mother goodnight after a date." He has a big grin on his face.

"Whatever, Dad!" She chuckles, and I feel grounded again.

"I'd love to show you the attic now," Julie says. "We've converted it into a grand apartment: a loft, complete with painted Sheetrock, skylights, and those old exposed rafters. The windows are what's so wonderful. You can see city rooftops all the way to the Verrazano-Narrows Bridge."

"Oh, I remember those windows." I turn toward Rose. "Andrew and I used to stick our heads through them and spit. We'd try to get our spit big enough to make a noise when it landed on the sidewalk."

"Gross, Mom! How disgusting!" She's laughing. "Wait'll I tell the girls: Mom, smoking and spitting out windows."

"I do have a key to the attic." Julie is talking to Peter. "But the renters are at work and I don't think it would be right to let you in."

"We understand," he responds. "Much as I'd love to see it, I agree with you, it wouldn't be right. I'll tell you though. Cathy and I spent many hours of our engagement cleaning that place out. Her parents used it for storage, except for a few years when her dad made space for a pool table. Cathy and I had lots of ideas about how it could be fixed up. Sounds like you and Brian came up with the ultimate."

"Thank you, Peter. I wish I could show you the basement too—it's a lovely garden apartment now—but I have the same problem. The renters aren't home."

I'm relieved.

"You can get a hint of it when we get back to the first floor and I show you the living room and kitchen," she continues, her tone helpful. "You can go out the kitchen door and down the stairs to the back yard."

Julie turns to lead the way downstairs. Peter and I follow but Rose lingers behind, looking at the skylight built into the roof at the top of the staircase to the attic.

"This place is *totally* awesome," she exclaims.

And I'm grateful that, to her, that's all it is.

Brian Murphy, a tall man of medium build with dark hair and eyes and bushy eyebrows, wearing a cranberry-colored short-sleeved cotton shirt, khakis, and a pleasant smile, greets us on the second floor. He's just returned from a meeting.

"Why don't you folks come on down to the living room and visit with Julie and me for a while before you leave?" he asks. "Have a glass of iced tea. Tell us stories about your family."

I smile, but don't answer his invitation. Julie leads us to the first floor while Brian follows from behind, chatting with Rose about her reaction to where her mother grew up.

First, Julie takes us into their modern kitchen.

"Look at the ceiling," she says, raising her head. "It was painted by a dear friend of ours who had AIDS."

"Cool," Rose says, looking up at painted blue sky with clouds interspersed. "My uncle Paul loved stuff like this."

"What a transformation," I exclaim. "My family called this the porch room, because there was a porch off the back. We had a Ping-Pong table in here when Dad's office was over on Garfield Place, and then later it was his secretary's room. I never imagined it as a kitchen, but this is great."

"Come toward the back, Catherine. This is my favorite area. I think you'll like it."

I walk into the section of the room that had been extended over our old porch and glassed in. It provides a luscious view of the back yard, which has been bricked and framed with raised brick planters filled now with red, pink, and white impatiens. A door opens to an iron spiral staircase with large pots of geraniums on each step, reminding me of Barbra Streisand's roof in the movie *On a Clear Day You Can See Forever*.

I walk down into the yard, remembering a green-canopied sandbox, and some happy times in a wading pool with Andrew when we were little, and later, family barbeques and playing with hula hoops.

"Be sure to peek into the basement apartment!" Julie calls to me.

At first I can't bring myself to look into the place that had once been a torture chamber for Dixie, Paul, and me. But I decide to force myself. *Perhaps new images would be good for you,* I tell myself. But I can't see much, and I feel nothing. I wonder what Mary Anne would say about all this.

Julie prepares a tray with glasses of iced tea, and Brian invites us to sit in the living room that had been the music room when I was a child and, later, Dad's office. Now it's filled with beautiful antiques, paintings, needlepoint cushions and pillows, and other fine accessories, including Julie's large collection of Delft.

I feel weak and queasy, ask for a glass of water, and sit for a while, attending to my feelings and deciding what to do with them. Rose, in a chair opposite me with her head down, peeks over the rim of her glasses. Peter, beside me on the couch, leans forward, watching me. Julie and Brian's faces are congenial, but now hold expectancy. After a few moments, I speak.

"I want to thank all of you for being so respectful while waiting for me to compose myself. . . . Julie and Brian, thank you for your generosity in giving us a tour of your home." I swallow, feeling resistant to the reality that it is now their home. "I know you want to know everything of significance that happened here, but right now I don't have what it would take to describe much in detail."

Peter moves back in his seat, extending his legs. I imagine he's more relaxed now, hearing that I've decided to limit what I'll share with them.

"I can tell you that my parents always talked as if they were very much in love at the time that they bought the house, two months before I was born. I have photographs that would attest to that. I have some happy memories of life within these walls. But Mom and Dad drank a lot. They had a fun-loving circle of friends when I was young. Mom was in a bridge club with the women. They met once a month for over twenty years. Cocktails, beer, or wine were always part of these gatherings, and my parents gradually became alcoholics. Also, Dad was manic-depressive . . . as far as I know, untreated during the time they owned the house. He was cruel to Mom, Andrew, Lucy, Paul, and me—a tyrant sometimes. And he sexually abused me, for many years." My heart is thumping in my chest and beads of perspiration are forming on my forehead and upper lip.

"Oh, Catherine, I am *so* sorry," Julie says, her voice tender. "You are very courageous to return here. Please, tell us what you need now. Brian and I would want to do anything we could to make this a healing experience for you."

Brian nods, his eyes fixed on mine. Peter reaches over and takes my hand, squeezes it. Rose grabs a tissue out of her camera bag and blows her nose. I know she doesn't have a cold; I suspect she's crying, but don't look at her face. I'm looking at Julie, her *Oh, Catherine, I'm so sorry* echoing through my head, calming the thumping of my heart.

"You've both been so kind, Julie and Brian. There's nothing more I need from you today . . . except, please accept the fact that I don't want to go into any details."

They nod, and I decide to reveal what I debated about telling them since our arrival: "Actually, all the details of abuse—the events that are, perhaps, the sources of the spirits you sense, and the cold spot—are in my book. I've been writing a memoir."

"That's wonderful," Julie exclaims. "Excellent. You are very brave. And you have such presence. I'm pleased to have met you, Catherine. And I hope—so much—that this day with us, in our home, will help."

I smile and stand to leave. "I'll send you a copy when it's published."

On the way out the door, I notice an old baby grand piano in the corner of the foyer, to the right of the door to the vestibule.

I glance toward Brian. "A baby grand?"

"Yes. It's shoved in this corner because someone's coming to pick it up tomorrow. None of us play, and we're finally getting rid of it. It was one of the first things we bought when we moved in."

"You bought a baby grand and none of you play?" I ask with a smile, teasing.

He nods. "The house seemed to be crying for one. No, begging us for one."

"Oh, I see." *Wow.*

I write a thank-you note to Julie when we return to Roswell:

Dear Julie,

While I was working hard to repair the damage done to my psyche, reno-vate my mind, and make my life my own, you were repairing the damage done to the tabernacle of my family's living space, renovating, and making the house your own.

We have both done great work, and we have met each other, and I bow to you in gratitude.

I mail the letter. But after absorbing the reality that the details of the house that had come to me in flashbacks were accurate, my grati-tude disappears under the weight of a deep and persistent sadness.

I decide to visit Mary Anne, now seventy and retired from her teaching position at the medical school. We're sitting opposite each other, in the same chairs we sat in during my first therapy session in her office in Auburn twenty years earlier, only now we're in a room of her home in Macon. A wall of built-in bookcases filled with marriage and family therapy texts is the backdrop to her soothing presence. There is no charge for this time with her. It has been over six years since I terminated therapy, and my termination process was carefully attended to by both of us. A therapist's own therapy has unique sensitivities to it, particularly concerning boundaries, and one thing for which I'll always be grateful to Mary Anne is how wisely she processed those things with me. Our relationship endures as a deep spiritual bond.

Always happy to see me, Mary Anne leans against the back of her chair, arms open by her side, and waits for me to tell her what's on my mind.

"I suppose there's still a part of me that wants to believe none of the abuse really happened," I tell her.

She nods.

"You know, the motivation to write and publish my memoir has always carried with it a secret wish that someone would make a movie version of the book."

She tilts her head and smiles. "Can you tell me more details of that fantasy, Cathy?"

This isn't difficult to answer. "A great producer buys back the house, reconstructs the interior to a replica of my family's living space, and actresses and actors resembling Mom, Dad, Andrew, Lucy, Paul, and me portray our lives on the screen, complete with an original soundtrack." The next part of the answer takes more effort: "I've been somewhat troubled by this fantasy, because I wouldn't want children to act in the scenes where I'm abused."

She squirms in her seat.

"But I hadn't realized, until I went back to the house, that under all those fantasies was my longing to have my family back again. Alive and well. Given another chance. Getting it right this time. Successful from beginning to end. Academy Award winners, every one of us. All dressed up and beaming with joy. That maybe if we became public figures, I could escape my private hell."

Her smile is gone.

"No such luck. Who would care?" There's anger in my tone now. "Anyway, it's not my house anymore. It belongs to the Murphys. It's so beautiful, Mary Anne, and it belongs to them. They're private people. They'd never agree to handing their house over to a movie producer."

"You're angry that it's not your house anymore?"

I nod. "I want it. I want it back."

"Do you really?" she asks. "Haven't you had enough of being haunted by that house and the atrocities you experienced in it?"

"It was just . . . so beautiful, Mary Anne!"

"I think you're making too much of its beauty, Cathy. Perhaps it was so devastating to return and erase all trace of denial that you've dissociated into its beauty again. It's only a house."

I stare at the Oriental carpet beneath my feet, feeling sad and fearful that I'll never be able to move on, something I haven't felt in a long time.

She looks at me over her trifocals. "I think you need to stop wondering at the beauty of that house and focus on the wonder of *you*."

Still sad, I return to staring at the floor.

"You fought hard for your life, Cathy." Her voice is insistent, urging. "Celebrate your marvelous *existence*. . . . Perhaps that sounds too difficult now, while every cell in your body is recovering from your pilgrimage. . . . Give yourself time to mourn. Be patient and compassionate with yourself, then *do it*: Cross over the threshold."

"I feel like I'm bidding one of my children goodbye," she says, leading me to the back door by her patio and driveway.

I smile. "You are, Mary Anne." We embrace, and kiss each other on the cheek. "You've been my *blessed* mother, and I thank God every day for leading me to your door."

That night I dream:

I stand across from 763 Montgomery Place. It is daybreak and I contemplate going to early Mass, but a voice inside me says, "No, we're having a different kind of liturgy today."

Strong and powerful angels descend on the stoop, huddling in a circle like a football team planning a strategy for the next play; then they enter the house in single file. Within moments, they exit the front door, carrying Dad's body outside. They lock his body inside a casket, while the Angel of Death escorts him and all his spirits to a place the angels assure me I need not be privy to, though I sense he'll be meeting the One who made us all.

A hearse pulls up; two men get out and swiftly move the casket inside of the vehicle. The task completed, they get into the driver and passenger seats, slam the doors shut, and depart.

I realize that the sun has come up and it's a beautiful spring day. 763 Montgomery Place is still. No inhabitants. No ghosts. No danger. And no real purpose for me to be here, because I know I don't live here anymore.

I notice a little bluebird sitting on the banister of the stoop. I walk over to look at him, thinking about how common it is to see pigeons in Brooklyn, and how extraordinary the sight of this little fella is. He turns to me, and in a strong and kindly voice says: "Go in peace!"

And I do. I release myself from the strong arms of pain and cross over the threshold, trusting the hard work of love to challenge and guide my way.

Epilogue

*December 2007. Peter and I enjoy a very different experi-*ence of family this year from the one we endured that fateful day years ago when we visited my parents after returning from Germany. Now, we are the grandparents. Claire is married and a mother of three children, ages six, three, and ten months. Her youngest looks like her at the same age, and is built so much like Peter, I'm awed by him. Beth is married and the mother of two girls, ages five and three. Her three-year-old has that same head of thick black hair Beth had as a little one. Our five precious grandchildren are healthy, bright, affectionate, fun, and adorable, and we enjoy being a regular part of their lives. Annie and Rose are both engaged. Our daughters have all chosen fine people for their mates, and we have taken them into our hearts.

Like any family we have problems and issues to wrestle with from time to time. And like those of many abuse survivors, war veterans,

holocaust survivors, and survivors of other traumas, some of our problems have been directly related to how my wounds have hurt the people I love the most. It grieves me to know this, but I have also learned
to trust the process of healing. Peter and I consistently witness, among
our daughters and their mates, a strong commitment to providing an
extended family network of love, respect, and support for the children. This family treasure adds sparkle to our days.

Andrew and Lucy are doing well. Our communications are pri-
marily through email, at a respectful distance. They have both expressed consistent support of my writing this memoir, and having
requested that I not use their real names, they are pleased with the
names I have chosen. Uncle Sean and Aunt Mary, whose names are
also fictitious, are now in their eighties. We communicate regularly,
through phone calls, letters, and visits, and our relationship continues
to be very loving.

Pat McCormick and Mary Anne and Rollin Armour told me to
keep their real names. Pat, happily married and teaching at a university, has written several books, and is very supportive of mine. Mary
Anne's hair, no longer gray, is now snow white. We have a treasured
friendship with mutual affection and admiration, visiting with each
other several times a year. She continues to radiate love and compassion. She keeps a copy of my manuscript in her bookcase and cheers
me on. Always, she wants to know how the girls are doing, each one
of them. I tell her, knowing that her exquisite psychological reparenting of me contributed to my parenting of them and how well they
are doing.

Peter and I enjoy the happiest years of our marriage. We cherish
each other. I have a wonderful life now, far richer than I dreamed was
possible when I was a young woman. There are moments, however,
when serenity escapes me still—abandons me as mercilessly as Mother
did on her drunken binges. They're precipitated by triggering events,
like a heightened terrorist alert in the airport while I'm checking in for
a trip to New York to visit family, or my youngest grandson being born
the same week a local pediatrician is arrested for child molestation.

Episodes like these have been infrequent and short-lived, but while they are happening, my sense of wholeness, strength, and place in the world rips away from me like the walls of a bungalow sucked up by the violent forces of a tornado. I have learned how to take care of myself when this happens. I reach out to Peter or a dear friend. They help me to put things in perspective, talk me through the trigger, and assist me in coming up with a plan to calm myself. Sometimes I get back into therapy, briefly, with a new trusted therapist, to process an event or prepare for something I know will make me susceptible to symptoms.

I maintain a clinical practice, enjoying the privilege of entering into the private worlds of individuals, couples, and families. Sometimes I'll hear myself say something in a session that sounds like Mary Anne, and it gives me a warm feeling. I also conduct marriage and parenting workshops for couples who are expecting their first baby. I want to help them get a good start. I want to help prevent child abuse.

Peter and I often talk about how critical my training and experience as a family therapist and our experiences in therapy have been for four generations of our family. In recent years, we have been able to draw from what we learned to administer care to several people in our extended family who have suffered from serious illness and loss. We were particularly grateful that Peter's mother, who lived to age ninety-two, and was so deserving of tender loving care, could reap some of the benefits of our previous work.

My six-year-old grandson, Claire's oldest, and our first grandchild, sits in the booster seat behind me in my white Volvo station wagon. We're going to spend the afternoon together. He's holding a clipboard filled with paper and a pencil; he carries it with him everywhere lately, says it's his journal and he has to bring it so he can write everything down.

We drive by the old cemetery in the heart of Roswell.

"Grandma," he says, "where is your father? Is he dead? Is he in one of those graves?"

I'd suspected these questions might come someday, but I'd never considered it would be this soon.

"No, he's not in one of those graves, but yes, my father is dead."

"Was he nice?"

"Well, sometimes he was nice, but sometimes he was very mean."

"Your father? He was mean?"

We're approaching a red light. I press my foot down on the break and ease the car into a stop. "Yes," I say softly, then look in the rearview mirror.

He's looking out the window, face all scrunched up like he's trying to figure it out. The light changes and I step on the accelerator and pull out through the intersection.

"Grandma," he says. "I don't know those fathers."

"I'm glad you don't. And I'm glad *you* have a very *kind* father."

"Me too," he says, then picks up his pencil, sits back, takes a deep breath, exhales. "I'm gonna make a picture for him."

"Good idea," I say.

Thank you, God.

Appendix

Dear Reader,

Thank you for reading my memoir. I realize that you may have intense reactions to what you've read, and, having asked you in the prologue to please make some good of it, I want to offer you a few suggestions about how you might do that.

First, listen to the children in your life. Are they saying anything by word, action, or inaction that gives you cause for concern? If so, explore it further, and if a child tells you s/he is being molested, look that child in the eye and say, "*Thank you* for telling me. Because I am an adult, I know what to do to help you." Contact your local child protective services organization, a mental health professional, or a pediatrician for guidance. The needs of abused children are too often compromised, even when reported. This makes it imperative for you to be proactive about consulting with competent professionals whose expertise can optimize opportunities for effective intervention.

Second, listen to yourself. If you are a sexual abuse survivor, you may be experiencing visceral reactions to the content of my story.

That's normal. Get help. Remember that you have already survived your own abuse. Your job now is to find a safe, healing environment with a competent therapist who will help you to integrate your experiences. There is a section on how to find a therapist in this appendix. Many communities also offer support groups for survivors of sexual abuse, sometimes with low or no fee. These groups can be tremendously helpful, if led by a licensed therapist who has specialized training in working with sexual abuse survivor groups.

If you're suffering from symptoms of bipolar illness, schedule an appointment with a qualified psychiatrist, and if you've been diagnosed bipolar and are undergoing treatment, don't alarm yourself with concern that you may be doomed to abuse children the way my father did. My father rejected treatment during his parenting years, and he also had sociopathic personality features. Remember, his psychiatric assessment concluded that in addition to being bipolar he also had zero ability to empathize. There are four excellent books on bipolar illness listed in the recommended reading section of this appendix, and two that deal with the makings of a psychopath.

Third, educate yourself. Look at the research data on the next two pages. Read some of the books I've recommended. *The Stop Child Molestation Book: What Ordinary People Can Do in Their Everyday Lives to Save Three Million Children* is one I think everyone should read. Are you the partner of a survivor? Perhaps *Allies in Healing* is the book for you? Maybe you're a parent of young children? The books about child development in the last section would be good for you. *Invisible Girls* is a must if you are involved with teenagers. There are also several excellent books about marriage listed, for those of you who want to learn more about strengthening yours. And if you work in a church setting, some of the books on feminist theology may expand your perspective, along with *Transforming a Rape Culture*, which could be a great Sunday school or book club catalyst.

I believe that our culture is in need of transformation. We are living in violent times. Our daily news is a litany of trauma from natural disasters to brutal combat. *Trauma and Recovery: The Aftermath of*

Violence—from Domestic Abuse to Political Terror is one of the finest books I can recommend to help you to understand the dynamics of trauma and healing. In the concluding chapter of the *International Handbook of Multigenerational Legacies of Trauma,* a large treatise of research, Yael Danieli explains that a "conspiracy of silence" often follows trauma, though most researchers agree that silence is profoundly destructive, in families and in society, and that it fuels the transmission of trauma to the next generation, while depriving survivors of social support, which is the most important factor in coping with traumatic stress. I think this is particularly true for sexual abuse survivors and their families. When survivors are prevented from articulating the words necessary to integrate their abuse, they are deprived of creating the meaningful dialogue through which the power of love dispels the power of evil, and their families are deprived of learning about courage, perseverance, redemption, and other important life lessons.

I implore you to become proactive. Help me to help my memoir become a call to arms—loving arms, the only kind of arms that should ever touch a child. Take what you've read, what you've learned, what you've been emotionally moved by, and let it motivate you to contribute to the safety of children, the healing of sexual abuse survivors, and the restoration of virtue.

Peace,
Catherine

Research Data

In a 2007 presentation to therapists in Atlanta, Nora Harlow, MFA, director of the Child Molestation Research & Prevention Institute, presented the following facts:

- ❧ Forty-two million Americans have suffered child sexual abuse.
- ❧ Three million of those are still children.
- ❧ One in every four families experiences child sexual abuse.

- In an average eighth-grade class of thirty children, four girls have been molested, two boys have been molested, and one boy has molested a younger child.
- 90 percent of sexual abuse is perpetuated on children in the family and children of trusted friends and neighbors.
- 10 percent of sexual abuse is perpetuated on child strangers.

The U.S. Department of Health and Human Services reports:
- One in ten children is sexually abused.
- Sixty-five million Americans are survivors of sexual abuse.
- Girls who are abused are three times more likely to experience psychiatric disorders and addictions than girls who are not abused.
- 35 percent of incarcerated women report being sexually abused.

The Rape, Abuse & Incest National Network (RAINN) reports:
- One out of every six American women and one out of thirty-three men have been the victims of an attempted or completed rape in their lifetime.
- 15 percent of sexual assault and rape victims are under age 12, 29 percent are 12–17, 44 percent are under age 18, 80 percent are under age 30.
- 93 percent of juvenile sex assault victims know their attacker—34.2 percent were family members, 58.7 percent were acquaintances, and 7 percent were strangers.
- Victims of sexual assault are three times more likely to suffer from depression, six times more likely to suffer from post-traumatic stress disorder, thirteen times more likely to abuse alcohol, twenty-six times more likely to abuse drugs, and four times more likely to contemplate suicide.

The Internet is a new and growing factor in the sexual exlpoitation of children:
- One in five children who use computer chat rooms has been approached over the Internet by pedophiles and only 25 percent of

youth who received sexual solicitation told a parent. (Top Ten Reviews, Inc., 2005)

ᔐ More than 20,000 images of child pornography are posted on the Internet every week. (National Society for the Prevention of Cruelty to Children, 10/8/03)

ᔐ Child pornography generates $3 billion annually. (12/2005, Internet Filter Review.com)

ᔐ 100,000 websites offer illegal child porn. (US Customs Service estimate)

ᔐ 140,000 child pornography images were posted to the Internet, according to researchers who monitored the Internet over six weeks. Twenty children were estimated to have been abused for the first time and more than 1,000 images of each child created. (National Society for the Prevention of Cruelty to children, 10/8/03)

ᔐ Demand for pornographic images of babies and toddlers on the Internet is soaring. (Prof. Max Taylor, Combating Pedophile Information Network in Europe, March, 2003)

Where To Get Help

The following organizations have websites with a wealth of information.

The Rape, Abuse & Incest National Network (RAINN)
2000 L St. NW, Ste. 406
Washington, DC 20036
(202) 544-3064
www.rainn.org; info@rainn.org
RAINN is the nation's largest anti–sexual assault organization and operates the National Sexual Assault Hotline at (800) 656-HOPE.

National Domestic Violence Hotline
(800) 799-SAFE (799-7233)
www.ndvh.org

Childhelp USA
National Child Abuse Hotline
(800) 4-A-CHILD (800-422-4453)
www.childhelpusa.org

Child Molestation Research & Prevention Institute
www.childmolestationprevention.org
You will find much relevant, useful material at this site.

Women's Resource Center to End Domestic Violence
www.wrcdv.org; info@wrcdv.org

Girlthrive
www.girlthrive.com
Wonderful, user-friendly website designed for teen girls and young women who have survived sexual abuse, with information, stories, and expert interviews.

Gift from Within
www.giftfromwithin.org
Post-traumatic stress disorder resources for survivors and caregivers.

Stigma
www.stigmatized.org
Support for children conceived through rape or incest.

Survivors of Incest Anonymous
www.siawso.org
(410) 893-3322

Child and Adolescent Bipolar Foundation
1000 Skokie Blvd., Suite 570
Wilmette, Illinois 60091
(847) 256-8525
www.bpkids.org; www.depressedteens.com

How To Find a Therapist

I think the best way to find a therapist is through the recommendation of a friend who knows a good one. Physicians and clergy are also good sources of referrals. Many people find therapists through their insurance company or managed care plan. Always do some research once you get a few names. Google the therapist, look at websites, and make sure the therapist is licensed and in good standing with his or her professional organization. My professional organization, the American Association for Marriage and Family Therapy, has an online referral service, noted below. Many therapists listed have extended listings, describing their practices. Feel free to call and ask questions before making an appointment. I think that within the first three sessions you will have a sense for whether or not this is the right therapist for you.

American Association for Marriage and Family Therapy (AAMFT)
112 S. Alfred St.
Alexandria, VA 22314
(703) 838-9808
www.aamft.org
www.therapistlocator.net

American Psychiatric Association
1000 Wilson Blvd., Ste. 1825
Arlington, VA 22209
(703) 907-7300
www.psych.org

American Psychological Association (APA)
750 1st St. NE
Washington, DC 20002
(202) 336-5500
(800) 374-2721
www.apa.org

National Association of Social Workers (NASW)
750 1st St. NE, Ste. 700
Washington, DC 20002
(202) 408-8600
www.socialworkers.org

Association for the Treatment of
Sexual Abusers (ATSA)
4900 S.W. Griffith Dr., Ste. 274
Beaverton, OR 97005
(503) 643-1023
www.atsa.com

Therapy Modalities

There are many avenues to healing in psychotherapy, and the therapy process is a sensitive one. Therapists work out of varying theoretical perspectives, belief systems, life experience, and clinical expertise, just as their clients present with their own unique symptoms, personalities, and contexts. Whether you work with a family therapist, social worker, psychologist, or psychiatrist, your therapist's integrity, intelligence, and ability to hear you accurately and with empathy will ground your work in safety, truth, and compassion.

Sometimes a therapist will call upon a particular modality during a phase of treatment that warrants it. Psychodrama, hypnotherapy, and psychomotor therapy were integrated into my treatment with Mary Anne over the years. The use of hypnosis for accessing repressed memories is controversial, should not be undertaken lightly, and should be considered only when practiced by a licensed mental health professional certified to do so. I had been in therapy with Mary Anne for ten years before undergoing hypnosis and found it helpful in managing memories that had been emerging through flashbacks. I requested it, researched it, discussed with Mary Anne whether, when, and how to approach it, and she was present for each session. This was expensive, because I paid both of them, but for me, it was the only way that made sense.

I had never done EMDR (eye movement desensitization and reprocessing), while in therapy with Mary Anne. But in recent years, I've called an EMDR-trained therapist when I've had a particular incident arise that stirs up my discomfort, and it's been very helpful.

To learn more about these modalities, log on to the following websites.

American Society of Group Psychotherapy and Psychodrama
www.asgpp.org

EMDR International Organization
www.emdria.org

National Board for Certified Clinical Hypnotherapists
www.natboard.com

Pesso Boyden System Psychomotor International
www.pbsp.com

Recommended Reading

The following books were helpful to me during my recovery and the writing of this book.

MEMOIRS
Angelou, Maya. *I Know Why the Caged Bird Sings.* New York: Bantam Books, 1969.

Daniell, Rosemary. *Fatal Flowers: On Sin, Sex, and Suicide in the Deep South.* Athens, GA: Hill Street Press, 1999.

Francisco, Patricia Weaver. *Telling: A Memoir of Rape and Recovery.* New York: HarperCollins Publishers, 1999.

Jamison, Kay Redfield. *An Unquiet Mind: A Memoir of Moods and Madness.* New York: Vintage Books, 1996.

Knapp, Caroline. *Drinking: A Love Story.* New York: Dell Publishing, 1996.

Lauck, Jennifer. *Blackbird: A Childhood Lost and Found.* New York: Pocket Books, 2001.

McCourt, Frank. *Angela's Ashes.* New York: Scribner, 1999.

Raine, Nancy Venable. *After Silence: Rape and My Journey Back.* New York: Three Rivers Press, 1998.

Silverman, Sue William. *Because I Remember Terror, Father, I Remember You.* Athens: University of Georgia Press, 1996.

Walls, Jeannette. *The Glass Castle.* New York: Scribner, 2006.

Wiesel, Elie. *Memoirs: All Rivers Run to the Sea.* New York: Alfred A. Knopf, 1995.

Wisechild, Louise M. *The Obsidian Mirror.* Seattle: Seal Press, 1998.

RECOVERY FROM SEXUAL ABUSE
Bass, Ellen, and Laura Davis. *The Courage To Heal: A Guide for Women Survivors of Child Sexual Abuse.* New York: Harper & Row, 1998.

Feuereisen, Dr. Patti, with Caroline Pincus. *Invisible Girls: The Truth About Sexual Abuse.* Emeryville, CA: Seal Press, 2005.

Finney, Lynne, JD, MSW. *Reach for the Rainbow: Advanced Healing for Survivors of Sexual Abuse.* New York: Perigee Books, 1990.

Mather, Cynthia, and Kristina Debye. *How Long Does It Hurt?: A Guide to Recovering from Incest and Sexual Abuse for Teenagers, Their Friends, and Their Families.* San Francisco: Jossey-Bass, 2004.

Thomas, T. *Surviving with Serenity: Daily Meditations for Incest Survivors.* Deerfield Beach, FL: Health Communications, Inc., 1990.

SPIRITUALITY

Brock, Rita Nakashima. *Journeys by Heart: A Christology of Erotic Power.* New York: Crossroad Publishing Company, 1991.

Flaherty, Sandra. *Woman, Why Do You Weep?* New York: Paulist Press, 1960.

Foote, Catherine J. *Survivor Prayers: Talking with God about Childhood Sexual Abuse.* Louisville, KY: Westminster/John Knox Press, 1994.

Fox, Matthew. *Sins of the Spirit, Blessings of the Flesh: Lessons for Transforming Evil in Soul and Society.* New York: Harmony Books, 1999.

Fox, Matthew. *Original Blessing: A Primer in Creation Spirituality.* Sante Fe, NM: Bear & Co., Inc., 1983.

Gluck, Louise. *The Wild Iris.* Hopewell, NJ: The Ecco Press, 1992.

Johnson, Elizabeth. *She Who Is: The Mystery of God in Feminist Theological Discourse.* New York: Crossroad Publishing Company, 1994.

Leehan, James. *Defiant Hope: Spirituality for Survivors of Family Abuse.* Louisville, KY: Westminster/John Knox Press, 1993.

Norris, Kathleen. *The Cloister Walk.* New York: Riverhead Books, 1996.

Osiek, Carolyn, RSCJ. *Beyond Anger: On Being a Feminist in the Church.* New York: Paulist Press, 1986.

Tutu, Archbishop Desmond. *No Future without Forgiveness.* New York: Doubleday, 1999.

Young-Eisendrath, Polly. *The Resilient Spirit: Transforming Suffering into Insight and Renewal.* Reading, MA: Perseus Books, 1996.

PROFESSIONAL BOOKS

Anthony, E. James, and Bertram J. Cohler. *The Invulnerable Child.* New York: The Guilford Press, 1987.

Blume, E. Sue. *Secret Survivors: Uncovering Incest and Its Aftereffects in Women.* New York: John Wiley & Sons, 1990.

Courtois, Christine A. *Healing the Incest Wound: Adult Survivors in Therapy.* New York: W. W. Norton & Company, Inc., 1988.

Danieli, Yael. *International Handbook of Multigenerational Legacies of Trauma.* New York: Springer, 1998.

Dolan, Yvonne. *Resolving Sexual Abuse: Solution-Focused Therapy and Ericksonian Hypnosis for Adult Survivors.* New York: W. W. Norton & Company, Inc., 1991.

Engel, Beverly. *The Right to Innocence.* Los Angeles: Jeremy P. Tarcher, Inc., 1989.

Fossum, Merle A., and Marilyn J. Mason. *Facing Shame: Families in Recovery.* New York: W. W. Norton & Company, Inc., 1986.

Herman, Judith L., MD. *Father-Daughter Incest.* Cambridge: Harvard University Press, 2000.

Herman, Judith L., MD. *Trauma and Recovery: The Aftermath of Violence—from Domestic Abuse to Political Terror.* New York: Basic Books, 1992.

Maltz, Wendy. *The Sexual Healing Journey: A Guide for Survivors of Sexual Abuse.* New York: HarperCollins Publishers, 1991.

Ochberg, F. M., MD, ed. *Post-traumatic Therapy and Victims of Violence.* New York: Bruner/Mazel Publishers, 1988.

Poston, Carol, and Karen Lison. *Reclaiming Our Lives: Hope for Adult Survivors of Incest.* Boston: Little, Brown and Company, 1989.

Salter, Anna C. *Transforming Trauma: A Guide to Understanding and Treating Adult Survivors of Child Sexual Abuse.* London: Sage Publications, Inc., 1995.

Schaefer, Charles, and Kevin O'Connor. *Handbook of Play Therapy.* New York: John Wiley & Sons, 1983.

van der Kolk, Bessel, MD. *Psychological Trauma.* Washington, DC: American Psychiatric Press, 1987.

van der Kolk, Bessel, MD., McFarlane, Alexander and Weisath, Lars, Eds. *Traumatic Stress: The Effects of Overwhelming Experience on Mind, Body, and Society.* New York: The Guilford Press, 1996.

Westerlund, Elaine. *Women's Sexuality After Childhood Incest.* New York: W. W. Norton & Company, Inc., 1992.

OTHER RECOMMENDED BOOKS

Abel, Gene, MD, and Nora Harlow. *The Stop Child Molestation Book: What Ordinary People Can Do in Their Everyday Lives To Save Three Million Children.* Philadelphia: Xlibris Corporation, 2001.

Black, Claudia. *It Will Never Happen to Me: Children of Alcoholics as Youngsters, Adolescents, Adults.* New York: Ballantine Books, 2002.

Buchwald, Emilie, Pamela Fletcher, and Martha Roth. *Transforming a Rape Culture.* Minneapolis: Milkweed Editions, 1993.

Burgess, Wes, MD, PhD. *The Bipolar Handbook: Real-Life Questions with Up-to-Date Answers.* New York: Avery/Penguin Group, 2006.

Crompton, Vicki, and Ellen Z. Kessner. *Saving Beauty from the Beast: How To Protect Your Daughter from an Unhealthy Relationship.* Boston: Little, Brown and Company, 2003.

Crosby, Michael H. *The Dysfunctional Church: Addiction and Codependency in the Family of Catholicism.* Notre Dame, IN: Ave Maria Press, 1991.

Davis, Laura. *Allies in Healing: When the Person You Love Was Sexually Abused as a Child.* New York: Harper Perennial, 1991.

Fast, Julie A., and John Preston, PsyD. *Loving Someone with Bipolar Disorder: Understanding and Helping Your Partner.* Oakland, CA: New Harbinger Publications, Inc., 2004.

Fast, Julie A., and John Preston, PsyD. *Take Charge of Bipolar Disorder.* New York: Wellness Central, 2006.

Gottman, John, PhD, with Joan Declaire. *Raising an Emotionally Intelligent Child: The Heart of Parenting.* New York: Simon & Schuster, 1997.

Hampl, Patricia. *I Could Tell You Stories: Sojourns in the Land of Memory.* New York: W. W. Norton & Company, Inc., 1999.

Love, Patricia, PhD, with Jo Robinson. *The Emotional Incest Syndrome: What To Do When a Parent's Love Rules Your Life.* New York: Bantam Books, 1991.

Magid, Dr. Ken, and Carole A. McKelvey. *High Risk: Children without a Conscience.* New York: Bantam Books, 1987.

Malone, Patrick, MD, and Thomas Malone, MD. *The Art of Intimacy.* New York: Prentice Hall Press, 1988.

Miklowitz, David, J. *The Bipolar Disorder Survival Guide.* New York: Guilford Press, 2002.

Miller, Alice. *Breaking Down the Wall of Silence: The Liberating Experience of Facing Painful Truth.* New York: Meridian, 1997.

Napier, Augustus. *The Fragile Bond: In Search of an Equal, Intimate and Enduring Marriage.* New York: Harper Perennial, 1988.

Napier, Augustus, and Carl Whitaker. *The Family Crucible: The Intense Experience of Family Therapy.* New York: Harper & Row, 1978.

Peck, Scott M. *People of the Lie: The Hope for Healing Human Evil.* New York: Simon & Schuster, 1983.

Schnarch, David, PhD. *Passionate Marriage: Love, Sex, and Intimacy in Emotionally Committed Relationships.* New York: Holt Paperbacks, 1988.

Shapiro, Francine, PhD, and Margot S. Forrest. *EMDR: The Breakthrough "Eye Movement" Therapy for Overcoming Anxiety, Stress, and Trauma.* New York: Basic Books, 1997.

Stout, Martha, PhD. *The Sociopath Next Door.* New York: Ballantine Books, 2005.

Terr, Lenore, MD. *Unchained Memories: True Stories of Traumatic Memories, Lost and Found.* New York: Basic Books, 1994.

Terr, Lenore, MD. *Too Scared To Cry: How Trauma Affects Children and Ultimately Us All.* New York: Basic Books, 1990.

Van Derbur, Marilyn. *Miss America by Day: Lessons Learned from Ultimate Betrayals and Unconditional Love.* Denver, CO: Oak Hill Ridge Press, 2003.

Weingarten, Kathy, PhD. *Cultural Resistance: Challenging Beliefs about Men, Women, and Therapy.* New York: Harrington Park Press, 1995.

Weingarten, Kathy, PhD. *The Mother's Voice: Strengthening Intimacy in Families.* New York: Harcourt Brace & Company, 1994.

Acknowledgments

There is a sense in which every person who ever loved me and treated me with respect has made a contribution to this book, for had they not, I would never have considered my story to be worth the paper it is printed on.

For teaching me to love reading, and years of urging me to write this book, I thank my dear friend Amandah Turner. For introducing me to the genre of memoir, for inspiring me to leave the novel version of my story behind and put the truth on the page instead, and for her intelligent, enduring support of the work and of me, I thank fellow-memoirist Rebecca Allard. For believing in this project and being the first to teach me the craft of writing, I thank Rosemary Daniell and the members of the Atlanta Zona Rosa writing group. For her generous hospitality after those late-night meetings, I thank my friend Susan Levy. The women in my Kaleidoscope writing group -- Rebecca Allard, Marsha Bailey, and Susan Stone – were the true midwives of this birth, without whom I may never have been able to bring my story into the world. I am deeply grateful to each of them, and I cherish their friendship.

The inspiration and learning I received from everyone at Bread Loaf 2003, particularly Patricia Hampl and Carol Houck Smith, who "got it" and gave me a working title, are gifts I treasure, along with Sally Mackay's pep talks. The power of Kathryn Harrison and Mary Karr's memoir presentation at the 2006 Mid-Atlantic Creative Non-fiction Workshop renewed my belief in the importance of this work, while Shanna Mahin's insights bolstered my waning courage. Thanks, to each of you.

Emmanuelle Alspaugh, my agent extraordinaire, shepherded both my manuscript and me with respect, wisdom, precision, enthusiasm, determination, and grace. Our connection has felt God-given and I am deeply grateful for it. She led me to Arlene Robinson, whose editing expertise helped me to make my work stronger, and then found for me an ideal publisher. Krista Lyons, my publishing editor, has been a delight to work with from the very beginning, as have all the folks at Seal Press. Thank you.

This project spanned ten years, and during that time col- leagues and friends read drafts and gave me feedback, or helped me to negotiate the balancing of my family life and psychotherapy practice with writing. Among them are Ann Carol Daniel, Deb Dawson, Linda Fredo, Peg McCaw Fiman, Elaine Gibson, Peggy Harrington, Gail Lyle, Patrick Malone, Patrick McCormick, Barbara Miller-Murphy, Bill Phillips, Nancy Rosenblum, Cheryl Simon, Polly Simpson, Kathryn Temple, Amandah Turner, and Geri Zilian. Their input is greatly appreciated.

Several health care professionals provided therapeutic treat- ments which enabled me to spend innumerable hours at the computer despite the chronic pain of my arthritic neck. Gayle Anthony,

Christine Arnold, Solomon Cohen, Cynthia Hastings, Kimberly Hughes, Gary Myerson, and Shirley Weyrich, I could not have written this book without your help.

There were musicians and vocal artists who influenced my creativity, as their music accompanied me through the fits and starts of the grueling process of writing, particularly Tracy Chapman, Charlotte Church, Ella Fitzgerald, Jewel, Bobby McFerrin, Sarah McLachlan, Audra McDonald, Luciano Pavarotti, Arthur Rubenstein, Barbra Streisand, and Art Tatum.

My sister's support was particularly loving, proactive, and insightful. It brought a level of healing into our relationship that I had never imagined was possible and I cherish. I am also grateful for my brother's consistent words of encouragement. Several members of the McCall clan – sisters-in-law, nieces and nephews – have also offered words of support which I appreciate.

I'd like to acknowledge three other people. They were not involved with the writing of the book, but contributed much to my healing process: friend and colleague Sandy Halperin, Karen Nash, and Jesse Harris Bathrick, the therapist who led the incest survivor support group I was a member of.

No vocabulary of thanks includes words sufficient to express my gratitude and deep appreciation to Peter, my husband and soulmate, whose fidelity, strength of character, and loving support are at the heart of every page. As this book goes to print, we are celebrating our sixtieth birthdays. Where would I be without his love?

Deo gracias

Group Discussion Questions

1. *When the Piano Stops* contains vivid scenes of sexual abuse, mental illness, and alcoholism. Has reading it altered your perspective on any of these issues?

2. Catherine and Peter faced many challenges in their marriage. Some of them were a direct result of wounds inflicted on her through her father's abuse and her mother's alcoholism and compliance. Some were a result of Peter's background. Some were related to the culture of the time, and some were challenges every married couple must grapple with. List their challenges, delineate which category you would put them in, and discuss their relevance in the context of your own life.

3. Has reading this book given you any ideas about how you can be a good support to a family member or a friend who has been sexually abused? How would you approach the topic with them?

4. Do you think there is a relationship between mental illness and evil? If so, what sense do you make of their connection?

277

5. Why do you think Catherine's father chose not to seek treatment for his mental illness? Why did her mother stay with him?

6. Catherine's memoir gives us an inside look at the dynamics of her therapy. She develops a strong attachment to her therapist, Mary Anne, and the power of their relationship is a driving force in her healing. What factors contributed to the richness of their relational bond?

7. The influences of religion, music, and education are consistent themes in Catherine's life. In your own life, how have these influences helped or hindered you?

8. Rituals, both those she is exposed to as a child and those she creates as an adult, are strong components of Catherine's healing process. What roles have rituals played in your life?

9. *When the Piano Stops* presents the reader with episodes related to the sexuality of several characters in the story. Have you developed any new insights as a result of this? If so, what are they?

10. This book also deals with end of life issues and eldercare. Did reading it stir up any new thoughts or feelings about these issues for you?

11. Did any aspects of this memoir move you to deal differently with a relationship in your own life?

12. At the end of the prologue Catherine pleads with you to make some good of having read her story. Name three concrete ways in which you can do that.